Loving and Hating the World

Loving and Hating
—— the World ——

Ambivalence and Discipleship

James Lawson

CASCADE *Books* · Eugene, Oregon

LOVING AND HATING THE WORLD
Ambivalence and Discipleship

Copyright © 2021 James Lawson. All rights reserved. Except for brief quotations in critical publications or reviews, no part of this book may be reproduced in any manner without prior written permission from the publisher. Write: Permissions, Wipf and Stock Publishers, 199 W. 8th Ave., Suite 3, Eugene, OR 97401.

Cascade Books
An Imprint of Wipf and Stock Publishers
199 W. 8th Ave., Suite 3
Eugene, OR 97401

www.wipfandstock.com

PAPERBACK ISBN: 978-1-7252-7661-1
HARDCOVER ISBN: 978-1-7252-7662-8
EBOOK ISBN: 978-1-7252-7663-5

Cataloguing-in-Publication data:

Names: Lawson, James, author.

Title: Loving and hating the world : ambivalence and discipleship / by James Lawson.

Description: Eugene, OR: Cascade Books, 2021 | Includes bibliographical references and index.

Identifiers: ISBN 978-1-7252-7661-1 (paperback) | ISBN 978-1-7252-7662-8 (hardcover) | ISBN 978-1-7252-7663-5 (ebook)

Subjects: LCSH: Church and the world. | Religion and culture. | Secularism. | Asceticism.

Classification: BR115.W6 .L37 2021 (print) | BR115.W6 (ebook)

12/17/21

Scripture quotations are from the *Common Bible: New Revised Standard Version Bible*, copyright © 1989 National Council of the Churches of Christ in the United States of America. Used by permission. All rights reserved worldwide.

An abbey cellarer testing his wine. Illumination from a copy of *Li livres dou santé* by Aldobrandino of Siena. British Library manuscript Sloane 2435, f. 44v. Public domain.

[T]he reduction of ambivalence is a problem of the discovery and application of proper *technology*: a *managerial* problem. Both factors combined to make modern times an era of particularly bitter and relentless war against ambivalence.

—Zygmunt Bauman

The world is the closed door. It is a barrier. And at the same time it is the way through.

—Simone Weil

We must hate the world as it is precisely because we must love the world as God willed it. Only thus can we give it the witness of that saving, recreating love with which God has never ceased to love it.

—Louis Bouyer

To Nana-Efua and Nana-Aba

Contents

Introduction | xi
Two Ways   xi
Two Humanisms   xiii
The Structure of the Book   xvi

1. **Communities of Ambivalence** | 1
   Flight from the world and the salvation of the world   1
   Seeking the welfare of the city, coming out of Babylon   2
   John: *in the world but not of the world*   5
   Paul: worldly asceticism   7
   The Christian Revolution   10

2. **A New Worldliness and a New Otherworldliness** | 12
   Resident aliens seeking to recompose the world   12
   A theology of ambivalence   18
   The world recomposed as "saeculum"   24
   Ascetic closure: the end of ancient Christianity?   27

3. *Contemptus Mundi* | 33
   A new paideia   33
   Vanitas vanitatum   37
   Temptation and detachment   47
   Contemptus and reform   49

CONTENTS

4. **The Reform of the World and the Making of a Secular Age | 54**
   Modernity as a mutation of Christianity   54
   Loving and hating the world: the Reform Master Narrative   55
   Worldlessness: the Intellectual Deviation story   68

5. **Ambivalence and the Critique of Modernity | 76**
   Amor mundi: Hannah Arendt and Hans Jonas   76
   Contemptus mundi: Theodor Adorno   94

6. **Ambivalence and Discipleship | 105**
   Kneeling before the world   105
   Ressourcement   110
   A faith more open, munificent, and sensuous: Dietrich Bonhoeffer   116
   Where do you go from the top of a thirty-foot pole? Thomas Merton   123
   The dilemma of mutilation: Charles Taylor   135
   Eutrapelia   148

   Bibliography | 151
   Index of Subjects | 165
   Index of Ancient Sources | 187

Introduction

Two Ways

This book has its origin in the not unreasonable anxiety with which one part of the church faces her future. The Church of England may be about to shrink rapidly or even vanish in certain areas unless urgent action is taken. The archbishops responded in 2015 with a reform and renewal program to reverse this decline. Their program was criticized for offering secular business-led, management-led, and growth-led ideologies without adequate spiritual or theological depth. But the program aimed not only to facilitate growth of the Church in numbers but also in depth of discipleship. As part of the program, the Archbishop's Council also published a report on the development of discipleship in the Church of England.[1] The report argued that both clergy and laity now need to think of themselves as missionary disciples to halt declining Church numbers in a global, secularized, and materialistic culture often experienced as a desert for the soul.

What constitutes true discipleship? This book attempts to contribute to a deeper understanding of what discipleship means in such a culture. It seeks to engage those drawn to the depth and authenticity of Buddhist or monastic spirituality, or to the new monasticism and the Benedict option.

It argues that authentic discipleship involves both embracing the world and pushing it away. Affirming the modern world can seem to be the response that Anglicans are more comfortable with—especially in a situation of rapid decline. Christian otherworldliness is then dismissed as "Platonism," or even Gnostic alienation from the goodness of creation, despite its association with the intriguing otherness of monastic spirituality.

---

1. Archbishops' Council, "Developing discipleship."

But, as the poet, novelist, and Anglican lay theologian Charles Williams taught, there are two ways by which souls come to God.[2] There is the way of negation as well as the way of affirmation. In the way of negation, God is defined in negative terms. He is to be reached by detaching the soul from love of all things that are not God—the things of the created world. This is the way of the rejection of images. But the Christian God is immanent as well as transcendent. Hence everything in the created world is also an imperfect image of him. The way of affirmation consists in the recognition of this, and in the acceptance, in love, of all things, not for their own sake, but as images of the divine.

Williams was a teacher of the way of affirmation, of the sacramental affirmation of images, as opposed to their ascetic renunciation. By "images" he meant romantic love, art, poetry, laughter, daily work, urban life, and all that follows from the sacredness of matter and the body. But he recognized that the two ways coinhere. He summed up his teaching about the two ways to God with the maxim, "This also is Thou: neither is this Thou."

Both ways are necessary, for different people and at different times. Each is incomplete without the other as a constant corrective. In this sense, Christian discipleship is essentially paradoxical. Each way requires the other to balance it.

Such a balance between the two ways is evident in T. S. Eliot's *Four Quartets*.[3] For the most part they oscillate between the Inferno of modernity, as Eliot saw it, and the Purgatorio of his ascetic call. This negative way is represented by John of the Cross. "Burnt Norton" calls the penitent to enter the dark night of the senses, which is the stage of active purgation ("descend lower, descend only/Into the world of perpetual solitude," III), while "East Coker" urges the more advanced phase of passive purgation, the dark night of the spirit ("I said to my soul, be still and let the dark come upon you," III). But the third movement of "Little Gidding" alludes to Julian of Norwich to gesture to a possible Paradiso by declaring "Sin is behovely, but/ All shall be well, and/ All manner of thing shall be well." The negative way converges at last with the affirmative way to cast a bright shadow back over all four quartets, bringing the two ways into balance, even though the negative way had predominated. Only after "Little

---

2. Williams, *The Descent of the Dove*, 58. David Fagerberg presents his studies *On Liturgical Asceticism* and *Consecrating the World* as treatments of Williams's ways of negation and affirmation respectively; Fagerberg, *Consecrating the World*, 2.

3. Newman, "Eliot's Affirmative Way."

INTRODUCTION

Gidding" could a reader of the *Quartets* realize that "the fire and the rose are one," that the two ways coinhere.

It was almost certainly Williams, teacher of the balance and coinherence of the two ways, who mediated his friend's reception of Julian. She was one of his favorite exemplars of the affirmative way, while he used John of the Cross to denote the negative way. Williams notes of John of the Cross, that "even he, towards the end, was encouraged to remember that he liked asparagus; our Lord the Spirit is reluctant to allow either of the two great ways to flourish without some courtesy to the other."[4] Part of what constitutes true discipleship then is our decision about where we place our point of equilibrium.

Two Humanisms

The two ways taught by Williams, the way of affirmation and the way of negation, correspond to two kinds of Christian humanism. These two humanisms are not mutually exclusive but were articulated in a lively debate in mid-twentieth century French Catholic theology between those who proposed an "incarnational humanism" and those who defended an "eschatological humanism."

Both humanisms seek the transformation of the world, but "incarnational humanism" affirms the continuity of this transformation—grace perfecting nature—while "eschatological humanism" emphasizes the discontinuity—the old self must die so that the new self may live. "Incarnational humanism" is presented in the work of Gustave Thils and Teilhard de Chardin and "eschatological humanism" in the work of Louis Bouyer.[5]

Both humanisms can be distorted and diminished. The optimism of "incarnational humanism" can seem a little excessive, conflating the spiritualization of earthly realities with the optimistic liberal idea of continual progress. "Eschatological humanism" can seem to present a contrastive account of the relationship between the church and the world that becomes dualistic.

---

4. Williams, *The Descent of the Dove*, 181.

5. Bouyer's use of this term expresses his ultimate preference for the eschatological orientation of the Eastern Patristic and of monastic traditions. He takes the expression "eschatological humanism" from Clement Lialine, a monk of Chevetogne Abbey, which has both Latin Rite and Byzantine Rite daily services. Lemna, *The Apocalypse of Wisdom*, 207–14; Ruddy, "What is the *Opus Dei*?"; Weill, *L'humanisme eschatologique de Louis Bouyer*.

INTRODUCTION

But both humanisms are attractive. The tension between them should be felt and not evaded. And so I respond that the balance between them needs to be maintained against the current dominance of an "incarnational humanism."

A celebrated essay by John Courtney Murray that set out the distinction between them prefigured this dominance.[6] He posed the basic problem as "affirmation of the worldly" versus "contempt for the world" and "participation in the world" versus "withdrawal." His framing—in its unacknowledged privileging of "incarnational humanism" and somewhat caricatured presentation of "eschatological humanism"—is inaccurate and slanted. It was such a privileging of "incarnational humanism" in *Gaudium et spes* that provoked the concerns expressed by Joseph Ratzinger and Henri de Lubac that the scandalous necessity of the cross was in danger of being obscured or put aside by the Council Fathers.

In fact, the "eschatological humanism" of Louis Bouyer offers a remarkably balanced account of the loving and hating of the world that is essential for true discipleship.[7] His ascetical and mystical theology is my starting point.

He balances what he calls a "metaphysical optimism" with a "historical pessimism."[8] Optimism in regard to the fundamental goodness of the created order, but realistic pessimism about the obvious fact of human sinfulness and the prospects of unaided human efforts to overcome this. As he puts it, "it is by losing love that we were lost." By closing in on ourselves we shut out the possibility of being loved. For Bouyer, "incarnational humanism" sees in the incarnation "only a sort of immersion, God disappearing into a purely human humanity."[9]

Thus he realized that the cross and creation must not be seen as competitive, zero-sum realities.

> The redemption has meaning only as restoring and perfecting the creation, in line with God's original and immutable plan for it. The Cross, therefore, with its culmination in the Resurrection, is not just something for which a place must, of course, be found in human life, but which is not to be allowed to permeate it through and through, for fear of the work of creation being retarded; quite the

---

6. Murray, "Is It Basket Weaving?"
7. Yap, "'Word' and 'Wisdom' in the Ecclesiology of Louis Bouyer," 252.
8. Bouyer, *Introduction to the Spiritual Life*, 183.
9. Bouyer, *Le Métier de Théologien*, 183.

contrary, it has become a necessity for the creation. Apart from the Cross, the creation is doomed to failure, and only by the Cross can it be saved, recovered, and brought to its true end.[10]

The cross is not an obstacle to human fulfillment; rather, it is the principal means of its fulfillment.[11] This is why Bouyer describes a properly Christian humanism as eschatological. It is only in the light of the eschaton of human history in Christ that the deepest human aspirations will be realized. Closed in on itself and, apart from an in-breaking of Divine Love, a fallen creation can only endlessly repeat its errors.

All the baptized, each according to his or her own vocation, are called to the ascesis of the cross, to hate and struggle against those things from within or without that oppose the realization of the ideal of perfection. For true, full humanity is found only in the death of the old self and the birth of a new self. Humanism and asceticism are not opposed. The cross is the key to Christian humanism, and so monasticism as living the gospel with particular intensity is the only true humanism, an integral and radically eschatological humanism.

This "eschatological humanism" does not demand withdrawal from the world or a devaluing of this life and its responsibilities and tasks. But they are to be seen in the light of eternal life, in the knowledge that eternal life is only promised to the Christian on condition that he or she makes a right use of this life.

> Life in the Church, of which baptism has made [the Christian] a member and to which every celebration of the eucharist leads him back, is not a life of escape. The Church is not outside the world, it is at the heart of the world. In fact, in order to save the world it must become *the* heart of the world.[12]

This book is informed by this "eschatological humanism." It attempts in turn to inform decisions about where we place our point of equilibrium between the way of affirmation and the way of negation, and so to equip contemporary Christians for true discipleship. It describes the source of these two ways: the ambivalence of the first Christian disciples about "the world." *God so loved the world that he gave his only begotten son*—but *friendship with the world is enmity with God*. It traces the history of this ambivalence

---

10. Bouyer, *Christian Humanism*, 101.
11. Heinitz, introduction to Louis Bouyer, *Introduction to the Spiritual Life*, 12.
12. Bouyer, *Christian Initiation*, 117.

in a survey of the history of Christianity from the New Testament to the present. It presents a revisionary account of a continuing and nonnegotiable tension between loving and hating the world, instead of a simple progression from world-denial to world-affirmation. It argues that this tension helped produce our own secular age as a mutation or corruption of Christianity. It considers modern Jewish and Christian philosophical and theological responses to this history and tries to suggest how Christians might negotiate this history and this tension.

By understanding the genealogy of our secular age more deeply we can understand our calling within it more clearly. And if discipleship is both a way of affirmation and a way of negation we can then decide: what should we love and what should we hate?

The Structure of the Book

The argument begins in chapter 1, "Communities of Ambivalence," with a consideration of how hating the world has become associated with a flight from the world into the desert or into a monastery. Loving the world has been opposed to hating the world like this as a choice between a fundamentally biblical love of the world as God's good creation and an attitude which is more gnostic or Platonic than Christian. But this monastic attitude to the world is not a simple one. It all depends on the point of view from which the world is considered: the world as it was made by God or the world organized against God by sin. Monastic communities can be characterized as communities of ambivalence about the world, and a survey of the texts of the New Testament shows that this attitude goes right back to the first communities of Christians, which were very far from being wholly world affirming.

Chapter 2, "A New Worldliness and a New Otherworldliness," describes how Christians came to articulate their affirmation of the truth, goodness, and beauty of the created world with a "sacramental ontology," a Platonist-Christian vision of the world as participating in God. But the early Christian tradition could still express a profound ambivalence about the "world." The original Christian suspicion of the "world" as the expression of values antithetical to the gospel came to be reconceived. For the new Platonist-Christian vision, material realities, being corruptible, occupied a lower place in this hierarchy than nonmaterial or spiritual realities. Material reality and embodied existence could now become objects of revulsion. New ways of loving and hating the world developed simultaneously.

Chapter 3, "*Contemptus Mundi*," offers an account of how a new revulsion developed into the medieval conception of the "world" as an object of contempt and renunciation. "*Contemptus mundi*" refers to both a world view and a literary genre particularly associated with the eleventh and twelfth centuries. It was informed by a reading of Ecclesiastes that took *vanitas* as its leading word. In this literature, Christian tradition continued to define itself as the carrier of transcendental visions and impulses over and against the vanity of the "world." The genre develops the negative side in the conflict and nonnegotiable tension in Christian tradition between loving and hating the world. But this development betrayed the earlier contempt of Christians for the dominant values of the world. *Contemptus mundi* became the ideology of a Latin Christendom in competition with the world on its own ground and for the same power.

Chapter 4, "The Reform of the World and the Making of a Secular Age," traces Charles Taylor's account in *A Secular Age* of how Christian ambivalence about the world comes to drive secularization. He presents secularization as the final outcome of Western Christianity's self-undoing through an effort that begins in Latin Christendom to dominate the world and to reform the lives of Christians and force them into conformity with the demands of the gospel. A form of love for the world also develops and determines the dynamic of this reform: "the affirmation of ordinary life," a positive vision of ordinary life as hallowed by God. The motivation of those who pursue the "higher" path of contemplation becomes suspect and this critique is later transposed and used as a secular critique of Christianity.

Taylor acknowledges that there is another story of Western "secularization" in addition to the "Reform Master Narrative" that he tells. It is the "Intellectual Deviation story," which deals with changes in theoretical understanding, mainly among learned and related elites. Hans Blumenberg presents a disturbing version of this story in *The Legitimacy of the Modern Age*. In obvious complicity with reform, these changes helped to destroy the medieval-Christian cosmos and bequeath a kind of "worldlessness" that became a hallmark of the modern age.

Chapter 5, "Ambivalence and the Critique of Modernity," turns to examine the work of two of Martin Heidegger's Jewish students, Hannah Arendt and Hans Jonas, which can be understood as responses to modern worldlessness and as critiques of a modernity that was characterized by

Jonas as a revival of Gnosticism. Jonas and Arendt present a school of resistance to modern Gnosticism that has a profound affinity with Christian attempts to love and to recompose the world. Arendt learns from as well as criticizes Augustine in her attempt to show modern persons how to love the world. By contrast with her *amor mundi*, Theodor Adorno resists the same "dark times" by adopting a radically secularized version of *contemptus mundi*. Both aspects of Christian ambivalence about the world, *amor* and *contemptus*, are parts of a repertoire of resistance to the "world" of modernity.

Chapter 6, "Ambivalence and Discipleship," considers how Christian discipleship is to be re-envisaged in relation to both the history of ambivalence about the "world" I have outlined and to the religious crisis of the 1960s. I consider Jacques Maritain's *The Peasant of the Garonne* and responses to secularization by theologians of *ressourcement* before offering a revisionary reading of Dietrich Bonhoeffer and Thomas Merton and returning to Charles Taylor to consider his own response to his account of the making of a secular age. One of the marks of Christian discipleship must surely be the need to continue to live with ambivalence about the "world." I argue that Bonhoeffer and Merton were faithful to this ancient ambivalence, instead of presenting them as simply moving from a world-denying to a world-affirming ethos; and so I show how they conceive of the balance between presence to the world and detachment from the world that authentic disciples must seek.

Chapter I: Communities of Ambivalence

Flight from the world and the salvation of the world

THERE IS A STRANGE paradox inherent in the gospel. The first disciples did not choose between loving and hating the world. They both loved and hated the world. Saint John says it most clearly: "God so loved the world that he gave his only Son so that anyone who believes in him will never perish but will have everlasting life" (John 3:16, NRSV). But he also says, "Do not love the world or anything in the world. If anyone loves the world, love for the Father is not in them. For everything in the world—the lust of the flesh, the lust of the eyes, and the pride of life—comes not from the Father but from the world. The world and its desires pass away, but whoever does the will of God lives forever . . ." (1 John 2:15–16, NRSV). He then says in 1 John 5:19 (NRSV): "We know that we are children of God, and that the whole world is in the power of the evil one."

Loving the world has been opposed to hating the world, and this opposition is seen as a choice between a fundamentally biblical love of the world as God's good creation and an attitude that is much more gnostic or Platonic than Christian. Hating the world has become associated with a flight from the world into the desert or a monastery, an attitude expressed by Peter Damian (1007–1072) in the opening of his life of Saint Romuald: "Against you, unclean world, I protest!"

But this monastic attitude to the world is not a simple one. It all depends on the point of view from which the world is considered. Which definition of the world are we talking about? Is it the world as it was made by God or the world as it is? In monastic theology, the world as it was in the beginning and as it is to become is God's creation, which he saw was very good. We should love it as he does to the point of sacrificing ourselves for it. But what about the world that has become unclean because of our sin?

This is not the world God willed; it is not the same world God made. It is a world that we have made by our sin, a world that is the enemy of God and our enemy too, and which can only be overcome by the victory Saint John also speaks of, *even our faith*.

Since our sinful or fallen world is organized against God, it imprisons us in the circle of its disobedience. We must begin by breaking out of this circle to find God again. We must flee the world to free ourselves. This cannot always be dismissed as escapism. Only by fleeing and keeping our distance from the fallen world will we be in a position to work at saving it. We are not being realistic unless we start by hating the world. Only by hating the world as it is can we love the world as God willed it. Only thus can we give it the witness of the saving, recreating love that God never ceases to give. And so our flight from the world is tied to the salvation of the world; loving and hating the world go together.[1]

If, as we shall see, it has not always been clear in this theology what is God's good creation and what is fallen, this later monastic attitude to the world still shows us something of the attitude of the early church. Carl Schmitt declared that the Catholic Church has never really decided to be entirely in the world or out of the world.[2] This attitude goes right back to the first communities of Christians. Like the later monastic communities, these early Christians can be characterized as communities of ambivalence about the world.[3]

Seeking the welfare of the city, coming out of Babylon

Paul, and other Christian writers after him, use metaphors of immigrant life to describe the engagement of the Christians in the cultural world around them. Christians are resident aliens in a city—the word used is *paroikeo* and its cognates (Eph 2:18; 1 Peter 2:11, NRSV). They are the *diaspora* or exiled people of God (1 Peter 1:1, NRSV). It is as if ancient Christians were made immigrants by their conversion, generating nonnegotiable tensions that still confront Christians today.[4]

They didn't fully belong to the city because they refused to participate in the civic cults that defined social identity. They claimed to be able to tell

1. Bouyer, *Introduction to Spirituality*, 186–88
2. Schmitt, *Roman Catholicism and Political Form*, 7–8
3. Meeks, *The Origins of Christian Morality*, 52–65.
4. Meeks, *The Origins of Christian Morality*, 50.

you who you are, independent of the ways in which the social and religious system of the city gives you your identity. They laid claim to a loyalty potentially at odds with that system. They made strong claims about the universality of their community and its normative status for the future of the whole human race. But where is their *politeia?* Is it somewhere in the sky (Phil 3:20, NRSV) or can it be established upon earth? The motley groups of Christians in urban households saw themselves as pilgrims seeking a city made by God (Heb 11:16, 12:22, 13:14, NRSV).

An anonymous second-century apology known as the *Letter to Diognetus* explains that Christians do not have their own land, language, or customs. There are no Christian cities for them to come from. But what the soul is to the body, the Christians are to the world. As the soul animates all the organs of the body, so Christians are present in all the cities of the world. They show forth the remarkable and unexpected nature of their *politeia* by living in their respective countries as resident aliens, taking part in everything as committed citizens, even though they are treated like foreigners. Every foreign land is their home and every home a foreign land. They find themselves in the flesh, but do not live according to the flesh (*Epistle to Diognetus* 5:4, 5, 8).[5]

Like a chameleon, which can focus its eyes in different directions at the same time, the first urban Christians were taught to develop both an earthly and a heavenly focus. They sought the welfare of the cities they lived in and at the same time also sought to come out of Babylon.

The prophet Jeremiah (29:7, NRSV) instructed the exiled people of God to *seek the welfare of the city*. Christians lived in societies that had long-established conventions by which the welfare of the city's inhabitants was secured with the help of leading citizens. First-century Christians were taught to embrace this tradition in order to help sustain and enhance the life of the cities in which they lived. Jeremiah's injunction provided a paradigm that enabled Christians as citizens to adopt and adapt the role of benefactor as they sought the city's welfare.[6] First Peter 2:11–3:17 (NRSV) in particular considers the theme of the welfare of the city in detail and exhorts its audience to let their light so shine before men that they would see their good works and glorify their Father in heaven: in civic life, in the households as Christian servants, in the marriage of Christians to non-Christian, and in

---

5. Blakeney, trans., *The Epistle to Diognetus.*
6. Winter, *Welfare of the City.*

the flash point situations where the Christian community appears to have been singled out for discrimination.

And yet the first churches were very far from being wholly world affirming. Their response to their context is mixed and ambivalent, if not contradictory.[7] At the same time they were seeking the benefit of the city, they defined themselves as carriers of transcendent visions and impulses against "the world," and so discipleship in the New Testament demands a very definite attitude towards the "world," that is, toward society as a whole and its fundamental values, means, and goals. This attitude always includes rejection of the world, although the specific object, form, and degree of that rejection vary from tradition to tradition.[8] It is at its most intense in John's Gospel, which draws a sustained and progressive contrast between the disciples and the Jews, and also in Revelation, with its uncompromising rejection of Rome and all the various aspects of its life and power. God's people are called to come out of Babylon so as not to share in her sins and receive her plagues (Rev 18:4), and this call in the last book of the Bible offers an interpretive key to the core message of all the others.[9]

A less intense position, although it is still austere, is present in Mark, which portrays an alternative social order with very different values and goals, as well as in Philippians, which proposes the surrendering of all personal entitlements despite the inevitable persecutions from the Jews. First Peter also presents the alternative social order of those who are called to follow Jesus through innocent suffering in a hostile Jewish and pagan context.

Ephesians and James present milder positions—an assimilation to God in and through ordinary, day-to-day tasks but one that is possible only to believers—and in James a full participation in the affairs of the world, but only as a friend of God. James 4:4 (NRSV), warns: "Adulterers! Do you not know that friendship with the world is enmity with God? Therefore whoever wishes to be a friend of the world becomes an enemy of God." In this plurality of traditions, increasing rejection of the world is associated with an emphasis on suffering as an essential part of discipleship.

---

7. Winter, *Welfare of the City*, 200–202, challenges Meeks's account of "ambivalence" as the best characterization of the mixed feelings of early Christians towards the Gentile cities in which they lived, feelings that were not and cannot be resolved. He shows that apostolic traditions created positive attitudes to the city but not that early Christians did not hate as well as love their cities.

8. Segovia, ed., *Discipleship in the New Testament*, 20–21.

9. Howard-Brook, *"Come Out, My People!"*

CHAPTER I: COMMUNITIES OF AMBIVALENCE

John: *in the world but not of the world*

This is clear in the Johannine texts of the New Testament in which the "world" plays a critical and ambivalent role. These texts allow us glimpses of the historical experience of some quite self-conscious communities. These groups came to retell the story of Jesus in a way that incorporated their own history of confrontation with other Jews, leading to hostility and alienation and finally to expulsion from the synagogue. What is remarkable is that this history is portrayed as the account of a crisis between the Logos, the Son of God, and the world, the *kosmos*, which was made through him and is the object of his love.

> The true light that gives light to everyone was coming into the world. He was in the world, and though the world was made through him, the world did not recognize him. He came to that which was his own, but his own did not receive him. Yet to all who did receive him, to those who believed in his name, he gave the right to become children of God. (John 1:9–12, NRSV)

In John 1–12, references to the world are mostly positive, while in John 13–20 and in 1 John they are mostly negative. The positive references relate largely to God's intention to save the world in the mission of his Son, and the negative ones to the situation of the community in the world after Jesus' departure. When considered in relation to God's will, the world can be redeemed and is the object of God's love; however, considered concretely, in its response to God's Son and to those who have become God's children through him, the world seems irredeemably hostile. John does nothing to explain or mitigate this paradox.

The world was created through the Logos who has now *become flesh*. He is the world's light and its savior (4:42, 12:47); he gives it life (6:33), for God loves it (3:16). The Savior comes into the world and then returns whence he came. Those whom he chooses, he chooses *out of the world* (15:19) and henceforward they are *in the world but not of the world*. Consequently the world hates them as it hated Jesus (15:18).

What is meant by the "world" is not something essential (matter or human nature) but something willed and willful. It is not the world of creation, of "nature," rather it is the world as it has been structured by human will and rationality, but also and especially by human self-absorption and selfishness in opposition to God and to the good of other people. Not everything human is evil; yet again and again men and women prefer the darkness.

The story of Jesus and the community's experience of hostility from neighbor and synagogue are transmuted into judgments about the world. Not merely the leaders in Jerusalem, but *the world* rejected Jesus. Not merely the local synagogue authorities, but *the world* hates his disciples.

The result of this understanding is to provide location and validation for a community disenfranchised by *the world* and its authorities. John's community has been compared to modern Black Christians for whom the world is also wrong because Jesus is right. Both groups believe that they are not who the world says they are; their true identity is to be found in the presence of Christ. Their alienation from their oppressor's world does not mean what the oppressor thinks it means, because Jesus himself experienced that same alienation. So it has been argued that for the Johannine Jesus to say, *They are not of the world just as I am not of world*, means the same thing as for James Cone, the founder of black liberation theology, to say that Jesus is Black.[10] In both cases a community's worth is affirmed against the denial of it by an oppressor through the group's knowledge that God stands with them, despite the strength and self-assurance of the world, and so they are able to withstand the world and resist its oppression. The whole tenor of the Farewell Discourse of John 14–17 teaches that presence of the Father and the Son in the Gospel of John enables both endurance and witness against the world. It enables struggle. John's Gospel is "spiritual" but that does not make it apolitical or escapist.

This community confronts the world in the solidarity of a sect. John's Gospel teaches the necessity for adherents to make a public choice between the world and the community of disciples. This choice is exhibited in some of the characters in the story. Nicodemus, who believes in Jesus but is secretly in fear of the Jews, remains in the night. The man born blind who is healed, boldly confutes the Pharisees, is expelled from the synagogue, and becomes a believer. The *work of God* is to believe (6:29, NRSV) and the one command of Jesus is *to love one another* (13:34–35, 15:12, NRSV). This commandment is directed to those who already believe that Jesus is the Messiah. Shockingly, it is restricted to love within the community, not to the neighbor or enemy. It is to be something among themselves, and precisely as such is to be the sign that they are his followers. A community of mutual love confronts the world. The community repeats again and again the confrontation of the presence of love in Jesus with the world's hatred, structured as violence and avarice. John calls this confrontation the world's

---

10. Rensberger, *Overcoming the World*, 122.

krisis, its judgment, a judgment it brings upon itself by its reaction to the light (3:19, NRSV). The community is called upon to bring about this crisis, a critical point of decision for or against love in the decision for or against God. God has acted to save the world; since the world refuses its salvation, God's act becomes its overthrow and defeat (16:33). The community of God's children perpetually endangers the world, and is perpetually endangered by it, precisely because it is a community of love.

Their mission is to *take away the sins of the world,* to draw people from darkness into light (1:29, 12:46, NRSV). The task of forgiving or retaining sins is given to the community by the risen Jesus in the context of their being sent as he was sent; it is orientated, not to community members only, but to *anyone* (20:21-23, NRSV). Like Jesus, the community is sent into the world with the revelation of God, and, like him, it meets with rejection. The function of John's Gospel, then, is to enable the community to step back from its situation of rejection, reflect upon it in the light of the fate of Jesus, and to be sent out again with its faith renewed. John's ambivalence about the world works not only to distance the community from the world but also both to affirm the community's identity and the possibility of conversion and salvation for people in the world.[11]

Paul: worldly asceticism

The Pauline churches did not confront the world with the passionate sectarian love of the Johannine communities. These fledging communities were invited by Paul to experiment with a new mode of existence in the world, a distinct expression of tension or ambivalence.

His discussion of the *kosmos* is concentrated in his letters to the Corinthians. The argument in 1 Corinthians starts out (1:18, NRSV) with a series of sharp contrasts between "the world" and "God." What is foolishness to one is wisdom to the other, what is weakness to the one is strength to the other, and vice versa. The synonyms of *kosmos* here include "this age," *houtos ho aion* (1:20, NRSV), but also "human beings" (1:25, NRSV) and perhaps "angels" as well. The "world" does not refer here to the physical universe, but to society, the human world, culture. The antitheses that Paul sets out, especially in the rhetorical climax of 1:26-31, assert an opposition between the values of the surrounding culture and the values implicit in God's action. For God has chosen the "foolish of the world," the "weak of the world,"

---

11. Rensberger, *Overcoming the World,* 144, drawing upon the work of Takashi Onuki.

the "common of the world," and the "despised [of the world]" to shame their opposites. God has chosen the things that are not *(ta me onta)* in order to bring to naught those that are *(ta onta)* (1:28, NRSV). Shaming his audience is merely a tactic incidental to Paul's real purpose. He wants to persuade them to change their thinking and their behavior. He writes to counter an incipient factiousness that derives from a competition for status and esteem in the Corinthian church (4:6–13). His argument implies a double irony. At one level he accuses humble people of behaving with comic hubris as if they were high and mighty. But there is a second, more serious level of irony. These no-accounts really have been made someone special by God's choice of them. However, they are in danger of throwing that away by acting as if the gospel had merely given them an advantage in the competition for status, now exercised in the microcosm of the Christian household, which they have polluted with the values of "the world."

Paul has one fundamental rule for all his communities: remain in the condition to which you were called. That is, "Let everyone lead the life which the Lord has assigned to him, and in which God has called him" (1 Cor 7:17, NRSV). In one passage he repeats the words *hos me*, "as if not" or "as not," five times.

> I mean, brothers and sisters, the appointed time has grown short; from now on, let even those who have wives be as though they had none (*hos me*), and those who mourn as though they were not mourning (*hos me*), and those who rejoice as though they were not rejoicing (*hos me*), and those who buy as though they had no possessions (*hos me*), and those who deal with the world as though they had no dealings with it (*hos me*). For the present form of this world is passing away.
>
> I want you to be free from anxieties. The unmarried man is anxious about the affairs of the Lord, how to please the Lord; but the married man is anxious about the affairs of the world, how to please his wife, and his interests are divided. And the unmarried woman and the virgin are anxious about the affairs of the Lord, so that they may be holy in body and spirit; but the married woman is anxious about the affairs of the world, how to please her husband. I say this for your own benefit, not to put any restraint upon you, but to promote good order and unhindered devotion to the Lord. (1 Cor 7:29–35, NRSV)

CHAPTER I: COMMUNITIES OF AMBIVALENCE

Paul is preaching what has been called a *meontology*, an account of the things that are not.[12] Furthermore, his is a double meontology: on the one hand, the form of the world is passing away and becoming nothing. But, on the other hand, what will take the place of the *god of this world* is at present nothing. It is simply the anguished vigilance of those who accept that Jesus is the Messiah and who await the Parousia, his return. How does one live this vigilance? One lives in it as if it were not, *hos me*. A waiting community, an anguished community, an abased community, an *ecclesia* of the wretched of the earth, living in the world as if it were not by attending to a call or demand that is not of this world. The messianic life is lived *hos me*, as if not.

What is required is an attitude of spiritual withdrawal, detachment. The world itself is not evil; thus, no complete renunciation of it is required. But it makes claims, demands commitment, the same kind of commitment the Lord requires. As long as one is in the world desiring to be pleasing to the Lord, a tension or division of commitment ensues. One is torn between the world and *the things of the Lord*. It is assumed by Paul that the supreme commitment must be to the Lord (1 Cor 7:35). What is required is an inner detachment, not physical withdrawal. Inner detachment is what is necessary, otherwise distraction and division will continue. What Paul recommends is a relativizing of all the things in the world, which relativizes Christian asceticism at the same time. It is an "inner-worldly asceticism" that does not renounce lower things but seeks to put them in their proper place, with clarity of purpose, steadfastness, and poise.[13]

At the center of Paul's rhetoric about the world is a set of analogies between the story of Jesus' crucifixion and resurrection and the desired dispositions and behavior of believers. Some are explicit, but they are more often implicit in metaphorical speech. Paul transforms what was for him the basic message of Christian faith into a malleable, polysemic trope. The implications of this trope for life in "the world" are summed up in Paul's sharp rebuke to the Galatian Christians: "Far be it for me to boast except in the cross of our Lord through whom the world was crucified to me and I to the world" (Gal 6:14, NRSV). This is not a warrant for rejecting and punishing the world and one's own body. For Paul to speak of the crucifixion is always to imply the resurrection. When we are dead to sin we are alive to God in Christ (Rom 6:11–13). Hence, Edwyn Hoskyns united the words Crucifixion-Resurrection with a hyphen as a slogan in his interpretation of Paul—and

12. Critchley, *The Faith of the Faithless*, 178.
13. Wimbush, *Paul the Worldly Ascetic*.

they are inscribed upon his gravestone in Grantchester churchyard. A Kierkegaardian "repetition," in which faith simultaneously gives up and gets back—transformed—the desired object, is closer to the double movement of Paul's concern.[14] But, unlike Kierkegaard, Paul is concerned with the integrity of a community: "For neither circumcision nor a whole foreskin is anything; what counts is a new creation" (Gal 6:15, NRSV). The trope, crucifixion of and to the world, declares that the social and religious division that for Jews was utterly fundamental, between those who were circumcised and those who were not, can no longer divide those who belong to the community that has been initiated into the death and resurrection of Jesus Christ.

The Christian Revolution

Louis Dumont and Marcel Gauchet have explained the distinctiveness and revolutionary significance of this ambivalence of the first Christians about the world. "What exactly is a believer in Christ?" Gauchet asks and takes his answer from Louis Dumont: "an individual outside-the-world." Dumont argues that the Western conceptions of equality and individualism that distinguish modern from traditional societies have their origins in early Christianity. Comparing Christianity at its inception with the Indian *sannyasin*, who renounce the world, and with later Christian monasticism, Dumont notices how the out-worldly individual in India never seems to have transformed his power into one that left the otherworldly religious sphere for a worldly one. But,

> What no Indian religion has ever fully attained and which was given from the start in Christianity is the brotherhood of love in and through Christ, and the consequent equality of all . . . Sociologically speaking, the emancipation of the individual through a personal transcendence, and the union of out-worldly individuals in a community that treads on earth but has its heart in heaven, may constitute a passable formula for Christianity.[15]

Christianity is life in the world outside the world. Nietzsche understood that Christianity consists of being in the world without being of the world. That is to say, it does not limit itself to adhering to inherence, to what is given. Two of Nietzsche's images illustrate what he sometimes claims to

---

14. Meeks, *The Origins of Christian Morality*, 64; and Gorman, *Apostle of the Crucified Lord*, chap. 5

15. Dumont, *Essays on Individualism*, 31.

be the experience at the heart of Christianity: the tightrope dancer and the child playing with dice. Neither relates to the world as a given by which she is surrounded; on the contrary, they relate to that in the world that makes an opening, rift, abyss, game, or risk.[16]

Gauchet argues that whoever scrupulously follows the message delivered by the incarnation becomes someone inwardly freed from any worldly affiliation by his or her secret dealings with an extra-worldly god. But he finds that Dumont's phrase, "an individual outside-the-world," does not take account of the dynamic tension inherent in the link between the here below and the beyond, a tension crucial to the development of the emergence of modernity from the inner logic of Christianity that he traces.

> Those individuals inwardly isolated from the world are still outwardly subjugated to it, both as corporeal and social beings. They had to win their spiritual autonomy by first turning against that part of themselves dependent on physical reality and controlled by it. Their individual liberty was won at the price of a personal split. In other words the religious division played itself out within them, it traversed and dwelt in them. But at the same time, God had willed and organized the sensory world from which we must separate ourselves in order to reach the heavens. How could the sensory be totally rejected when it was judged worthy for the Word-Made-Flesh? So if we are to radically distance ourselves from the sensory, we must also to some extent consent to it. We cannot completely reject the world, however impossible it may be to accommodate ourselves to it. We must reach a compromise between acceptance and rejection, a compromise that cannot be definitively defined. We find ourselves in a vicious circle of obligations: we must hold ourselves outside the world while admitting we live in it. The true originality of the relation to the world established by Christianity lay in this axiomized ambiguity, which was a direct refraction of the union of two natures in Christ. It made the Christian into a being torn between a duty of belonging and one of distancing, between forming an alliance with the world and being estranged from it. But also a being in whom this shuttling between worlds is to come to an end—a being who will one day reconcile choice for the beyond and systematic commitment to the here-below.[17]

This axiomized ambiguity in relation to the world will develop into a new worldliness and a new otherworldliness in patristic theology.

16. Alexandrova and Devisch, eds., *Retreating Religion*, 2–3.
17. Gauchet, *The Disenchantment of the World*, 131.

Chapter 2: A New Worldliness and a New Otherworldliness

Resident aliens seeking to recompose the world

THE "WORLD" IS NOT simply a synonym for created reality. It is both a material and a linguistic reality. As such it is not simply a given. It is also something that human beings fashion and contest. And the theology of the New Testament does not rest upon a fixed "Jewish background." It is caught up in the trajectory of changing Jewish understandings of the "world" that are expressed in a transition from the language of apocalypticism to that of Gnosticism.[1] Thus the generative moment of Christian language is one of dissonance and difficulty. Early Christianity is fundamentally disruptive of pre-existing forms of religious meaning and social belonging. It dissolves earlier worlds of symbolic understanding, and its foundational texts are filled with images of paradox and irony, and also by a pervasive suspicion of the appearances of the sacred and the orderly. Jesus fulfills prophecy but reconstructs it in fulfilling it. To be acceptable in the sight of God now requires only fellowship with Jesus; to be holy requires not separation from the impure but association with the impure: with the polluted corpse of the crucified and with those whom the crucified welcomed into his company. Paul, the emissary of Jesus, appears as a "fool," as a prisoner displayed in another's triumph, as a shining example of inarticulacy, squalor, and helplessness—this is how Paul describes himself in his letters to the Corinthians.

The initial Christian proclamation in the New Testament strongly suggests that the given environment—ritual, social, and political—is inherently unreliable or deceptive. The question thus posed to the emergent Christian institution is whether its language is to survive as a constant

---

1. Robinson, "'World' in Modern Theology," 105.

CHAPTER 2: A NEW WORLDLINESS AND A NEW OTHERWORLDLINESS

reenactment of the disruption in which it begins, suggesting a lasting and unhealable schism in the order of things, between the empirical world and the truth of revelation, or whether there is another level of unity to be sought and discerned at a deeper level than hitherto considered. The latter option will, in effect, argue that the world can be "reassembled" and that the appearance of rupture reflects prior error or distortion: now there is a new synthesis. The self-consistency and self-continuity of the community itself act as a kind of reassurance that order is somewhere restored and honored; the unity of the community and its history affirms the unity and of the divine source of its meaning.

If this reading is correct, second-generation Christianity has a particularly strong investment in tackling issues of continuity and stability, if only to explain how it locates itself in a world decisively disrupted and contradicted by what has been revealed, yet manifestly continuing: "the Christianity that emerged as the predominant voice was consistently anxious to put Humpty-Dumpty together again." The Christians wanted to reestablish a vision of the universe and its history that made one story, one system.[2]

It is in this context that the theological polarizations of the second century begin to make more sense. The cluster of systems identified as "gnostic" generally represent a commitment to the unreliability of the empirical environment and of the god responsible for it (for contingency, matter, history and human authority, including the human authority involved in Christian community life). They remained with the disruptive moment, but systematized it into a theory of "anti-history": there is always and necessarily a gulf between the world and the truth, between appearance and reality, between wisdom and convention or communal life. In contrast, the strategy typified in the apologists of the second century such as Justin Martyr, for example, insists upon unsuspected unities, not only the unity of Christian revelation with the law of Moses but also its unity with the theism of Socrates and Heraclitus: the history of divine action is one. This dovetails with an insistence on the unbroken witness of teaching and practice in the Christian community itself. Episcopal authority and "rules of faith" evolve side by side. The formulae of these rules invariably insist upon the unity of the Christian God with the God of "the law and the prophets," and also frequently appeal to their own unbroken ancestry and universality.

"Heresy" thus emerges as a concept in a specific historical situation. Not only is there a problem of a community or network of communities

---

2. Williams, *Why Study the Past?*, 41; and see Williams, "Defining Heresy."

faced with critical questions of self-definition, but the community itself deploys a set of foundational stories and images identifying it as disruptive or discontinuous, and its social patterns are separatist, subversive, and universalist. For such communities to maintain a continuous and coherent social presence over time, this disruptive foundation had to be supplemented with a different conceptuality that allowed the basic ruptures to be resolved in some way. And in this process, those who appeared to be reinscribing the primitive separatism in radical ways were inevitably the cause of anxiety to the emergent institution. Those who were struggling to establish a normative Christianity were struggling to recompose a world and a trustworthy social and ritual environment; heresy comes to be defined, tacitly or explicitly, as what splits this precariously achieved unity or coherence.

So it is that Irenaeus confronts gnostic otherworldliness with a new Christian worldliness, a doxological theology of the mutual glorification of God and creation. Against the gnostic separation of the old and new covenants, he taught the unity of the testaments in Christ: they were different because they were different stages in the one divine education of the human race. Against a gnostic separation of soul and body, spirit and flesh, spiritual and material existence, Irenaeus counters with the incarnation of God. The fact that God has become man, indeed flesh, proves that the redemption and resurrection of the entire earthly world is not just a possibility but also a reality. His doctrine of recapitulation teaches that, in Christ, God was involved not just in redeeming but also in restoring and recreating his world afresh. The incarnation and enfleshment of God in Christ means that the entire material world has already been transfigured and become a kind of sacrament through which the eyes of faith can see all things shining with the light of God in their endless beauty. Thus Irenaeus asserts not only the goodness and integrity of the created world but also the goodness and integrity of the God who created and sustains it.

Central to the development of a distinctly Christian cosmology was the idea of the *logos* or the Word of God. The prologue of the Fourth Gospel had already clearly expressed the essential role of the *logos* in the creation of the cosmos: "Through the Word all things came into being" (John 1:1, NRSV). Tertullian and Clement of Alexandria took this idea and used the Stoics' profound sense of the *logos* as the animating principle of the cosmos to develop a Christian cosmology. Responding to the gnostic claim that God is remote from the created world, Tertullian cited the Stoic teaching that through the *logos* God permeates the cosmos in the same way as honey in the comb. The

CHAPTER 2: A NEW WORLDLINESS AND A NEW OTHERWORLDLINESS

way the divine *logos* permeates the created world without losing its divinity is like the sun's relationship with its own rays, which are a portion and extension of their source. For Clement of Alexandria, the *logos* has three distinct but related dimensions: it is utterly transcendent, being identical with the totality of the ideas or powers of God; it is also the principle and pattern of everything that has been created; and it is the *anima mundi*, or world soul, the law and harmony of the universe, the power that holds it together and permeates it from the center to its uttermost limits.

Such ideas sustained the capacity of Christians to believe in and experience the presence of God in the created world. In the *fiat lux* of the account of creation in the book of Genesis, as well as in the luminous golden background of ancient Christian mosaics, the *logos* is expressed as light. According to Irenaeus, the word that speaks through the cross also speaks through the cosmos: because Christ is the Word of God, who in his invisible form pervades us universally in the whole world and encompasses its length and breadth and height and depth; and because the Son of God was crucified, this was imprinted in the form of the cross upon the universe.[3] This idea is later expressed in a Byzantine mosaic at the Mausoleum of Galla Placidia in Ravenna. The cosmic cross appears in a shallow dark blue dome in the midst of stars, which are arranged in concentric circles. Their diminishing size towards the center gives the viewer the impression of gazing up into the night sky.

Origen taught that a Christian could experience encounters with the *logos* that sustains the cosmos. One of the privileged places of this encounter was the reading of Scripture. Here the *logos* comes to light as an ardent love for the world within us. In the prologue to his commentary on the Song of Songs, Origen claims that if a person considers the grace of all the things that have been created in the Word, the shining beauty of them will so strike him that he will be wounded by Christ like an arrow and kindled with the blessed fire of his love. Here is a sensual, palpable *logos*, present to us, says Origen, much as touch, fragrance, sound, vision, and taste are present to us.

Within the Christian monastic tradition, tasting and chewing upon the *logos* became a way of life. For the monks of the Egyptian desert the *logos* arose from the silence as a powerful and numinous presence. To ruminate on, digest, and absorb such a word was to be brought into the presence of the Holy One. Nor was the natural landscape of the desert itself an

---

3. Irenaeus of Lyons, in Ladner, *Cosmos and Humankind*, 99.

insignificant part of this process. According to Athanasius's *Life of Antony*, the Word of God not only called Antony to withdraw into the desert, but also called him to a particular wild place in the remote desert simply named, "the inner mountain." For three days and nights, in the company of "a band of Saracens," he made his way across the harsh open landscape of the Galala Plateau to finally arrive at "a very high hill. Below the hill there was water—perfectly clear, sweet and quite cold, and beyond that were plains and a few untended date palms." Athanasius writes that, on seeing it for the first time, Antony immediately loved this place. He found the inner mountain so alluring that he remained on the mountain alone, planting a garden, giving himself fully to the life of the place, and spending the rest of his life there. The inner mountain became "his own home," the place where he learnt to keep his heart awake. There, Antony became: "one who as Scripture says, having *trusted in the Lord, was like Mount Sion* keeping his mind unshaken and undisturbed." The account of the experience related in *The Life of Antony*—of a monk living in the deep solitude of the desert at home in the world, in himself, and in God—became an emblem of what the early monks sought: a kind of paradise. The subsequent tradition of monastic stability, or devotion to place, owes much to this early sense that places like the inner desert are alive with the power of the *logos*, that they speak to us with a particular voice, and that rumination upon the word and the spirit of a place are integral elements in the rhythms of spiritual life.[4]

Christians thus developed a tradition of an *amor mundi* through a vision of a recomposed created world participating through Christ in the mystery of God. This tradition came to take the shape of a Platonist-Christian synthesis expressed in a "sacramental ontology."[5] This synthesis allowed for an affirmation of the truth, goodness, and beauty of the created order while safeguarding the infinite difference between creation and God. The participatory anchoring of the created order in the eternal Logos meant the recognition of a tremendous surplus value in created objects. At the same time, the tradition avoided assigning ultimate value to creation, since its being is *derived* from the Creator. This sacramental ontology conceived of being in terms of the relationship of the sensible world around us to ultimate spiritual reality and understood the Eucharist as the intensification of Christ's sacramental presence in the whole of creation: while the church

---

4. See Burton-Christie, "Christianity (4)," 324–26; and Burton-Christie, *The Blue Sapphire of the Mind*, 41–53.

5. Boersma, *Heavenly Participation*, 19–39; and Tyson, *Returning to Reality*.

CHAPTER 2: A NEW WORLDLINESS AND A NEW OTHERWORLDLINESS

fathers looked to the bread and wine of the Eucharist as the sacrament in which Christ was really present, they also believed that Christ was mysteriously present in the entire created order.

Everything in the world of nature is meant to lead us back to God. In that sense, created matter is meant to serve eucharistically. By treating the world as a eucharistic offering in Christ, received *from* God and offered *to* him, we are drawn into God's presence. The entire cosmos is meant to serve as a sacrament: a material gift from God in and through which we enter into the joy of his heavenly presence.

And yet the early Christian tradition could still express a profound ambivalence about the "world"—the natural, the bodily, profane culture, the public, and the political. The original Christian form of unworldliness was that of Jewish apocalyptic defined in relation to the Parousia or the second coming of Jesus. This unworldliness also came to be redefined in relation to a Platonic ontology of transcendence. The New Testament suspicion was of the "world" defined as an expression of values antithetical to the gospel. In patristic exegesis this suspicion could also became fear and revulsion in relation to the world defined as material reality, embodied existence, and even the cosmos itself.

The original Christian ambivalence about the world was thus redefined. The new Platonist-Christian synthesis allowed theologians to recompose their world and to assert its unity and coherence in relation to the divine using the resources of philosophical ontology; however, this synthesis generally meant accepting the Platonist hierarchy of values. Material realities, being corruptible, occupied a lower place in this hierarchy than nonmaterial or spiritual realities, which through their affinity with God, the supreme spirit, were seen as having eternal value and significance. A new worldliness and a new otherworldliness developed simultaneously, new ways of loving and hating the world.

Even for a sacramental ontology there was the danger of an imbalance. For example, Gregory of Nyssa's anagogical (or heaven-directed) approach doesn't always seem to do sufficient justice to the goodness of the material, created order. He consistently seeks anagogical progression in the divine life and this almost always implies a turn away from the material toward the spiritual. Thus, while he affirms the goodness of the physical body and of the institution of marriage, he teaches that marriage and sexuality are inevitably bound up with the passions, which hinder our upward journey. Participation is a spiritual rather than a material reality. In his work *On*

Virginity, even as he acknowledges that material beauty participates in intellectual beauty, in the same breath he adds that the soul is supposed to "forget the matter in which the beauty is encased."[6] While Gregory frequently speaks about participation, he doesn't talk very often about participation of physical, created realities in the life of God. As a result, he sometimes gives the impression of wanting to leave behind the *sacramentum* in favor of the *res*. A sacramental ontology could encourage this impatience to turn from the *signum* to the *res*, from the sign to the reality.[7]

A theology of ambivalence

Augustine offers the supreme patristic account of Christian ambivalence about the world. This ambivalence is evident in his dominant image for the human life: *peregrinatio*, which at once signifies a journey to the homeland (a pilgrimage) and the condition of exile from the homeland. For Augustine, all human beings are, in the earthly life, exiles from their true homeland: heaven. Some, but not all, become pilgrims seeking a way back to the heavenly homeland, a return mediated by the incarnate Christ. Becoming a pilgrim begins with attraction to beauty. The return journey therefore involves formation, both moral and aesthetic, in loving rightly.

This image has occasioned anguish in ethical thought in the last century. Critics such as Hannah Arendt allege that Augustine's vision of Christian life as a pilgrimage casts a pall of sorrow and longing over this life in favor of happiness in the next. Augustine's eschatological orientation robs the world of beauty and ethics of urgency.

But Augustine's portrayal of the journey to the heavenly homeland does not make a desert out of this world. Attraction to beauty initiates the journey. Ongoing confirmation in love to beauty—Christ's and our neighbor's—sustains the pilgrim. The full glory of this beauty waits in heaven. The satisfaction of the desire for beauty that drives the pilgrim's journey is, indeed, deferred. And yet the necessary interplay of earthly and eschatological love and beauty means that persevering along the road to the homeland requires developing a taste—the right taste—for earthly things. Guided by the eschatological end, our perceptions of and responses to earthly things are reformed according to the beauty that truly fulfills desire. The pilgrim

---

6. Gregory of Nyssa, "On Virginity," 11.292.12–13, in St. Gregory of Nyssa, *Ascetical Works*, 39.

7. Boersma, *Embodiment and Virtue in Gregory of Nyssa*, 9.

CHAPTER 2: A NEW WORLDLINESS AND A NEW OTHERWORLDLINESS

formed in and by truth, goodness, and beauty itself thus experiences the truly good beauty of the earth. This foretaste is real; its reality rests on its heavenly source. Only in light of that earthly eschatological continuity is beauty rightly and truly loved. The eschatological orientation of loving beauty opens the Christian pilgrim to true experiences of beauty and true relationships of love with others in this life. The continuity between earthly and eschatological beauty that creates the continuity between earthly and eschatological love rests on the mediation of Christ. As incarnate God, Christ is both the way and the end. He is the way because he is the end, simultaneously. Adhering to Christ, we have at once grasped the end even as we travel the way.[8] As Catherine of Siena was later to declare, "All the way to heaven is heaven because He said I am the Way."[9]

Augustine exemplifies a new worldliness in his use of Platonic ontology to recompose the world and assert its unity and coherence in his response to Manichaean Gnosticism. Plotinus had rejected a form of Gnosticism and his teaching served to deny the darkest strand of the Manichaean view of the world, the conviction that the power of the Good was essentially passive, the conviction that it could only suffer the violent impingement of an active and polluting force of evil. He had argued in his *Ennead* VI that the spiritual world was fundamental to the world of place and time, while still remaining distinct from it. He also argued that the power of the Good always maintained the initiative: the One flowed out, touching everything, molding and giving meaning to passive matter, without itself being in any way violated or diminished.

> Evil is not alone: by virtue of the nature of Good, the power of Good, it is not Evil only: it appears, necessarily, bound around with bonds of Beauty, like some captive bound in fetters of gold; and beneath these it is hidden so that, while it must exist, it may not be seen by the gods, and that men need not always have evil before their eyes, but that when it comes before them they may still be not destitute of Images of the Good and Beautiful for their Remembrance. (*Ennead* I.viii.5)

Plotinus's cosmos is a continuous, active whole that could admit no brutal cleavages and no violent irruptions. Each being in it drew strength and meaning from its dependence on this living continuum. Evil, therefore, was only a turning away to separateness: its very existence assumed the

---

8. Stewart-Kroeker, *Pilgrimage*, 2.
9. Cited by Day, *On Pilgrimage*, 161.

existence of an order, which was flouted while remaining no less real or meaningful. It was the self-willed part that was diminished by losing contact with something bigger and more vital than itself.[10]

Augustine writes in the *Confessions* that he no longer desired a better world, because he was thinking of creation as a whole: in the light of this more balanced discernment he had come to see that higher things are better than lower, but that the sum of all creation is better than the higher things alone (VII.xiii.19). He was able to make this cosmological affirmation and develop a view of evil as insubstantial, as an absence or lack, and on which he later elaborates, only after reading the *libri platonicorum* that he encountered in Milan.

Augustine also exemplifies the new otherworldliness in his commitment to the radical interiority of the spirituality significant and in his complex attitudes to human embodiment and sexuality. "Among modern thinkers, he is more feared than loved. Rumors about Augustine and Augustinianism abound. Some of them are true."[11] In particular there is the question of how much or little his Christianity was shaped by Manichaean thought.[12]

Manichaeanism positioned itself as an alternative, and indeed "true," Christianity. Manichaeans regarded Nicene-Catholics as crude semi-Christians. Their theology can be understood in terms of the initially distinct "Eastern" and "Western" trajectories of the Christian movement. These two rival forms of Christianity were separated at birth, acculturated in different environments, each in their own way shaped by and adapted to local conditions. In the West, the Christian movement entered into a Hellenistic milieu that played a large role in defining its modes of expression, the context of assumptions within which it would possess meaning, and its terminology and practices. In the East, the Christian movement developed on the basis of different cultural traditions and assumptions. Just as Augustine found concordance between Christ and Plato, so Mani found key alignments between Christ, Zoroaster, and the Buddha, producing the quite distinct form of Christianity that we call Manichaeanism. Each developed selected features of the shared root tradition, and then collided in their differences.

For this reason, Augustine could not just treat Manichaeanism as a rejected "other," a non-Christian heathenism. He had to deal with

---

10. Brown, *Augustine of Hippo*, 99.
11. Gregory, *Politics and the Order of Love*, 13, cited in Kiess, *Hannah Arendt*, 114–16.
12. BeDuhn, "'Not to Depart from Christ,'" 7.

CHAPTER 2: A NEW WORLDLINESS AND A NEW OTHERWORLDLINESS

Manichaeans referencing Christian authorities (Jesus, Paul), and Christian themes (evil, world as prison, enslavement to sin, the soul's desire for "return" to "another world"). The Nicene tradition he adopted had partially defined itself as against "heresies," including Manichaeanism, and had made certain contrasting choices, in particular emphasizing God as the creator and providential orderer of the world, and free will. It had downplayed or set aside features of the earlier Christian movement that had become too closely associated with its rivals, just as those rivals likewise represented developments of selected Christian themes.

Augustine originally adopted this developed Nicene set of positions in all their contrast to the Manichaeanism he had abandoned. Then, for reasons that he does not expressly identify, he gradually appropriated from Manichaeanism elements of the Christian tradition that the former emphasized, but had been neglected in the Nicene-Catholic tradition. While his motives remain uncertain, the context of his shift is clear: his ongoing struggle with the Manichaeans of North Africa and his effort to convert them. This continuing encounter with Manichaeans brought to Augustine's attention certain elements of the Christian tradition that Catholics had previously downplayed, in particular Paul's witness to the debility of the will, the mind's struggle against the "flesh." With reference to the same Pauline passages cited in his public debate by his antagonist, the Manichaean presbyter and missionary Fortunatus, Augustine constructs a very similar concept of salvation by grace that involves some sort of predetermining election quite similar to what Fortunatus and the Manichaean bishop Faustus argued Paul meant in speaking of the birth of the New Man as coming out of a mixed mass of good and bad elements in the Old Man who is not really a conscious and responsible human being at all.

> If today Christian theologians find in Paul the apostle of grace, it is due to the powerful influence of Augustine, the doctor of grace. And even though there are distinctive qualities to Augustine's doctrine of grace that have nothing to do with Manichaeanism, the degree to which he found in Paul a source of such an idea derives from his unique position between Manichaean and Christian theology.[13]

A sense of the heaviness of material existence pervades Augustine's thinking about the meaning of sin. He often imagines sin as an experience of being "weighed down," unable to move. This is consistent with the

---

13. BeDuhn, "'Not to Depart from Christ.'"

Manichaean understanding of embodied existence and their attention to the "battle for the body," which they believed to be congenitally antagonistic to the good.[14]

The Manichaean community was part of a diverse Christian movement that, in Augustine's lifetime, was being distilled through normativizing processes consolidating Catholic dominance. It fell to individual leaders such as Augustine to determine what would be included within the "Catholic" product of those processes, whether derived from within, (for example christological positions, or traditions of biblical exegesis), or without (for example Platonic ontology), the larger Christian movement. Thus, Augustine was in a position to make normative judgments that identified some aspects of Manichaeanism as suitably "Christian" and justified appropriating and adapting them for the "Catholic" synthesis, while rejecting others as foreign bodies within Christianity as he and his colleagues were defining it. His theological engagement with Manichaean doctrine was both a boundary-forming and boundary-crossing activity, an intrinsic part of the development of his account of true Christianity. In certain respects Augustine fashioned a historical synthesis out of the two conflicting traditions, Manichaean and Nicene-Catholic Christianity, that had successively claimed his allegiance.

It was this synthesis that determined Augustine's response to the reinforcement of the new Christian worldliness by the beginning of *tempora christiana*, Christian times.

The basic tensions in Christian theology, which express themselves in opposed Christian postures towards the created world, became manifest in Christian political theologies.[15]

Islam conquered its empire self-consciously with a confident tradition of political theology that provides a rich legal tradition for governing social life. By contrast, Christianity acquired its empire accidentally, beginning with the conversion of Constantine, and was forced to derive the principles of its political theology under the changing press of circumstances.

Christ had gone up on high; he had led captivity captive. So the nations and rulers of the world were confronted with the rule of God, triumphantly present in a community that owned no other rule. The first Christians saw themselves riding on the wave of the future, conquering society with the word of truth and the blood of the martyrs, God's own

---

14. BeDuhn, "'The Metabolism of Salvation.'"
15. Lilla, *The Stillborn God*, 40.

strategy for success. It was only a matter of time before the pagan empire, too, with its repellent idolatry, would yield before Christ's army. And so it happened (as it seemed) with Constantine's victory at the Milvian Bridge. To his legitimator, Eusebius, it seemed like the victory of God. Structurally it even seemed to fill the place of the Parousia.[16]

In the Platonist-Christian theology of Eusebius, the social order is now part of an all-embracing cosmic order, grounded in the ultimate rationality of the world. The head of the colossus of Constantine preserved on the Capitoline Hill in Rome is an overpowering cult object that depicts him with his eyes uplifted in the posture of prayer, as he is also depicted on his coinage. In his speech in praise of Constantine, Eusebius presents him as the reflection and counterpart in the visible world of God's invisible *logos*.[17] The emperor lifting his eyes to heaven is an intermediary between the terrestrial empire and the heavenly kingdom. He is the representative of the heavenly kingdom placed at the head of the terrestrial empire. In his sacred countenance, human affairs are drawn into the cosmic order.

Augustine's response to the Christianization of the Empire, by contrast, is ultimately a healthy ambivalence that expresses the disruptive Christian vision still articulated by his Manichaean antagonists.

His political theology is implicit in his rereading of Paul in the mid-390s AD after his debate with Fortunatus. This rereading is the key to his sense of the power of sin over our lives, of our powerlessness to free ourselves from its control, of our need for the grace of God for the least initiative to achieve salvation. Human life becomes a chronic conflict between sin and grace, and history the theater in which this conflict is played out on a large scale. Salvation is no longer, as he had once thought, an ordered progression to a distant goal. It is a sustained miracle of divine initiative. His previous confidence in man's moral capabilities collapsed; the notion of a justice attainable by human effort or through the arrangements of social living was revealed as illusory.

For a brief period in the 390s he had joined the chorus of his contemporaries in their triumphant jubilation over the victory of Christianity. But Augustine's mind changed. By the time he began writing the *City of God* in late 412 or 413 AD he had reinterpreted the need for political authority and institutions in terms of this new vision of human existence: social life too has to be seen as radically fallen and infected with

---

16. O'Donovan, *The Desire of the Nations*, 198.
17. Eusebius, *Oration in Praise of Constantine*, sections 4–5.

sin. Pride, rooted in self-love, often turns into *libido dominandi*—the lust for power. He reinterprets the authority of government and its coercive mechanisms. Their object is no longer to embody an overarching divinely rational order of society, but to secure its fabric against the forces of disintegration, helping to check conflict and to minimize its disruptive power. Christians are to be disenchanted but not disengaged from this task, and Augustine presents an account of the "ideal statesman" that bridges the concepts of *ecclesia* and *res publica*.[18]

There can be no identification of the Roman order with the Christian one—no *imperium christianum*. Augustine's Eusebian enthusiasm for, or wonder at, the success of the once persecuted church and the apparent demise of paganism gives way to a profound ambivalence. Persecutions may return. The church is filled with pagans. Do not the same people who fill the churches also fill the theaters for pagan festivals? For all the worthy qualities of Rome that Augustine praises without irony, the Christian must remain ambivalent. The so-called virtues of pagans are not genuine virtues at all for they are vitiated by their pride.

This ambivalence delivers Augustine from both the apocalyptic hostility to Rome as an apostate demonic order found in Hippolytus and a Eusebian acceptance of the ideology of empire for which Rome is a sacramental vehicle of grace. Augustine resisted the growing coincidence of the church and the world. Between incarnation and consummation, history is still an interim that is dark in its ambivalence.

The world recomposed as "saeculum"

Augustine's refusal of the ideology of empire in turn informs his account of the world as *saeculum*. There does not have to be a final and sacred political order created in order for the integrity of the church to survive.[19]

Augustine used the words *mundum* and *saeculum* to refer to the world.[20] He uses the word *mundum* to refer to what is to be used rather than enjoyed. For example, in his *On Christian Doctrine* he says, "If we wish to return to our homeland, where alone we can be truly happy, we have to use this world, not enjoy it" (1.4:4). He explains that he means only

---

18. Markus, *Saeculum*, xi; Dodaro, "Ecclesia and Res Publica"; Dodaro, *Christ and the Just Society*.

19. Williams, "Secularism, Faith and Freedom," 23–36.

20. Clark, "World."

CHAPTER 2: A NEW WORLDLINESS AND A NEW OTHERWORLDLINESS

that one should not live "for this world" so as to make its enjoyment one's main aim in life (2.3.3). When John said, "And the world did not know him" (1:10, NRSV), Augustine says that he refers to those "human beings greedy to enjoy the creature instead of the creator [who] had taken on the fashion of this world (*configurati huic mundo*)" (1.12.12). His frequent use of the "world" in this pejorative sense is derived from Scripture, where Satan is spoken of as the prince of this world.

For Augustine, *saeculum*, as he makes clear in *City of God*, means "in this passing age" (1.Preface), an age beyond the sacred history related in Scripture, between the incarnation and the Parousia, the last age before the end of the world. And life in the last *saeculum* is ultimately for Augustine an obscure and mysterious tension between the ends of two types of cities and two types of love. "We see then that the two cities were created by two kinds of love: the earthly city was created by self-love reaching the point of contempt for God, the Heavenly City by the love of God carried as far as contempt of self" (14.28). Both are forced to share the common goods necessary to this mortal life, though each city "uses" these goods in very different ways according to their two different loves. The key division between these two types of citizens is the nature of their love. Augustine believes that every person in history can be separated by the quality and direction of his love: either the love of God (*amor dei*) or the love of self (*amor sui*), either humility or pride. Love is either good and directed outward toward God or bad and directed inward towards the self.

These two different loves are symbolically represented by Augustine in the two scriptural cities of Jerusalem and Babylon. The whole of history is a conflict between these two cities, a tension of forces that will only appear in their naked reality beyond time and history. The sphere in which all human institutions have their being is radically ambiguous and they are all infected with this ambiguity. The city of God is not identified with the church nor is the earthly city identified with Rome. In this world (*saeculum*) the two cities are entangled (*permixtae*) and mingled (*perplexae*) with one another and they will remain so until the Last Judgement shall separate them (*City of God* 1.35). The church is on pilgrimage toward the heavenly city yet is inextricably mixed and bound to the necessities of this mortal life. The ambiguity and confusion of life in the last age not only affects institutions but also individuals who find themselves at war with themselves: the two types of love exist within each individual.

Augustine's concept of the "secular," originating in this temporal and historical use of *saeculum* as "age," gradually shifts to include a new spatial sense of the secular as "worldly."[21] In the classical world, *saeculum* meant simply "an age," as in the period of a single generation, or the period covered by the longest duration of person's life, up to a century. There is no precedent in the uses of the word "*saeculum*" in classical literature for Augustine's spatiotemporal sense of the word. The first departure from traditional usage comes from Augustine's contrast of "secular" classical literature of paganism with sacred Scripture (*City of God* 18.40). In chapter 6 of book 10 of the *City of God*, Augustine describes the inordinate love of things that pertain to this present age as "worldly desire" or "secular love" (*concupiscentia saecularis*), in contrast to a right desire for imperishable things. In the first book of his *On Christian Doctrine* he asserts the need for an *ordo amoris* in distinguishing between enjoying something and using it to make the point that God is to be enjoyed but other things ought only to be used.[22] These temporal things are not inherently bad but must be loved with reference to their true end in God (who is the true source and origin of all that is good and beautiful) if they are to be loved appropriately. Augustine refers to this ephemeral and perishable sense of "the allurements of the world" (*blandimenta saeculi*) as "the perversity of this world" (*perversitas saeculi*) (5.17–18). In these uses, both temporal (the allurements and perversity "of this age") and spatial ("of this world") senses of the *saeculum* are expressed.

Augustine's conception of worldliness is complex. Augustine contrasts the *civitas caelestis* with the *civitas terrena* but never with a *civitas saecularis*. Neither city nor their citizens are fully manifest in the present age, nor is either fully embodied in Rome or the church. *Saeculum* names the time of the inextricable and confusing mixture of the two cities, an age of competing loves in which loyalties are constantly being negotiated. There is no such thing as a separate *civitas saecularis*. There is only the time of the secular, the time that remains before the end. The spatial sense of the word *saeculum* is secondary and derivative. It begins to refer to the space occupied by the two cities on their way to their final destinations. That is, the "world." But *saeculum* continues to primarily denote a period of time or an age, not a space or sphere. Only in a secondary or derivative way does *saeculum* refer to a space or place. In this secondary way, the

---

21. Clair, "The Concept of the Secular."
22. Gregory, *Politics and the Order of Love*, 335–50.

eschatological and temporal sense of the deferral of the two cities is transposed into a new spatial concept of the *saeculum* as a worldly domain. But this is not the modern conception of the "secular" as a neutral and absolutely autonomous domain. The spatial sense remains dependent upon and inseparable from Augustine's temporal sense: *in hoc saeculo* could be translated, "during the world."[23]

Life in the last age is characterized not only by the obscure and perplexing mixture of the two cities but also by a pervasive sense of the instability and mutability of time itself. The last *saeculum* is a transitory, inconstant age in which *homines temporalis* (*City of God* 12.15) are subject to frailty, fear, and sorrow (*City of God* 19.8). The significance of the final *saeculum* for Augustine, then, is ultimately that human life is time-bound, mortal, contingent, and vulnerable. The "world" in which Rome was sacked by the Goths has become a *senectus mundi*, an "old world." Thus his account of the *saeculum* is related to his stated aim in writing the *City of God*: "to persuade the proud how great is that virtue of humility, which, not by human achievement, but by divine grace bestowed from on high, raises us above all the earthly pinnacles of this inconstant age" (1.Preface). Humility is constantly espoused in the *City of God*. The refrain, "God resisteth the proud but gives grace to the humble," which merges two crucial scriptural citations for Augustine (Jas 4:6 and 1 Pet 5:5), is repeated from the first pages to the last. This espousal of humility informs his insistence on the temporal sense of the secular. In book 19 he argues that, given the frailty of time-bound human life, the ancient philosophical searches for *felicitas* through the rational acquisition of virtue only represent different forms of denial. Recognition of this sense of the vulnerability of life in the *saeculum* opens the possibility of radical hope in a future replenishment and restoration, in resurrection. This is the insight of humility and Augustine's response to the earthly.[24]

Ascetic closure: the end of ancient Christianity?

Augustine's *City of God* is far from being a book about flight from the world, and the ascetic models of Christian life that were later to efface his teaching. It is a book about being otherworldly in the world.[25] In his

23. Matthews, *A Theology of Public Life*, 10.
24. Clair, "The Concept of the Secular," 348.
25. Brown, *Augustine of Hippo*, 324.

sermons he gave his hearers in city congregations a sense of identity. He told them where they belonged and to what they must be loyal. They are citizens of Jerusalem homesick like the Jews in Babylon, set apart in their exile by what they love and what they hate. Preaching on 1 John 3:2, "We shall be like him, for we shall see him as he is," he said, "The whole life of a good Christian is a holy longing ... that is our life, to be trained by longing, and our training through the holy longing advances in the measure that our longings are severed from the love of this world."[26] And in a sermon on Psalm 137 he warned:

> But take heed how you dwell among them, O people of God, O body of Christ, O high-born band of wanderers (for thy home is not here, but elsewhere), lest when you love them, strive for their friendship, and fear to displease such men, Babylon begin to delights you and you forget Jerusalem. In fear then of this, see what the Psalmist directs, see what follows. *If I forget you, O Jerusalem*, amid the speeches of those who hold me captive, amid the speeches of treacherous men, amid the speeches of men who ask with ill intent, asking, yet unwilling to learn ... What then? *If I forget you, O Jerusalem, let my right hand forget me. Let my tongue cleave to my jaws, if I do not remember you.* That is, let me be dumb, he says, if I do not remember you. For what word, what sound does he utter, who does not utter the songs of Sion? That is our tongue, the song of Jerusalem. The song of the love of this world is a strange tongue, a barbarous tongue, which we have learnt in our captivity. Dumb then will he be to God, who forgets Jerusalem. And it is not enough to remember: for her enemies too remember her, desiring to overthrow her. "What is that city?" say they, "Who are the Christians? What sort of men are the Christians? Would that they were not Christians." Now the captive band hath conquered its capturers; still they murmur, and rage, and desire to slay the holy city that dwells as a stranger among them. Not enough then is it to remember: take heed how you remember. For some things we remember in hate, some in love. And so, when he had said, *If I forget thee, O Jerusalem*, he added at once, *if I prefer not Jerusalem in the height of my joy*. For there is the height of joy where we enjoy God, where we are safe in united brotherhood, and the union of citizenship. There no tempter shall assail us, no one be able so much as to urge us on to any allurement: there nothing will delight us but good: there all want will die, there perfect bliss will dawn on us.[27]

---

26. Augustine, *Homilies*, 69.
27. Augustine, *Expositions*, 168–73.

CHAPTER 2: A NEW WORLDLINESS AND A NEW OTHERWORLDLINESS

But the *peregrinus* is also a temporary resident in the cities of the Empire. He or she must accept an intimate dependence on the life around him and understand that it was created to provide conditions that he or she is glad to share with others.

> So the heavenly City, too, uses the earthly peace in the course of its earthly pilgrimage. It cherishes and fosters, as far as it can without compromising its faith and devotion, the orderly coherence of men's wills concerning the things that pertain to the mortal nature of man; and the earthly peace it directs to the attainment of heavenly peace (*City of God*, 19.17).

Political institutions, social practices, customs—are all radically relativized but allowed a relative autonomy within this restricted sphere. For a Christian, they are ambivalent; they can be used rightly, directed to the enjoyment of eternal peace by members of the city of God, or wrongly, directed to the enjoyment of lesser goods, the earthly peace (19.14). This emphasis flows from Augustine's understanding of the *saeculum*, not as a no-man's-land between the two cities, or an autonomous *tertium quid*, but as their temporal life in their interwoven, perplexed, and only eschatologically separable reality.

The *civitas peregrina*, the strange pilgrim city that humbles the ultimate significance of extra-biblical history and extra-ecclesial politics, even when it brings Christian social domination, also creates an ambivalent this-worldly space for a shared public culture with pagans, the beginning of a "secular" space. Both the sacred and profane were familiar in antiquity, but until it was imported by Christianity, there was no notion of the "secular" in the ancient world. From the Christian point of view the secular is roughly what can be shared with non-Christians. It is not simply a realm of sin cut off from the ecclesial. But in Augustine's spatiotemporal account of the *saeculum*, the secular is only relatively autonomous and it is not neutral.[28] Nothing is neutral for Augustine. The world is saturated with God. All politics is about fellowship and worship. Politics is either towards or away from God and our souls are always being shaped in accord with one of the two cities in agonistic struggle. Ambivalence rather than hostility is his attitude to the world and to the secular.[29]

---

28. Guarino, "For the Secular."

29. Gregory, *Politics and the Order of Love*, 322, contra both Markus and John Milbank; and Bruno, *Political Augustinianism*, 222.

It is this assertion of the ambivalence of the *saeculum* that has been said "to protect the merciful opacity of human affairs. In declaring the *saeculum* to be largely opaque to human scrutiny, Augustine protected the richness of human culture from the hubris of those who wanted to relate every aspect of the world around them directly to the sacred."[30]

But this part of Augustine's legacy was effaced in the decades after his death. Ascetic models of Christian life became increasingly significant. Ascetic discipline drew upon Stoic and Platonic conceptions of human flourishing and upon late antique psychological and medical knowledge. It aimed at achieving self-control, at controlling and contracting a range of the "passions," from appetitive passions for food and sex to states such as anger, jealousy, and avarice. Asceticism was not primarily dualistic and it was not considered an end in itself. Bodily discipline was deeply implicated in the transformation of the soul. Ascetics sought to become vehicles for the divine will and to realize the intended nature of human existence as the image of God.[31]

Pro-Nicene theologians promoted ascetic models of Christian life in their accounts of the purification necessary for all Christians. They interpreted non-Nicene theologies as the result of failures to maintain appropriate attention to the mysteriousness of God and so too as evidence of inappropriately trained souls. There is a conscious attempt in their homilies, not simply to encourage people to join ascetic communities, but to encourage those who continue to live in non-celibate families to adopt practices that stem from ascetic contexts. Describing and encouraging the "portability" of ascetic practice can thus be seen as intrinsic to pro-Nicene theology and catechesis.[32]

The promotion and appeal of asceticism as a means to define authentic Christians as distinct from Christians in name only grew out of a crisis of identity for the church in the decades around 400 AD.[33] A century of growing respectability and privilege, to which were added before the end of the fourth century the forces of urban mob violence now directed against pagans and of imperial legislation, did nothing to check a flood of half-converted Romans into Christian congregations. Christians in *tempora christiana* needed to reassure themselves that their church was the heir of

---

30. Brown, "Introducing Robert Markus," 184.
31. Elm, *Virgins of God*, 13–14.
32. Ayres, *Nicaea and its Legacy*, 342–43.
33. Markus, "Church Reform and Society in Late Antiquity."

CHAPTER 2: A NEW WORLDLINESS AND A NEW OTHERWORLDLINESS

the persecuted church of the martyrs, and did so partly through the cult of the martyrs and partly through the increasing significance of ascetic models of Christian life. The ascetic succeeded the martyr and became, like him or her, an exemplar of true Christianity and intercessor. What is it to be a Christian? The new form of martyrdom was a life of self-denial. This raised the question of how much renunciation being a true Christian demanded. The spectrum of permissiveness contracted. It was not enough to be baptized and to profess Christianity. To be a Christian had become too easy; one needed to be one *Non nomine sed opere*—"not in name but in action"—if the church was to continue to stand out in relief in the society around it. This was a refrain in Pelagian literature. Perfection was demanded of all. The reformers wanted the line which divided committed authentic Christianity from mediocrity to become the boundary of a reformed Christianity. Augustine opposed the rigorism of Pelagius but, despite Augustine, the appeal of ascetic ideals intensified. Monasticism, which had originated as a flight from the city to the desert, now returned to the cities of the Empire: monastic formation was increasingly considered to be the proper training of a bishop, especially in Gaul in the fifth and sixth centuries. This in turn meant attempts to impose ascetic norms on the life of the aristocratic laity. In sixth-century Arles its bishop Caesarius aspired to a regime of moral surveillance and a literal policing of desire in his city with the help of informers, to whom he appealed in his sermons to denounce adulterers to him.[34] A new worldliness, that of *tempora christiana*, again provoked a new otherworldliness.[35]

It has been claimed that this increasing significance of ascetic models of Christian life signals the end of ancient Christianity, at least in the West.[36] The predominance of asceticism caused a contraction of horizons. The development of a "culture of the Theopolis" was eclipsed.[37] A Christian culture, subordinated to a religious ideal, but keeping the continuity of its link with the classical origins from which it derived, which had existed briefly between the classical *paideia* and the culture of medieval Christendom, is succeeded by more narrowly biblical culture in a drastic human impoverishment. The cosmopolitan and pluralistic culture of diverse and sophisticated cities was certainly eroded by barbarian invasion. But it is

---

34. Leyser, *Authority and Asceticism*, 93.
35. Brown, *The Rise of Western Christendom*, 220.
36. Cameron, "Ascetic Closure and the End of Antiquity."
37. Marrou, *Saint Augustin*, 695.

difficult to judge the extent to which an "ascetic closure" was responsible, and the degree to which lay Christians internalized ascetic ideals; and of course, Christian culture still coexisted with a profane classical culture.[38] The largely Christian sources may give a misleading impression. But men in whose hearts the profane ancient city had been allowed to die now dominated the churches.[39] There was less room in their minds for the ambivalence of the world as Augustine had conceived of it. "The Devil was close, always ready to swallow up the world and the flesh."[40]

---

38. Rebillard, *Christians and Their Many Identities*; and Bowes, *Private Worship, Public Values*.

39. Brown, *Power and Persuasion in Late Antiquity*, 158.

40. Markus, *The End of Ancient Christianity*, 228.

Chapter 3: *Contemptus Mundi*

A new paideia

"Traditions, when vital, embody continuities of conflict."[1]

THE EXPRESSION CONTEMPTUS MUNDI refers to both a world view and a literary genre, particularly associated with the eleventh and twelfth centuries, which reflect on the evils of pride, the transitory nature of the material world, the permanence of heaven, and the spiritual and corporeal suffering of fallen humankind. This world view originates in elements of a conflict, a nonnegotiable tension, within Christian tradition. Its disruptive, subversive, and separatist foundation was supplemented with different conceptualities that allowed the founding ruptures to be surpassed or resolved in some way. Nonetheless, the radical conversionism, the witness to disruption, present in a Paul or a Mark continued to be present as an endemic mistrust of the world and its prince (and princes).[2] Christian tradition continued to define itself as the carrier of transcendental visions and impulses over and against the "world."

The historiography of Christian representations and politics of these elements of this tradition has tended to condemn them, or to explain away or apologize for them. Thus, a narrow and negative view of otherworldliness has been asserted or assumed. The continuity of this conflict within Christianity has been ignored by accounts that present a tradition developing naturally and inexorably from a world-rejecting to a world-affirming ethos. But a rather different view is defensible.[3] This view traces

---

1. MacIntyre, *After Virtue*, 221.
2. Rowan Williams, in Kreider, ed., *The Origins of Christendom in the West*, 325.
3. Corrington-Streete, "Trajectories of Ascetic Behaviour"; and Bellah, "Religious Evolution."

the continuing tension within Christian tradition in the ambivalence of its responses to the "world."

This ambivalence is not always reducible to a world-rejecting ethos, even in extreme examples of ascetic self-abnegation. In the sayings of the Desert Fathers it was told that:

> Once when Abba Silvanus was living on Mount Sinai, his disciple Zacharias went away on an errand and said to the elder, "Release the sluice and water the garden." When the elder came out, he covered his face with his hood and only saw his footsteps. At that time a brother came to visit him, and seeing him from a distance, noticed what he was doing. When the brother came up to him, he said, "Tell me, Abba, why did you cover your face with your hood and water the garden like that?" The elder said to him, "My child, so that my eyes should not see the trees and my mind become distracted from its work by them."[4]

In other sayings Zacharias sees Abba Silvanus falling into repeated ecstasies and being baptized in the light of God. This strange act of covering his face is not the result of paranoia or hypochondria. He himself admitted that, with the contemplation of uncreated light, he was indifferent to the world of transitory things and wanted only to gaze on the spiritual world. But in this way he was not simply escaping from created reality. He was doing something else: in preventing his senses from turning towards created things and then returning to him, he was neutralizing the mechanism of self-assertion at its source. If nihilism is the overturning of established values, so too is the decision of Abba Silvanus to water the garden without looking at the trees. By dwelling on the spiritual world, he wants to give material things their highest possible value. His nihilism rejects sensible objects in their simple utilitarian form. In nullifying the senses, however, he was nullifying himself.[5]

This deliberate effacing, even destruction, of self was seen as the only path of self-affirmation and formation, of transformation into a human person instead of an egocentric individual. The ascetics knew all too well the words "whoever will lose his life for my sake shall find it." They lived this fundamental dialectic of death and life in Christian experience.

---

4. Ward, trans., *The Sayings Of The Desert Fathers*, 233.
5. Ramfos, *Like a Pelican in the Wilderness*, 253–55.

CHAPTER 3: CONTEMPTUS MUNDI

The *schola* and the world of the *paidagogos* was a milieu that these Christian ascetics wished to capture, to colonize, and to redefine.[6] The "culture of the Theopolis" was redefined by a new kind of teacher and a new kind of *paideia*. This new *paideia* was bound to a concept of repentance as a path of perpetual submission to Scripture and to the commandments of Christ, in which a way of humility and obedience could be learned and lived out.[7]

The monastic culture of the Western Middle Ages that developed from this new *paideia* has been interpreted in completely opposed ways. Jean Leclercq (1911–1993) described monastic culture as an integral humanism that cultivated an increase of the influence of Jesus, as the one perfect man, in a process that will be completed outside of history. Leclercq insisted that monastic culture reconciled this eschatological humanism with a love of learning oriented toward contemplation and lifelong conversion. Its doctrine of the human person increasingly centered on the heart rather than the mind alone.[8] The religious gained from the classics a sensibility attuned to worldly and metaphysical beauty and also acquired a refinement of speech and sentiment needed for self-examination. This humanism assumes a *reductio artium ad theologiam* (leading of secular disciplines back to theology), according to which Christianity fulfills and completes earlier, fragmentary understandings of the universe. The partial truths (*logoi*) of pagan knowledge are incorporated into the wholeness of Christ the Logos.[9]

Robert Bultot challenged Leclercq's construal of monastic culture as part of a polemical account of Christian *contemptus mundi*, which gave rise to what has been characterized as "una *querelle* di vaste proporzioni" among medievalists.[10] He withholds the term "humanism" from any Christian culture that fails to uphold the autonomy of secular disciplines and at the least the provisional finality of human values. Bultot finds that the Middle Ages spectacularly failed to produce a positive theology of worldly realities and activities. Monastic theologians see no intrinsic worth in created things, including humanity; their perpetual counsel is one of rejection of the material world. The total range of human affairs—marriage, politics, business, power, education, and wealth—as portrayed in their

---

6. Rousseau, "Ascetics as Mediators and as Teachers," 55.
7. Torrance, *Repentance in Late Antiquity*.
8. Appleby, "'Bodily Need is a Kind of Speech,'" 125.
9. Appleby, "Humanism, Christian," 617.
10. Forsanar, cited in McCready, *Odiosa sanctitas*, 167.

writings only leads to corruption, misery, and perdition. Any involvement in terrestrial realities must be avoided; in a practical sense, the monastery is the only refuge for those whose contempt of the world is genuine. Bultot finds that an overpowering love of God engenders an utter disdain for what does not fully share in divine perfection. The lay state of life is not only seen as less than perfect but almost as a life without grace, and its specific features as obstacles to salvation. It seems as if the tension between loving and hating the world has been lost in a fateful confusion of the "world" as terrestrial reality with the "world" as the reign of Satan.[11] The polyvalence of the "world" in Christian tradition has been forgotten. The devil has swallowed up the world and the flesh.

Bultot sometimes seems to aiming at sitting targets, especially in his presentation of eleventh-century texts. Peter Damian, who incessantly decries the "miserable condition of man," concludes a sermon with an exhortation to "scorn all that is visible." John of Fecamp writes of *haec pessima vita, ista infelicissima vita:* "Miserable life, decrepit life, impure life sullied by humors, exhausted by grief, dried out by heat, swollen by food, mortified by fasts, dissolved by pranks, consumed by sadness, distressed by worries, blunted by security, bloated by riches, cast down by poverty . . ." The monk Herman Contract writes an *Exhortatory Poem on the Contempt of the World* where he catalogues the worries, sadness, problems, sicknesses, ills, and sufferings that fill existence. The same pessimism is found in the *Carmen de contemptu mundi* of Roger of Caen. Life is short and full of evils. It begins with the tears and wailing of a newborn child and continues with the sufferings caused by heat and cold, by hunger and thirst, by flies and fleas (which do not even spare kings), by the exile and death of loved ones, by infamy and prison. Man is vulnerable to unhappiness. Can one speak of health when illness is stronger? Can one speak of life since death ends it? Earth is a "vale of tears," a "desert," an "exile" compared to "sure life, tranquil life, beautiful life, pure life." In an anonymous hymn of the twelfth century, a poet speaks of, " . . . Worldly life, evil thing/Never worthy of love . . . /Worldly life, foul life/Pleasing only to the impious."[12]

But the world that so repelled the authors of the morbid and sensational texts cited by Bultot is no longer that of the cities of late antiquity with their baths and public spaces. It is a world created by the barbarian invasions, and its "profane values" were not attractive. Few marriages were

---

11. Delumeau, *Sin and Fear*, 12.
12. Delumeau, *Sin and Fear*, 13–15.

based on love. The monks can hardly be blamed for having been unable to develop a spirituality for lay people when there was as yet no laity, for lack of a world in which its specificity could have been grasped.[13] The *mundus* was not secular. It was a rival sacred order to the *ecclesia* culminating in the person of the king or emperor, the Lord's anointed and his representative on earth. *Contemptus mundi* could express a refusal to compromise with an unjust, violent society that was perhaps less Christian than the most secular of modern states, rather than a systematic disparagement of secular realities.[14] This attitude is found in Anselm's treatise, *Exhortatio ad Contemptum Temporalium et Desiderium Æternorum*, which severely criticized the domestication of prelates by the king of England and the uncontrolled violence of the knights, and in Abbot Hugh of Cluny, who is said to have preferred the monastic life to the aristocratic page's normal training in cattle stealing and robbing the peasantry. And it can be seen in the illuminated capitals of Romanesque art, where human figures enmeshed by coiling monsters biting them and drawing blood "are the images of an age hardened to unalleviated pain."[15]

And Leclercq can respond to Bultot that this theme of *contemptus mundi* was never a dominant element in monastic literature. It was part of an ensemble and so its true meaning cannot be seen in isolation. A florilegium of extracts from some of the same literature could also be gathered to express the theme *admiratio mundi*. It is not a matter of trying to decide between *contemptus mundi* or *admiratio mundi* as characterizations of monastic theology but of accepting that they are complementary.[16]

The tension between loving and hating the world was not utterly lost. It was even expressed with a new sophistication governed by the necessity for the purification of the heart in the monastic search for God.

Vanitas vanitatum

Peter the Venerable Abbot of Cluny (1092–1156) reminisced to his secretary that they spoke together "more frequently and intimately than others . . .

---

13. Batallion and Jossua, "Le Mepris du Monde," 23–38.

14. Batany, "L'Eglise et le Mepris du Monde," 218–28.

15. Boase, *English Art, 1100–1216*, 89, cited by B. Smalley in her review of Bultot, *Christianisme et Valeurs Humaines*, 235.

16. Leclercq, in *Aspects of Monasticism*, "Postface."

about contempt of the world and love of heavenly things" (Ep. 58).[17] The medieval literature of *contemptus mundi* has a source in patristic readings of Proverbs, Ecclesiastes, and the Song of Solomon, which were all believed to have been written by Solomon, the exemplar of scriptural wisdom. Origen located Ecclesiastes between Proverbs and the Song of Songs, at the second stage of the soul's spiritual itinerary. His lost commentary on Ecclesiastes is likely to have been the first instance of this reading. In the prologue to his commentary on the Song of Songs, he writes:

> Therefore if a person completes the first subject by freeing his habits from faults and keeping the commandments—which is indicated by Proverbs—and if after this, when the vanity of the world has been discovered and the weakness of its perishable things seen clearly [in Ecclesiastes], he comes to the point of renouncing the world and everything in the world, and he will come quite suitably also to contemplate and to long for the things that are unseen and are eternal.[18]

This prepares the soul for the intimate union with God as taught in the Song of Songs. The Solomonic itinerary presented by Origen becomes commonplace within the *contemptus mundi* tradition as it develops in patristic and medieval texts. This happened especially through the influence of Jerome, who brought Origen's exegetical work to the attention of his fellow Latins, and who adopts Origen's scheme, offering what becomes the most influential interpretation of Ecclesiastes, propagating the reading of its *leitwort* (leading word) *hebel* as *vanitas*.

Thus, when in the twelfth century Bernard of Clairvaux (1093–1153) comes to preach on the Song of Songs, he can assume this interpretative framework:

> Now, if I am not mistaken, you have been taught well enough by the words of Ecclesiastes to know and despise the vanity of the world. And what about Proverbs? Surely your life and conduct have been sufficiently amended and directed by the teaching found there? ... Come for the third loaf too, so that perhaps you may recognize what is best.[19]

---

17. Peter the Venerable, *Epistle* 58, cited by Giles Constable, *The Reformation of the Twelfth Century*, 130

18. Origen, *The Song of Songs*, 45, 46.

19. Bernard of Clairvaux, *Selected Writings*, 210–11.

Ecclesiastes is Solomon's manual for penitents.[20] Once a promising and sagacious ruler who was given wisdom by God, Solomon departed from the fount of wisdom and became a fool. But he still had a remnant of his former wisdom, which allowed him to recognize his misdeeds and confess them. Ecclesiastes is his act of penance. Confessing his errors is necessary for retracing his steps back to Jacob's ladder, by which he may once again make his contemplative ascent. The Song of Songs illustrates his experience at the top of the ladder. Yet, one may not climb the ladder without first confessing one's folly. Thomas à Kempis was taught by this tradition of reading Ecclesiastes that: "This is the highest wisdom: through contempt of the world, to strive for the kingdom of heaven."[21]

Origen had observed in *de Principiis* (1.4.5), "Solomon appears to characterize the whole of corporeal nature as a kind of burden, which enfeebles the vigour of the soul in the following language: '*Vanity of vanities*, saith the Preacher; *all is vanity* . . .' To this vanity then is the creature subject . . . subjected to vanity not willingly."

For Jerome, vanity represents what is to be despised of the world: *contemptus mundi*. He makes this theme clear in his response to Qoheleth's first words in chapter 1 of Ecclesiastes (NRSV):

> Vanity of vanities [vanitas vanitatutum] Vanity of vanities all is vanity. If all things that God made are truly good then how can all things be considered vanity, and not only vanity, but even vanity of vanities? . . . [H]eaven, earth, and the seas and all things that are contained within its compass can be said to be good in themselves, but compared to God they are nothing. And if I look at the candle in a lamp and am content with its light, then afterwards when the sun has risen I cannot discern any more what was once bright; I will also see the light of the stars by the light of the setting sun, so in looking at the world and the multitudinous varieties of nature I am amazed at the greatness of the world, but I also remember that all things will pass away and the world will grow old, and that only God is that which has always been. On account of this realization I am compelled to say, not once but twice: Vanity of vanities, all is vanity . . . All things are and will be in vain, until we find that which is complete and perfect.

---

20. Atkinson, *Singing at the Winepress*, 79, summarizing Bonaventure's account of the penitential provenance of Ecclesiastes.

21. Thomas à Kempis, *The Imitation of Christ*, book I.1.3.

Jerome develops the *vanitas* theme in a qualified, nuanced way. In this he is followed by numerous later Christian commentators on Ecclesiastes.

Augustine only includes a brief exposition of Ecclesiastes in his account of the ambiguity of the *saeculum* in *City of God*. In book 20.3, his subject as he comes to the culmination of the work is the last judgment. He refers to Ecclesiastes 8:14, "There is a vanity that takes place on earth, that there are righteous people who are treated according to the conduct of the wicked, and there are wicked people who are treated according to the conduct of the righteous. I said that this also is vanity." Augustine sums up his interpretation of Ecclesiastes: "The wisest man devoted the whole book to a full exposure of this vanity, evidently with no other object than that we might long for that life in which there is no vanity under the sun, but verity under him who made the sun." He goes on to contrast God's present judgment of this vain life under the sun with God's future judgment in which those who have clung to the eternal truth in these transitory days will receive permanent goods, while those who have faded away with its vanity will become nothing, receiving only evil things.

Augustine's key distinction is between the transitory and the permanent. To place one's love in the transient things of this world is to become dispersed among them, forfeiting the self which is the image of God, while to direct one's love to the eternal things of God is to regain one's true self as that which has its goodness and being in God. In such a context, the message of Ecclesiastes can only be the negative counterpart of the positive attraction of the love of God.

Yet this reading is not necessarily antithetical to an affirmation of the world in all its embodied particularity, *contra* critics like Bultot who condemn the whole *contemptus mundi* tradition. Augustine's brief response to Ecclesiastes is illuminated by relating it to the account of this world and the otherworldly that he presents in book I of *De doctrina christiana*.[22] This account is informed by his distinction between *frui* and *uti* (enjoyment and use, respectively). He distinguishes between

> things that are meant to be enjoyed, others that are meant to be used, [and] yet others which do both the enjoying and the using. And he goes on to define enjoyment (*frui*) as "clinging to something lovingly for its own sake, and use (*uti*) as "referring what has come your way to what your love aims at obtaining." He concludes that the only proper "object" of enjoyment is God, while all else

[22]. See Ticciati, "Ecclesiastes, Augustine's *Uti/Frui* Distinction."

is to be used for the end of the enjoyment of God: "if we wish to return to our home country, where we alone can be truly happy, we have to use this world, not enjoy it, so that we may behold the invisible things of God" (1.4.4).[23]

This may sound like the advocacy of an instrumentalization of the temporal world for the sake of eternal life with God. But Augustine also brings another set of concepts into play alongside the *uti/frui* pairing, through which this latter pairing is to be interpreted. This is the distinction between *res* (things) and *signa* (signs), things being considered in their own right, and signs signifying something else besides themselves (1.2.2).

Augustine goes on to call God, the "supreme thing" (*summa res*) (1.5.5). He invites us to map enjoyment (*frui*) onto things (*res*) and use (*uti*) onto signs (*signa*): to enjoy is to treat as a thing, while to use is to treat as a sign. If God is to be enjoyed as the "supreme thing," then creatures are to be used as signs of God. This changes the meaning of *uti*. Singling out God as a thing to be enjoyed means that, unlike creatures, God cannot be used or referred to anything beyond himself. God cannot become a sign. God needs no larger context of interpretation. The divine provides the context for the interpretation of everything else. Augustine argues that my enjoyment of God cannot involve the subordination of God to my own agenda, which would make me the context for the interpretation of God. Rather, to enjoy God is to relinquish my partial agenda, allowing myself to be defined by God. But it follows that to use another creature for my enjoyment of God cannot involve instrumentalization or subordination of that creature to my agenda. Rather, it will involve our mutual subordination to our common good, which is God. God as the supreme thing is "shared in common by all who enjoy it" (1.5.5).

Thus to treat another creature as a sign of God is to refuse to give it a finite significance determined by me, allowing it to have meaning beyond what I give it, and even beyond what I can conceive of. In a paradoxical way this reinstates it, in all its irreducibility, as a thing. By contrast, when I improperly enjoy a creature, rather than using it for God, I define it in terms of its ability to satisfy my desire, which means reducing it to its significance for me. To use for the end of enjoyment of God is to safeguard other creatures against selfish and reductive use for my own ends. To treat something as a sign of God is to acknowledge a creature's infinite significance, rather than reducing it to its finite significance as determined by me.

23. Ticciati, "Ecclesiastes, Augustine's *Uti/Frui* Distinction," 257.

This is the lesson of the story that Augustine tells in the *Confessions* (4.4.9–4.7.12) of one of his darkest moments—his grief over the death of an unnamed close friend. His lament is not just about his grief, or the love of the finite as a distraction from the love of God. The problem is also his own lack of self-control. Properly ordered love is the operative mode of Augustinian *caritas*. When he loved his friend as if he would never die he had tried to take possession of his friend as his own—as belonging to him rather than to God. He loved what he lost as if it was his not to lose. The sin that corrupts love is the lie that God and God's creation exist for one's own private possession.[24] And so he loved a mortal person as if he would never die, "pouring out his soul onto the sand." His friend became a kind of substitute for God, and this was "a vast myth and a long lie."

> At this sorrow my heart was utterly darkened, and whatever I looked upon was death . . . . I hated all places because he was not in them . . . I became a vast problem to myself, and I questioned my soul . . . *o dementiam nescientem diligere homines humaniter!* O madness, which know not how to love men as men should be loved![25]

Augustine's summary of the teaching of Ecclesiastes in the *City of God* 20.3 was that the transitory world is exposed as vain in order that we might long for eternal life in God. Though he does not himself do so in the *City of God*, if this is translated back into his *uti/frui* terminology then it means that the transitory world is to be used for the end of the enjoyment of eternal life with God. But then the vanity of the world must consist in its being an improper object of enjoyment, such that when it becomes the focus of one's desire, it cannot deliver; it becomes the site of reductive and destructive relations in which the true significance it has in God is forfeited. When, by contrast, it is used for the sake of God, it is redeemed from this vanity in the negative sense. If *frui* interprets the transitory world as vain or futile, then *uti* renders the transitory world as ephemeral, honoring God's creatures precisely as creatures. As Augustine goes on to say, "But in these days of vanity it makes an important difference whether [man] resists or yields to the truth, and whether he is destitute of true piety or a partaker of it" (20.3).

In other words, the world is vain when considered in abstraction from its end in God, but regains its true radiance when directed towards that end. This ambivalence plays havoc with the distinction between this world

---

24. Gregory, *Politics and the Order of Love*, 286.
25. Augustine, *Confessions* 4.4.9, p. 50.

and the otherworldly. To focus one's gaze on the otherworldly is precisely to give this world its full and true significance; instead of the distinction between this world and otherworldly it might be better to speak instead of the creator and the renewal of creation.

In the *Confessions* Augustine says to God, *sed bonorum omnium largitor affluentissimus tu es*: "But you are the most generous giver overflowing with good things."[26] Augustine makes a claim about God in order to make a claim about how to love the world most deeply and pleasurably. To love the world with the deepest amount of love and pleasure possible, one needs to love the entire world as a gift from a loving giver. In this way religious faith is not a means of frustrating our love for this world and our lives in it; rather faith becomes a means of loving the world with the most possible joy. Augustine thinks that in faith we come to love the world with the maximal love possible and come to feel grateful for the world with the maximal gratitude possible. For Augustine, loving the immanent world maximally and with maximal pleasure means believing in a transcendent, generous God; if we want to love this world as much as we can, with as much pleasure as we can muster, we must believe in, love, and thank God as its creator. Thus he writes at the very beginning of the *Confessions* that, "to praise you is the desire of humankind. . . . You stir humankind to take pleasure in praising you, because you have made us for yourself, and our heart is restless until it rests in you."

Far from arguing that we should focus our attention solely on God at the expense of the world and our lives in the world, Augustine proposes that a significant aspect of what it means to praise God is to thank God for the world and thereby love the world maximally and with maximal pleasure.[27]

Bonaventure's (c. 1217–1274) commentary on Ecclesiastes uses this understanding to respond to the claim that contempt of the world is contempt for its creator. He presents an Augustinian account of *contemptus mundi*, using the simile of a wedding ring.[28]

> To despise a work reflects back on the worker. So the person who despises the world, despises God . . . Likewise . . . [S]omething directed towards its goal [i.e., creation directed towards God]

---

26. Augustine, *Confessions* 4.4.9, as translated by McCurry, "To Love the World Most Deeply," 50.

27. Augustine, *Confessions* 4.12.18, 1.1.1; and McCurry, "To Love the World Most Deeply."

28. Atkinson, *Singing at the Winepress*, 87.

> should not be despised but rather accepted and loved. Therefore, this world, with all that is in it, is to be loved. I reply: It should be said ... that the world is like a ring given by the bridegroom to the soul itself. Now the bride can love the ring given her by her husband in two ways, namely with a chaste or an adulterous love. The love is chaste when she loves the ring as a memento of her husband and on account of her love for her husband. The love is adulterous when the ring is loved more than the husband, and the husband cannot regard such love as good ... Contempt for a ring by treating it as a poor and ugly gift reflects on the husband, but contempt of a ring by regarding it as almost nothing compared to the love of the husband, gives glory to the husband ... It is of such contempt that we are speaking and so the matter is clear.[29]

Chaste love for the world means recognizing its emanation from God, while proper contempt for the world means recognizing its consummate end in God, an end that should likewise bring those who are made in the image of God and who delight in the creator of the cosmos to beatific similitude (Works of St Bonaventure 9.28).

Leclercq writes "in praise of nuances" and against the oversimplification of complex data in discussions of medieval texts.[30] The nuanced *contemptus mundi* of Bonaventure is not contempt for the beauty and goodness of creation and of the creator, but an alienation from an already alienated world. It is contempt for a false and destructive vision of the world suggested supremely by covetousness. The eighth-century abbot Ambrose Autpert, in his treatise *Conflictus vitiorum atque virtutum (Combat between the vices and the virtues)*, sets *contemptus mundi* against *cupiditas* (greed). Autpert observed that the acquisitive greed of the rich and powerful in the society of his time also existed within the souls of monks, and he wrote a treatise entitled *De cupiditate* in which, with Paul, he denounced greed as the root of all evil: "In the earth's soil various sharp thorns spring from different roots; in the human heart on the other hand, the stings of all the vices sprout from a single root, greed" (*De cupiditate* 1: CCCM 27B, 963).[31] Autpert imagined the objection that the rich and powerful might raise, saying: but we are not monks; certain ascetic requirements do not apply to us. And he answers:

---

29. Bonaventure, cited in Christianson, *Ecclesiastes Through the Centuries*, 32; and Karris and Murray, *Commentary on Ecclesiastes*, 77–79.

30. Leclercq, *Aspects of Monasticism*, 146.

31. Pope Benedict XVI, *Church Fathers and Teachers*, 88–90.

> What you say is true, but for you, in the manner of your position and in accordance with your strength, the straight and narrow way applies because the Lord has proposed only two doors and two ways (that is, the narrow door and the wide door, the steep road and the easy one); he has not pointed to a third door or a third way (*De cupiditate* 1: CCCM 27B, 978).

He concludes his penitential homily, "I have not spoken against the greedy but against greed, not against nature, but against vice." The vice of avarice was the sin of worldliness par excellence in early medieval thought, which in general thought that humanity would become more avaricious in the last days and that this deterioration was a sign of the approaching end.[32]

The authors of the *contemptus mundi* tradition consistently affirm that all God's creations are good, in accordance with Psalm 150 that all spirits and each creature praise the creator. They dialectically affirm, too, the dignity of man, as even Innocent III intended to do in a sequel to his *De miseria humane conditionis*, as he relates in its prologue. They disparage nature and the delights of the world not because they are bad but because they are transitory. This attitude to all material things is exemplified in one of John of Fecamp's poems in which declares that, as in the third chapter of Ecclesiastes, the transient glories of the world are just not enough:

> Woe to man
>
> Woe to man
>
> Woe to you unhappy man!
>
> Why do you love the goods of this world that are going to perish?
>
> Vanity of vanities, all is vanity.
>
> Everything existing under the sun is vain.
>
> All the glory of the world is like the flower and the grass.
>
> The world will pass away with all its desires.[33]

The tone of the *De vanitate mundi* of Hugh of St Victor (1096–1141) is a poignant ambivalence about the love-worthiness of the ephemeral beauty of creation: all things are vanity because, just as each creature comes into being out of nothing, so too its daily changes show that, of itself, it also tends to nothing. The wonders of the visible world, marvelous though they

---

32. Newhauser, *The Early History of Greed*, 131.

33. John of Fecamp, *De Vanitate Mundi*, cited in Howe, *Before the Gregorian Reform*, 202.

are, are fleeting, ephemeral, and transient. Their mutability makes them ultimately incapable of offering a stable object for the soul's knowledge (and ultimately its love). This mutability is evoked repeatedly in the image of flowing water. "While this life lasts, you should think of the entire world, because of the mutability of everything, as if it were a flood of down-coursing waters." These dissipate both themselves and the souls of those whose loving attachment to such things provokes an inappropriate attachment. If "the soul through cupidity immerses itself in all that is borne down by the flood, it is forthwith torn by countless distractions, and, being somehow divided from itself, it is dispersed abroad." Perceiving "the mutability of present things" the soul feels "contempt of the world" and loses its "esteem for all that seems fair in the world." Visible beauty now provokes Christian minds to seek both within themselves and God "the loveliness of their creator all the more ardently." This desire is the olive branch in leaf, which the dove brings back to Noah in the ark.[34]

The extravagant attention of the *contemptus mundi* tradition to flesh and decay is not a "flight from" the body but a "submersion in" the body.[35] But in the phenomenon of "dilation," early medieval visionaries sought to transcend the world, to see it as they believed God sees it. The seer stands outside and above him or herself—and above the world itself which now appears very small as an image from the Wisdom of Solomon: "Because the whole world before you is like a speck that tips the scales, and like a drop of morning dew that falls on the ground" (11:22, NRSV). An early medieval image of the world transcended in this way in dilation is the story of the vision of Benedict told by Gregory the Great. While praying in a tower Benedict saw a celestial light poured out from above, "which brought the whole world before his eyes, as if gathered in a single ray of sunlight" (Gregory, *Dialogues*, II.35). Benedict does not cease to be himself in the world, but the world appears in its totality and from afar, within a new horizon. The world has lost its status as his horizon. He has transgressed the distinction between world and kingdom, occupying a non-place that exceeds the totality of all places, like the non-place of the monk in the liturgy where it was believed that eschatology had a place on earth. He is in a place but without being in the world. The world is bracketed for a moment so that the eschatological kingdom, the eternal depth of the world, can appear

---

34. Hugh of St Victor, *Archa Noe*, cited in Coolman, *The Theology of Hugh of St Victor*, 186–87.

35. Bynum, "Why All the Fuss about the Body?"

more clearly. This vision is a "liturgical subversion of the topological," and an anticipation of the eschaton.[36]

Temptation and detachment

If the medieval conception of the "world" as an object of contempt and renunciation was informed by a reading of Ecclesiastes that took *vanitas* as its leading word, it was also determined by the idea of the three temptations that are presented in the first epistle of John: "Do not love the world or the things in the world. The love of the Father is not in those who love the world; for all that is in the world—the desire of the flesh, the desire of the eyes, the pride in riches—comes not from the Father but from the world" (1 John 2:15-16, NRSV).

In the *Confessions*, Augustine wrote that the things of the "world" were to be held in contempt, and he describes the "world" in terms of the three temptations of 1 John 2:16. Each vice is stigmatized as the antithesis of a virtue that in turn characterizes the excellence of a part of the human soul seen as an image of the Trinity. *Ambitio seculi*, which embraces avarice as well, defeats humility, the virtue of the self as created being, counterpart of God as creator. *Concupiscentia oculorum* seeks illicit knowledge to the detriment of *sapientia*, wisdom, the authentic knowledge that marks in us the illumination of the divine Word. And *concupiscentia carnis* runs amok in love of created things without reference to God, and thus destroys the *caritas* that comes of the Spirit. Thus, even in sin, for Augustine, we reflect the image and likeness of God.[37]

Medieval Christians present these three temptations as daily luring them toward damnation: *the lust of the flesh, the lust of the eyes, and pride of life*. They testify to feeling besieged by the lures of the world, the *mundus*, the suggestions of their appetites, and the snares of Satan—"the world, the flesh and the devil."[38] They also understand John's list of three sins or "lusts" as describing the psychological process by which sin occurs. Gluttony, the lust of the flesh, had been the initial suggestion of the tempting serpent. Avarice, the lust of the eyes, had appealed to Eve and caused delectation. And vainglory, the pride of life, had brought Adam to consent to sin. Gregory the Great, in the *Moralia*, develops this understanding by saying

---

36. Lacoste, *Experience and the Absolute*, 23–26.
37. Augustine, *Confessions*, 10.30.41; and see O'Donnell, *Augustine*, 203.
38. Howard, *The Three Temptations*, 43–76.

that "suggestion is made by the Adversary, delectation by the flesh, consent by the spirit."[39] The *mundus* and the *saeculum*, which became its synonym among monastic writers, were thus associated with the temptations of Adam and also of Christ. The *mundus* was not intrinsically evil but it was suggestive because of the three temptations.

And so the monastic vows of poverty, chastity, and obedience appear to correspond to these three temptations. Poverty is opposed to the desire for riches (lust of the eyes), chastity to the desire for pleasure (lust of the flesh), and obedience to the desire for power and status (pride of life). When he had made these vows a monk was said to have "died to the world" and this "world" that the monks renounced was the world as defined by 1 John 2:16.[40] From the third century, the "world" had already been named in baptismal rites as among those things that all Christians must renounce.

The tradition of *contemptus mundi* thus offers an account of the "world" as a source of temptation that is characterized by *vanitas*. It emphasizes the corruption and the transience of the world. Detachment might be an apt synonym for this contempt.[41] In its cultivation of detachment this tradition has affinities with Buddhist meditative practices, which identify our predicament as one of *dukkha*, of suffering, satisfaction, and disease, an account whose only biblical precedent is the pessimism of Ecclesiastes.[42] When we fail to see that nothing within *samsara*, the "world," is substantial and enduring we grasp at and become attached to what is fluctuating, transitory, and insubstantial. It is this grasping and attachment that cause us to suffer. One of the Paali words of Buddhist teaching that is sometimes translated as "detachment," *viveka*, can mean separation, aloofness, or seclusion. *Upadhiviveka* means the absence of lust, desire, and craving for existence. So *viveka* might be better translated as "nonattachment" when attachment connotes possessiveness in relationships, defensiveness, jealousy, covetousness, and competitiveness. *Saraga*, "attachment," also leads to biased and false perceptions since objects are seen through a veil of predispositions to attraction or aversion. Nonattachment is a movement towards seeing the true nature of things more clearly. Through nonattachment, destructive dispositions are attenuated and overcome, allowing "a self without selfishness" to exercise *karunaa*, "true compassion," for all beings. It may

39. Gregory the Great, cited in Howard, *The Three Temptations*, 59.
40. Howard, *The Three Temptations*, 55–56.
41. Shaw, "Contemptus Mundi and the Love of Life."
42. de Lubac, *La Rencontre du Bouddhisme et de l'Occident*, 28.

be that without the "fullness" of charity no one will ever realize the "void" of detachment.[43] But compassion and detachment are not incompatible.[44] And, as in the *contemptus mundi* tradition, Buddhist meditative practice also includes the morbid and sensational. In the *Satipatthana Sutta*, the discourse on the foundations of mindfulness, the monk is encouraged to undertake "cemetery contemplations" and to view the decaying naked body of a woman in order to experience sexual stimulus without reacting with lust and so to cultivate nonattachment.

Contemptus and reform

The civilizations of Theravada Buddhism and medieval Catholicism are similar in their "decentered centrality." Virtuoso ascetic elites who defined themselves as marginal or opposed to the dominant forms of social life were still able to establish themselves in positions of cultural prestige, corporate wealth, and relative ascendancy in both civilizations. But the Christian interpenetration of worldliness and otherworldliness is radically different from their neatly segregated and hierarchized coexistence in canonical Buddhism. The lay world, however spiritually inferior, is allowed a significant degree of autonomy. The renouncer has transcended its troubles, obsessions, and vices. It is never conceived of as the locus of salvation. It is not expected to model itself after the highest Buddhist ideals. *Samsara*, mundane life, is *dukkha*, painful and unsatisfactory. And so it is to be escaped rather than dominated. The image of the ascetic virtuosi emerging from the canonical Scriptures of Buddhism is of an elite that combines ultimate superiority with a narrowly defined involvement in and lack of control of worldly life on the other. And so the Cluniac alliance between monasticism and the papacy, together with the systematic attempt in at least some phases of the Gregorian era to impose asceticism beyond the walls of the monastery, represent a phenomenon unknown in the history of Theravada monasticism.[45] A monastic church merged with the universal church and sought to dominate all Christian society, and all humankind.[46]

This distinctive attempt is the context of the corruption and abuse of the tradition of *contemptus mundi*. A new thing had come into the world

43. de Lubac, *Aspects of Buddhism*, 52.
44. Harris, "Detachment and Compassion in Early Buddhism."
45. Silber, *Virtuosity, Charisma, and Social Order*, 70, 168.
46. Iogna-Prat, *Order and Exclusion*.

with Christianity: the idea of reform. Paul exhorted the Romans, "Be not conformed to this world, but be transformed in the renewal of your mind" (Romans 12:2, NRSV). *Reformatio* in the early centuries of the church came to refer to a way of behaving and feeling that had never been known before. The classical world had known renewal and rebirth as one phase of the eternal cycle of the stars and the seasons, but this was nothing like the idea, which had spread throughout the Empire and beyond by the fourth century, of a conversion that could sweep away the culture of the convert and leave them in a new state determined by their repentance. In the patristic era, especially before the conversion of Constantine, reform was essentially personal. It was conceived of as the moral effort to restore the damage done to the image of God in the soul through sin. In the early Middle Ages it was also the idea informing the Benedictine vow of *conversatio morum*, a conversion of behavior in fidelity to monastic life.

In the eleventh century the idea of reform was extended from the reform of monastic institutions to that of the *ecclesia* and even the *mundus*. A papally directed movement sought to restore moral purity to the clergy and right order to church governance by insisting on prohibitions against simony, clerical marriage, and lay control over churches and ecclesiastical appointments. This movement reinforced papal status and authority by placing the papacy at the heart of eschatological events. It seems to command energies released by the hope and fear of the apocalyptic year 1000;[47] medieval Christians could relieve their anagogical longing, their impatience, for another world by embodying that world in their determined action upon this one.[48] A sense of the imminence of the end, of the reign of Antichrist, and the imminent dominion of God over the *mundus*, which is absent in the writings of Augustine, is joined to an explicit program of institutional reform in the writings of Pope Gregory VII:

> From the moment when by divine inspiration Mother Church raised me, unworthy and God knows unwilling, to the apostolic throne, I have labored with all my power that Holy Church ... might come again into her own splendor and might remain free, pure and catholic. But because this was not pleasing to our ancient enemy, he stirred up his members against us to bring it to nought ... And no wonder! For the nearer the day of Antichrist

---

47. Landes, Gow, and Van Meter, eds., *The Apocalyptic Year 1000*.
48. Dumont, *Essays on Individualism*.

approaches, the harder he fights to crush the Christian faith (*Collected Letters* 9.46).

Like Augustine, medieval Catholics believed that the number of the saved was very small. They were a small elite among the mass of the damned. But, unlike Augustine, they now saw a dispensation in which the elect would rule and discipline the whole of society.[49]

The reform movement has been interpreted as a response to the danger that *ecclesia* could lose its distinctive identity in relation to the *mundus* of medieval Christendom. The Church and lay society became increasingly symbiotic and mixed in the late tenth and eleventh centuries, establishing a equilibrium. *Ecclesia* and the *mundus* ruled by anointed kings and emperors were even treated as identical and synonymous. But losing its distinctive identity would entail *ecclesia* losing its leadership of Western society as well. Once again, as in the ascetic closure of late antiquity, a new worldliness seems to provoke a new otherworldliness, a new urge to come out of Babylon. If the Church and the world are now identical and synonymous then how can asceticism and reform stop within the limits of the Church? For the Church has no limits, or at least its limits are those of the world itself. Therefore the reformers began to seek to carry the ascetic, purifying impulse into the world itself, refusing to accept the old equilibrium in their struggle to establish what Gregory VII called *Christianitas*.[50] All Christians must meet higher standards of dedication and commitment. An effort began to align the masses on the religion of the elites. For example, the Lateran Council of 1215 lays down the requirement of auricular confession for all the laity, at least once a year.

The corruption and abuse of the tradition of *contemptus mundi* is a symptom of its deployment in this campaign of reform of the world, and which had limited success. "Contempt of the World" becomes a set theme for treatises at the end of the eleventh and beginning of the twelfth centuries that are characterized by a new tone of scorn and disillusionment, as described by Robert Bultot. The background is of a separation of *ecclesia* and *mundus* but also of restlessness, malaise, and disintegration in the monastic system, which was losing its intellectual and moral dominance.[51] Treatises and poems *de contemptus mundi* not only impose the spirituality of monks upon all but now also urge "contempt" and rejection of the world

---

49. Berman, *Law and Revolution*; and Nemo, *What is the West?*
50. Cantor, "The Crisis of Western Monasticism, 1050–1130."
51. Miccoli, "Monks," in Le Goff, *Medieval Callings*.

in far more violent language than had been used before. These writings begin with those of the reformers themselves. Peter Damien, in his *Apologeticum de contemptu saeculi,* written in the late eleventh century as a letter addressed to the hermit Albizo and the monk Peter, argues that because the integrity of the monastic profession has weakened, the world has fallen even deeper into an abyss of sin and corruption and is rushing headlong to destruction. Let monks and hermits take refuge within the walls of the monastery, he urges, while outside the advent of Antichrist seems imminent. He arranges his points according to the three monastic vows—poverty, obedience, and chastity. He castigates monks for their interest in money, their habit of leaving the seclusion of the monastery, and their fondness for rich garments and other vanities. He blames their anger, drunkenness, loss of fervor, hypocrisy, and lechery. But he then turns his attention to offenses outside the monastery in lay society: illicit and incestuous marriages, the selling of justice, avarice. He ends the letter by warning sinners against the horrors of the tomb and the snares of worldly life:

> And so you will see how quickly this short life will pass away. You will see how the world declares with clear indications its coming end ... Wherefore as the apples of a hollow tree brought forth too soon fall before they are ripe, so shall men in their bitter exile die before coming to the fullness of age.[52]

A line is drawn by the end of time and in particular the terrible image of the Antichrist, to criticize the present. The world is made worldly by eschatology. Otto of Freising, in his *Chronicle of Two Cities* of the 1150s, a history of the world up to his days, is written, as he says, "in bitterness of spirit," and gives clear expression of this bringing into history of the last things. "We, however, placed at the end of time as we are, have our knowledge of the afflictions of mortal men and women not by reading about them in books but by meeting them among us in what we have lived through in our own day." But what seems like a sense of the end time is, as *contemptus mundi,* a specifically medieval form of historical experience, in which disappointment and hope struggled with one another over how the world should be depicted and shaped.[53]

The most celebrated example of this kind of treatise *De contemptu mundi* is the *De Miseria Condicionis Humane,* written in 1194/5 by Cardinal Lotario dei Segni shortly before he became Pope Innocent III. The text

---

52. Damian, *Letters,* 225.

53. Rauh, "Eschatologie und Geschichte."

is divided into three parts. The first part, entitled "The Miserable Entrance of the Human Condition," describes the wretchedness of the human body and the various hardships one has to bear throughout life. Book two, "The Guilty Progress of the Human Condition," lists man's futile ambitions: affluence, pleasure, and esteem. The third book, "The Damnable Exit from the Human Condition," deals with the decay of the human corpse, the anguish of the damned in hell, and the day of judgment, ending with a chapter entitled, "That Nothing Can Help the Damned."

Innocent's commitment to the reform of the Church and the world helps explain why the same person who could write a such a harshly otherworldly treatise could go on to rule Italy and Europe like an worldly emperor. The reformers' zeal demanded political power for a reformed and reforming Church. And the world's corruption is exactly what makes it subject to ecclesiastical power. In the *De miseria*, Innocent says much less about the Church's inadequacies than those of the world. His contention that the temporal order is transitory, vain, and corrupt does not therefore contradict his belief in papal authority and the power of the Church; rather, it supports it. The "world" represents a rival power structure. Contempt for the world has become not contempt for the objectives of the world, but competition with the world on its own ground and for the same power.[54] A significant change has occurred. The *sacerdotium*, the spiritual function, now seeks to rule in worldly matters and has thus entered the "world." The difference between the realms, the *sacerdotium* and the *imperium*, is now conceived as one of degree, not of kind, so that the spiritual power, as it was now called, was deemed to be superior to the temporal even in temporal matters.[55]

It is one thing to cultivate a *contemptus mundi* that implies a sense of liberation, detachment, and unconcern because one has completely abandoned the cares of the world through a life of poverty and renunciation. It is quite another thing to remain very much in the world as a decisive influence upon its affairs, and to bring that influence to bear with "contempt"—while at the same time, in practice, seeking worldly power and wealth oneself. A conception in the service of liberation from the world is now a weapon of domination and suppression. *Contemptus mundi* has become "the ideology of Latin Christendom."[56]

---

54. Merton, *Conjectures of a Guilty Bystander*, 46–51.
55. Buss, "The Evolution of Western Individualism," 11.
56. Howard, *The Three Temptations*, xxiv.

Chapter 4: The Reform of the World and the Making of a Secular Age

Modernity as a mutation of Christianity

In ORTHODOXY, G. K. Chesterton wrote about how the church went in for dangerous ideas. He describes how ideas such as otherworldliness and worldliness had to be deliberately balanced against one another in "her experiment of the irregular equilibrium." Let one idea become less powerful and some other idea would become too powerful. "It was no flock of sheep the Christian shepherd was leading, but a herd of bulls and tigers, of terrible ideals and devouring doctrines, each one of them strong enough to turn to a false religion and lay waste the world."[1] In *A Secular Age*, Charles Taylor tells the story of how this laying waste happened when the medieval equilibrium between otherworldliness and worldliness was lost. The result was a corruption or mutation of Christianity whose final outcome is modern secularity.

Marcel Gauchet describes the originality of the relation of Christianity to the world as its "axiomized ambiguity." The Christian is a person torn between loving and hating the world, between a duty of belonging and a duty of distancing, between alliance with the world and estrangement from it. A transcendent God has willed a sensory world from which Christians must separate themselves in order to reach heaven. But how can the world be totally rejected when it was judged worthy of the Word made flesh? So they cannot completely reject the world, even if they find it impossible to accommodate it. They must find equilibrium between acceptance and rejection, an equilibrium that cannot be definitively defined.[2]

---

1. Chesterton, *Orthodoxy*, conclusion of chap. 6.
2. Gauchet, *The Disenchantment of the World*.

CHAPTER 4: THE REFORM OF THE WORLD AND THE MAKING OF A SECULAR AGE

For Gauchet this tension and instability is essential for the story he traces of the emergence of modernity from the inner logic of Christianity, "the religion for departing from religion,"[3] and the final working out of a problematic that originates with the advent of transcendent gods in the Axial Age. A "recalcitrant logic" inevitably leads Christianity to put an increasing distance between divine power and human activity and leads the world towards its secularization. Taylor agrees with Gauchet that modernity did not begin as a reaction against Christianity but arose out of the inner logic of Christianity. But for Taylor this development is defined less strictly in terms of a logical essence. He distinguishes what a he calls a "linear master narrative" from his own "reform master narrative" and so presents his nuanced "total history of a specific contingency."[4] There is no straightforward path of inevitable progress. Instead there are multiple shifts and turns, zigs and zags that could have gone otherwise but which—given certain historical contingencies—generated the possibility of secularity.[5]

Loving and hating the world: the Reform Master Narrative

Taylor traces how Christian ambivalence about the world comes to drive secularization. He presents secularization as the final outcome of Western Christianity's self-undoing through its effort to reform the lives of Christians and force them into conformity with the demands of the gospel. His account of the rage for reform that has gradually brought us to where we are now begins not with the Protestant Reformation but with Latin Christendom, specifically with the reforms of Pope Gregory VII (Hildebrand) in the eleventh century. For Taylor, the project of reform started with a laudable attempt to fight back the demands of the "world" and then make it over. He notes the Christian ambivalence about the "world (cosmos)" expressed in the New Testament, where the world has both a positive and a negative meaning. The latter negative sense of "world" can be understood as the present sacralized order of things and its embedding in the cosmos. Taylor refers to Rene Girard's account of God's nonviolent kingdom defeating the evils of sacrifice and scapegoating in Girard's *I See Satan Fall Like Lightning*. It was this sense of "world" that Hildebrand clearly saw when he

---

3. Gauchet, *The Disenchantment of the World*, 101.
4. John Milbank, cited in Storey, "Charles Taylor's *A Secular Age*," 201.
5. Cloots, Latre, and Vanheeswijck, "The Future of the Christian Past," 4.

fought to keep episcopal appointments out of the invasive power field of dynastic drive and ambition in the Investiture Controversy.

> It might have seemed obvious that one should build on this defensive victory with an attempt to change and purify the power field of the "world," to make it more and more consonant with the demands of Christian spirituality. But naturally, this didn't happen all at once. The changes were incremental, but the project was somehow continually re-ignited in more radical form, through the various Reformations, down to the present age. The irony is that it somehow turned into something quite different; in another, rather different sense, the "world" won after all. Perhaps the contradiction lay in the very idea of a disciplined imposition of the Kingdom of God. The temptation of power was after all, too strong, as Dostoevsky saw in the Legend of the Grand Inquisitor. Here lay the corruption.[6]

Taylor asks: "Why was it virtually impossible not to believe in God in, say, 1500 in our Western society, while in 2000 many of us find this not only easy, but inescapable?"[7] The answer he gives contends that the secular is more than subtraction.[8] The secular is not just the neutral, rational, areligious world that is left once theism is rejected. The secular is not just unbelief. What characterizes secularity and the secular age is not merely privative. The emergence of the secular is bound up with the production of a new option: the possibility of "exclusive humanism" as a viable social imaginary or background—a way of constructing meaning and significance without any reference to the divine or to transcendence. It wasn't enough to stop believing in the gods or in God; significance also had to be imagined within an "immanent frame," in which meaning has no relation to transcendence.

The basic transformation of Western Christianity that Taylor describes begins in medieval society. He names this, after Weber, an "enchanted world" inhabited by spirits and demons, in which "moral forces" are felt to be embedded in the lived environment. Human agents are embedded in society, society in the cosmos, and the cosmos incorporates the divine.[9] "Sacramental ontology" had constituted the natural world as a cosmos that functioned semiotically, as a sign that pointed beyond itself,

---

6. Taylor, *A Secular Age*, 158.
7. Taylor, *A Secular Age*, 25.
8. Smith, *How (Not) to be Secular*, 26.
9. Taylor, *A Secular Age*, 152.

CHAPTER 4: THE REFORM OF THE WORLD AND THE MAKING OF A SECULAR AGE

to what was more than nature. Society itself was understood as something grounded in this higher reality. Earthly kingdoms were grounded in a heavenly kingdom, in the medieval balance between conceptions of a Christian world order and of alienation from the world.[10] This metaphysical picture, supported by both the Aristotelian account of the cosmos of Aquinas and by popular belief, implies that religious meaning is not merely "in the mind" but is actually "out there." An inhabitant of this world can identify experiences that confirm that even the most everyday objects are "charged" with supernatural power. Relics or holy places of pilgrimage and healing were commonly understood to have power independently of the minds of human beings and their experience of such objects and places.[11] Atheism comes close to being inconceivable, because in a world so constituted the world is seen as suffused with presences that are not natural. Forces that can penetrate the self, whether by demonic possession or the Holy Spirit, populate the environment and so selfhood is not experienced as "buffered" and ontologically distinct or walled-off from its surroundings and able to disengage and disbelieve more easily. The self is instead "vulnerable" and "porous."[12]

Taylor explains how medieval Christendom lived with a unique tension between "self-transcendence"—a "turning of life towards something beyond ordinary human flourishing"—and the this-worldly concerns of human flourishing and creaturely existence. It was a tension between what was required by "eternity" and the demands of mundane domestic life, otherworldliness and worldliness, hating and loving the world. It was assumed that human life found its ultimate meaning and *telos* in a transcendent eternity and that securing this *telos* demanded an ascetic relation to the pleasures and cares of the mundane. It was a tension between "the demands of the total transformation which the faith calls to" and "the requirements of ordinary ongoing human life."[13]

This tension was not resolved, but inhabited. The social body makes room for a certain division of labor. In the entirely religious vocations of monks and nuns the church created a vicarious class who devoted themselves to the demands of eternity on behalf of the wider social body. Monks are not individualists devoting themselves to a solely personal pursuit of

---

10. Ladner, "*Homo Viator.*"
11. Taylor, *A Secular Age*, 32.
12. Taylor, *A Secular Age*, 35.
13. Taylor, *A Secular Age*, 44.

salvation. They pray for the world, in the world's stead. So the social body lives this tension between the demands of transformation and of the mundane by a kind of division of labor.

Two-tiered medieval Christianity was characterized by a divergence between, on the one hand, a faith in which the doctrinal element was more developed, and in which devotional life took to some degree the form of inner prayer, and later even meditative practices; and on the other hand a faith in which the belief content was very rudimentary, and devotional practice was largely a matter of what one did, "une religion du faire, non du savoir."[14]

But the social body in Christendom had a sense of time that allowed even those engaged in domestic life to know rhythms, seasons, and rituals that allowed them to inhabit the tension between the mundane and the transcendent. This could be as simple as not eating meat on Fridays or during Lent. Rituals also dealt with this tension in order to foster equilibrium. Taylor's most extensive example is Carnival, when the ordinary order of things was inverted and what was ordinarily revered was mocked. The demands of virtue were not compromised or relaxed but they were periodically suspended. Boys wore miters, fools were made kings, and people permitted themselves various forms of license. "The weight of virtue and good order was so heavy, and so much steam built up under the suppression of instinct, that there had to be periodic blow-outs if the whole system were not to fly apart."[15] Here again, the equilibrium between sacred and profane demands is maintained, not by resolving the tension but by inhabiting it.

So, in this world, God and society are mixed and intertwined. From the local parish to the universal church, medieval persons are embedded within a complex web of personal, economic, political, and ecclesiastical arrangements, which reinforce a sense of society itself as a locus of divine power. These arrangements are plural and highly differentiated. The celibate clergy prays and fulfills priestly and pastoral functions for a married laity, which in turn supports the clergy. Monks pray for all, from the thirteenth century onwards, new mendicant orders preach, and others provide alms and hospitals. Over time the tension between different roles had been overlaid with an equilibrium, based on complementarity of functions.[16] The millennium-long emergence of the secular world involved the gradual

14. Taylor, *A Secular Age*, 63, citing Pierre Chaunu.
15. Taylor, *A Secular Age*, 46.
16. Taylor, *A Secular Age*, 44.

CHAPTER 4: THE REFORM OF THE WORLD AND THE MAKING OF A SECULAR AGE

breakdown of this integrated religious society and the rise of a new social imaginary in which people no longer conceived of themselves as necessarily embedded within a holistic network of institutions and beliefs.

This transformation was manifold and its preparation required hundreds of years. The story as Taylor tells it centers on the matrix of what he calls the work of "Reform": the "Reform Master Narrative."[17]

Taylor builds upon Ladner's account of the idea of reform to argue that Reform arises from "a profound dissatisfaction with the hierarchical equilibrium between lay life and the renunciative vocations."[18] From the perspective of Reform, these interdependent multiple "speeds," of belief and practice, like those of integration into the European Union, are problematic, for the "equilibrium involved accepting that masses of people were not going to live up to the demands of perfection. They were being 'carried,' in a sense, by the perfect."[19]

Differences of "speed" can end up being unambiguously accepted in terms of relationships of complementarity and exchange. In many Buddhist societies the laity feed the monks and thereby gain merit against better future rebirths. In medieval Christendom aristocratic patrons endowed monasteries and the monks prayed for the repose of their souls. But what seems peculiar to Latin Christendom is the deep and growing dissatisfaction with this two-"speed" model. Serious attempts were made to narrow the gap between the fastest and the slowest. The dissatisfaction grew and manifested itself in different movements, some among elites, and some among the people—at both levels.[20]

Taylor emphasizes that this movement of Reform is quite different from "small 'r'" reform, through which the higher speeds work through proselytism and renewal movements "to convert more people from these [slower speeds] to the higher 'speeds.'"[21] Whereas small "r" reformers sought to spread their "forms of practice and devotion, by preaching, encouragement, and example," Reformers sought to *delegitimize* the slower speeds. Taylor identifies motivating factors that underlie the attempts of both reformers and Reformers to restore and revitalize the lives of the faithful, including new forms of piety and a suspicion of "magic." But unlike

17. Colorado, review article on *A Secular Age*.
18. Taylor, *A Secular Age*, 61.
19. Taylor, *A Secular Age*, 62.
20. Taylor, *A Secular Age*, 62.
21. Taylor, *A Secular Age*, 62.

groups like the Brethren of the Common Life, a confraternity which aimed to reduce the distance between the two "speeds" by integrating the life of prayer more closely into everyday life—thus remaining at the level of "small 'r' reform"—"large 'R'" reformers felt compelled to "smash the old dispensation" of multispeed hierarchical religious life.[22]

A fundamental part of the smashing the multispeed dispensation was the suppression of "magic," including what was considered to be a misuse of the sacraments. To explain the primacy of magic before a secular age Taylor describes a shift in our conceptions of subjectivity. For moderns in the context of secularity, meaning is situated exclusively within the human mind, "in the sense that things only have the meaning they do in that they awaken a certain response in us, and this has to do with our nature as creatures who are capable of such responses, which means creatures with feelings, with desires, aversions, i.e., beings endowed with minds, in the broadest sense."[23]

This stands in stark contrast to conceptions of meaning in the enchanted medieval world where a "porous self" is open to the causal powers of demons and spirits and enchanted or "charged" objects. The modern "buffered" self has sharp boundaries. Porous selves turned to "good magic"—to relics, or to the eucharistic host—for magical protection. Reform confronted and undermined such popular piety. Under its influence the faithful were pulled "towards a quite different form of liturgy and church life, in which the sacraments tend to become purely symbolic, authority slides away from a hierarchy, and is placed back in Scripture, and the visible church is more sharply distinguished from the true community of the saved."[24]

Taylor notes that, though these historical shifts have been referred to as a series of "Proto-Reformations," a fundamental element of the Reformation is absent—Luther's doctrine of *sola fide*. Taylor contends that justification by faith found fertile ground in the field of fear that characterized the late Middle Ages, as believers were inundated by the dread of damnation that went with the corrupt system of the sale of indulgences, which added to the already significant fears of demonic agencies that impinged on the porous selves of that "enchanted" era. By articulating a doctrine that could assuage these fears, Taylor argues that "Luther was touching on the neuralgic issue of his day . . . In raising his standard on this issue, Luther was

---

22. Taylor, *A Secular Age*, 76.
23. Taylor, *A Secular Age*, 31.
24. Taylor, *A Secular Age*, 74.

CHAPTER 4: THE REFORM OF THE WORLD AND THE MAKING OF A SECULAR AGE

on to something which could move masses of people, unlike the humanist critique of mass piety, or the rejection of the sacred."[25]

The contribution of the Protestant Reformation to the earlier history of Reform that Taylor traces is twofold. First, the Reformation had a massive role in the disenchantment of the world; and second, chiefly through its Calvinist streams, the Reformation gave rise to a new order of discipline that sought the remake the world. Taylor argues that disenchantment contributes to a change in the "center of gravity of religious life," with an increased internalization.

> The power of God doesn't operate through various "sacramentals," or locations of sacred power which we can draw upon. These are seen to be something we can control, and hence are blasphemous. In one way, we can see that the sacred/profane distinction breaks down, insofar as it can be placed in person, space, time, gesture. This means that the sacred is suddenly broadened: for the saved, God is sanctifying us everywhere, hence also in ordinary life, our work, in marriage, and so on.
>
> But in another way, the channels are radically narrowed, because this sanctification depends entirely now on our inner transformation, our throwing ourselves on God's mercy in faith.[26]

As the Reformation deepened its disenchantment of Christendom, it eventually reached a point where the sacraments themselves are redefined: the movement moves away from the "magical" sacramentality associated with the corrupt hierarchical church to a conception of sacraments as purely symbolic. The Reformation can be understood as subjecting Christianity to a movement towards "excarnation," away from more enfleshed forms of piety, which included practices such as lighting candles blessed in churches at Candlemas, ringing church bells when lightning threatens, or "creeping to the cross" on Good Friday and other practices that accompany the liturgy. This movement towards "excarnation" included, for some Protestants, a rejection of the celebration of Mass as well as belief in the real presence.

This "Reform Master Narrative" is thus the story of the loss of the medieval equilibrium between otherworldliness and worldliness. It is the story of an attempt to relieve the tension between loving and hating the world that paradoxically results in both a broadening of the sacred and in a movement towards "excarnation."

---

25. Taylor, *A Secular Age*, 75.
26. Taylor, *A Secular Age*, 79.

The teaching of *contemptus mundi* had been directly used in the effort of Reform to raise the level of religious devotion and practice of the whole society. In particular the action of mendicant preachers had a destabilizing effect on the hierarchical church when they preached *contemptus mundi* and fear of the last judgment to the laity. A "pastoral of fear" fostered a spirituality of death that was an important step towards undermining the multispeed system. A previously ascetic stance towards death, as in Jerome's depiction with a skull, became a mass phenomenon. The pleasures of the flesh pass and are barely real and in turning to these pleasures we are neglecting what is really important, the issue that we face beyond death, the judgment of God upon our whole life. And our response to this judgment is our own individual responsibility. Contempt for the world, dramatization of death, and the insistence on personal salvation emerge together. All Christians are called to live for something beyond ordinary human flourishing, compelled by a new guilt and fear, and not just a top tier.[27]

But a form of love for the world also comes to determine the dynamic of Reform: "the affirmation of ordinary life."[28] The original form of this affirmation was theological, and it involved a positive vision of ordinary life as hallowed by God. Work and family life are seen as having a higher significance conferred on them by God. This is what grounds the affirmation. None of this is to be considered profane. In their ambivalence about the world, medieval Christians experienced life in diverse ways and, alongside the literature of *contemptus mundi*, there are also repeated reforming attempts to bring a more intense devotional life closer to everyday life where it had previously been absent. Thus the mendicant friars took on some of the disciplines of monasticism, including poverty and celibacy, but took them out of the cloister into the world.

A connection can be seen between this aspiration and profound shifts in representation, which can be seen in Western painting after the High Middle Ages; between the Franciscan movement and a new "realism," a new interest in portraying the particular people around one in religious painting, which begins with Giotto. In the centuries that follow Renaissance Italian and later Netherlands art, painting moves out of the orbit of the icon, which tends to portray Christ, Mary, and the saints as almost archetypal figures, dwelling in higher time, and paints them as human beings, present in their own time, people whom their viewers could meet in their

---

27. Taylor, *A Secular Age*, 65–69, citing Aries and Delumeau.
28. Taylor, *Sources of the Self*, Part III.

CHAPTER 4: THE REFORM OF THE WORLD AND THE MAKING OF A SECULAR AGE

own world. This painting indicates a "strong Incarnational spirituality" that attempts to see "Jesus and Mary as having really been among us." It is not a "turning away from transcendence" but "an attempt to live it more fully by bringing it completely into our world."[29]

The perennial tension between loving and hating the world, between the demand to love God on the one hand, to be ready to renounce everything, and the demand to affirm ordinary life and flourishing on the other hand, remained. The two come together in the path of giving to God that often takes the form of feeding, healing, clothing; fending off suffering and death, and thus making human flourishing possible.

The tension intensifies when it comes to determining what the Christian life is for those who are engaged in human flourishing, through work, family, civic life, and friends. The holy renouncer puts the two together in that his or her renunciation can directly serve works of mercy and healing. But what about the person engaged in ordinary life, married with children, living from the land or from trade? Taylor submits that an answer can be given that is valid in theory for everyone:

> Go beyond the kind of affirmation of the good of life which the ordinary *homme moyen sensuel* makes, which is very much focused on my own good, my own life, and might even be willing to sacrifice endless others to this; and connect to the affirmation of God, his agape, which loves all humankind, and is ready to give without stint, to let go of what I hold in order to be part of a movement of love.
>
> For the ordinary householder this answer seems to require something paradoxical: living in all the practices and institutions of flourishing, but at the same time not fully in them. Being in them but not of them; being in them, yet at a distance, ready to lose them. As Augustine put it: use the things of this world, but don't enjoy them; *uti*, not *frui*. Or do it all for the glory of God, in the Loyola-Calvin formulation.
>
> The big problem is working out what this means. Any attempt to tie it down faces two opposite dangers. One is to set the element of renunciation so high as to make the life of flourishing a travesty of itself, as in medieval teaching to the laity about married sexuality, which totally excluded any sexual joy. The other is to set a bare minimum, keeping only certain important commandments. Even these will often be broken; so in the end the minimum demands simply that you repent in time.

---

29. Taylor, *A Secular Age*, 144.

> The end result here is that the inherent danger built into this tension itself now befalls us. We clearly set the renunciative vocations above the ordinary lay ones. There are first—and second—class citizens; the second in a sense being carried by the first. We fall back into hierarchical complementarity. Whereas the crucial truth we wanted to hold on to was the complementarity of all lives and vocations, where we all serve under God and can't put some above others.[30]

So for Taylor there seems a dilemma here for discipleship, between demanding too much renunciation from the ordinary person on the one hand, and relaxing these demands, but at the cost of a multispeed system, on the other hand.

Radical Protestantism utterly rejected the multispeed system, and in the name of this abolishes the supposedly higher, renunciative vocations; but also builds renunciation into ordinary life. It avoids the second horn of this dilemma, but comes close to the first danger of loading ordinary flourishing with a burden of renunciation it cannot carry. It fills out the picture of what a properly sanctified life would be with a severe set of moral demands. This seems to be unavoidable in the logic of rejecting complementarity, because if we really must hold that all vocations are equally demanding, and don't want this to be a leveling down, then all must be at the most exigent pitch. Protestantism is in the line of continuity with medieval reform here, attempting to raise standards, not satisfied with a world in which only a few integrally fulfilled the gospel, but trying to make certain pious practices absolutely general.

Peter Damian had written of the eleventh-century monastic reformer Romuald that "his ardent desire was that he might make the whole world a hermitage or convert them [the laity] to monastic order and save the whole multitude of the populace."[31] Romuald's desire was realized in the *magna monasterium* of Calvin's Geneva (and prefigured in the Arles of Bishop Caesarius). "Having overthrown monasticism [Calvinism's] aim was to turn the world into a gigantic monastery, and in Geneva, for a short time it almost succeeded."[32]

Protestant Reform affirmed ordinary life as a way to holiness. But ordinary lives, and whole societies, were now to be disciplined by a puritan "rage

---

30. Taylor, *A Secular Age*, 81.
31. Damian, *Vita Romualdi*, 37.78.
32. Tawney, *Religion and the Rise of Capitalism*, 115.

CHAPTER 4: THE REFORM OF THE WORLD AND THE MAKING OF A SECULAR AGE

for order" that sought to relieve the tension between loving and hating the world with what Weber described as an "inner-worldly asceticism."[33] Carnivals and dancing are suppressed. Laxity and disorder are punished. Taylor argues that closely connected to the progress of Reform was the rise of the "disciplinary society" and the emergence of the modern moral order.

Grounding both developments was a radically altered view of nature, the origins of which he traces especially to Nominalist philosophy. This replaced the old view of nature as endowed with intrinsic purpose and essence with a new view of it as indeterminate and possessing only extrinsic purpose. In this sense nature was no longer simply viewed as a given but became, at least in principle, infinitely malleable. When turned inward this stance of instrumental reason had far-reaching effects. For rather than passively accepting his own nature, man began the process of actively remaking himself. Crucial to this was a voluntarist understanding of the will as the engine of moral change—another legacy of Nominalism.

Taylor traces this voluntarist understanding through diverse movements including the Renaissance culture of civility, late medieval Reform, and the Calvinist Reformation, arguing that all of these manifest in different ways a shared desire to transform the "raw nature" of humanity.[34] He sees its culmination in the movement of Neo-Stoicism, embodied by Lipsius and Descartes. The Stoic norm of detachment, which led both to a new ethic of rational control and discipline and a transformed view of "buffered identity." Applied to the political sphere this led to an unprecedented attempt to transform, or discipline, society through the application of instrumental reason. As Taylor suggests, it was this disengaged, disciplined stance that became "an essential part of the defining repertory" of modernity. In the long term, its effect lay in what he terms the "great disembedding."[35] Where before men and women were unable to imagine themselves outside of a particular social and cosmic context, now for the first time the stance of detachment made this possible. Disembedded, society fragmented from a unified whole into a collection of buffered individuals.

An older conception of the self as embedded in a holistic but differentiated natural-social-theological order slowly gave way to a "disembedded" selfhood understood to be ontologically prior to and independent of its surroundings. A realist conception of the world as the bearer of intrinsic

33. Weber, *The Protestant Ethic*, chap. 4.
34. Taylor, *A Secular Age*, 112.
35. Taylor, *A Secular Age*, 156.

meanings to which we must conform was supplanted by the notion that the only orders we must acknowledge are those we construct for ourselves. The result was a new conception of atomistic individuals who are responsible only to themselves and only contingently responsive to those around them. This new model of the human being came to be shared across a wide spectrum of early modern philosophers (notably, Descartes, Locke, and Kant) and eventually solidified in the "buffered self." The buffered self is assertive, rationalistic, and stakes a claim to autarky that shuts down its experience of intimacy even in relation to its own bodily passions.

Living in a disenchanted world, the buffered self is no longer open, vulnerable to a world of spirits and forces that cross the boundary of the mind, and indeed, negate the very idea of there being a secure boundary. "The fears, anxieties, even terrors that belong to the porous self are behind it."[36] This sense of self-possession, of a secure inner mental realm, is all the stronger, if in addition to disenchanting the world, unbelief expands to question the existence of God. For the first time the very idea of human dependence upon a transcendent or nonhuman order came to seem potentially dispensable. The way was now clear for the appearance of an "exclusive humanism" that no longer felt the urgency of an appeal to transcendence. A secular age is close.[37]

In the disciplinary society, the good order of civility and the good order of piety to some extent merged and inflected each other.[38] Expectations were lowered. Where Christians had once preserved a tension between the pursuit of supernatural perfection and the promotion of worldly flourishing—distinguished as "perfect" and "imperfect" vocations—reformers wished to make spiritual ideals more accessible. This led them to de-emphasize the goal of divinization in favor of habits of self-control, industry, and thrift. Bonaventure had interpreted Ecclesiastes within the thousand-year-old tradition that came down from Origen and Jerome as a penitential guidebook and thus a step towards the union of the soul with God. Martin Luther's lectures on Ecclesiastes in 1526 condemned and broke with this tradition. He responded to the text with an extended commentary on the meaning of Christian vocations in the world and the need for moderation.

---

36. Taylor, *A Secular Age*, 301.

37. Gordon, "The Place of the Sacred in the Absence of God," 662; and Gregory, *The Unintended Reformation*.

38. Taylor, *A Secular Age*, 105.

CHAPTER 4: THE REFORM OF THE WORLD AND THE MAKING OF A SECULAR AGE

Two things followed from this new Protestant emphasis.[39] First, Christianity became increasingly identified with a bourgeois moral code. Taylor chronicles the ways in which Christianity was transformed from a message of salvation into a bulwark of "civilization" and a guarantor of social order. Second, the idea that God has intentions for human life infinitely beyond worldly flourishing went into eclipse. For many, the answer to "What are God's purposes for us?" was simply "To preserve life, bring prosperity, and reduce suffering."

The collapse of Christianity into a conventional ethics midwifed something new: the ability to interpret the world nontheistically. As the goals for life became immanent, Christians began asking if appeals to God were necessary to ground morality and pursue human flourishing. Aren't reason and natural human desires sufficient to motivate us to preserve life, bring prosperity, and reduce suffering? In pressing these sorts of questions, Taylor argues, Christians slowly discovered the ability to conceive of themselves and the natural world apart from divine purposes. Life without God became imaginable, and some even wondered if Christian faith might be an obstacle to human well-being. The idea of a Supreme Being who issues commandments and promises salvation needlessly complicated utilitarian calculations. The self-undoing of Western Christianity was underway. Soon, all striving for something beyond human welfare—the pursuit of holiness—came to be regarded by many as fanatical or absurd.

Protestants had promoted "the affirmation of ordinary life" to dethrone the supposedly higher activity of contemplation and put the center of gravity of goodness in ordinary living, production, and the family. But their earthly critique of contemplatives was later transposed, and used as a secular critique of Christianity. Something of the same rhetorical stance adopted by Reformers against monks and nuns is taken up by secularists and unbelievers like Nietzsche against Christian faith itself. Faith allegedly scorns the real, sensual, earthly human good for some purely imaginative higher end, the pursuit of which can only lead to the frustration of the real, earthly human good, to suffering, mortification and repression. The motivation of those who espouse this "higher" path is suspect.[40]

---

39. Rose, "Tayloring Christianity."
40. Taylor, *A Secular Age*, 370.

Worldlessness: the Intellectual Deviation story

Taylor tells the story of the Reform Master Narrative. Reform demanded that everyone be a real 100 percent Christian. Reform not only disenchants but also disciplines and reorders life and society. Persecuting societies arise and become colonial empires. Along with civility, this makes for a notion of moral order, which gives a new sense to Christianity, and the demands of faith. This collapses the distance of faith from the social order of Christendom. It induces an anthropocentric shift, and hence the breakout from the monopoly of Christian faith.[41]

But Taylor acknowledges that there is another story of Western "secularization" in addition to the one that he tells, the "Intellectual Deviation story." He doesn't think this story can suffice as the main story behind secularity but he sees the two stories as complementary. "ID" deals with changes in theoretical understanding, mainly among learned and related elites. It clarifies some of the crucial intellectual and theological connections. In obvious complicity with Reform it helped to destroy the medieval-Christian cosmos and bequeath a kind of "worldlessness" that became a hallmark of the modern age.

One disturbing version of the "ID" story is that presented by Hans Blumenberg in Part II of *The Legitimacy of the Modern Age*.[42] He presents an apologia for modern worldliness, that is, of the emergence of what he terms "human self-assertion" as the fundamental existential attitude of the modern age. What he has in mind is a radically active, even reconstructive, orientation to the world, in which the world now appears as something to be mastered and reality as something to be constructed or reconstructed according to a human order. According to Blumenberg, this shift in self-understanding had as its precondition the theological absolutism of late medieval Nominalism. By taking the thesis of divine omnipotence to its logical conclusion, Blumenberg argues, Nominalist theology rejected any claim for the necessity of a rational and providentially ordered cosmos on the grounds that it would limit God's power. This led to an "*Ordnungsshwund*," a loss of ordering, that so radically transformed the way the world was experienced that it prepared the way for a radically new stance within that world—the creative, world-transforming activity of modern

---

41. Taylor, *A Secular Age*, 744.

42. Blumenberg, *The Legitimacy of the Modern Age*, Part II; Kroll, *A Human End to History?*; and Bielik-Robson and Whistler, eds., *Interrogating Modernity*.

CHAPTER 4: THE REFORM OF THE WORLD AND THE MAKING OF A SECULAR AGE

self-assertion. The world ordained by God's unbounded will no longer presented itself as ordered to human reason and human needs. It is an indifferent and essentially arbitrary reality. In opposition to a new form of Gnosticism, modernity attempted to establish a ground for human well-being in human self-assertion.

Blumenberg claims that "the modern age is the second overcoming of Gnosticism."[43] Catholic Christianity rejected gnostic dualism in the process of its formation. "[T]he Christianity that emerged as the predominant voice was consistently anxious to put Humpty-Dumpty together again," to show that the world can be "reassembled" and that the appearance of rupture reflects prior error or distortion; now there is a new synthesis which defines itself against the disruption of "Gnosticism."[44] But for Blumenberg, Humpty Dumpty has another great fall and now Christians couldn't put him together again.

According to Blumenberg, the formation of the Middle Ages can only be understood as an attempt at the definitive exclusion of the gnostic syndrome. To retrieve the world as the creation from the negative role assigned to it by the doctrine of its demiurgic origin, and to salvage the dignity of the ancient cosmos for its role in the Christian system, was the central effort all the way from Augustine to the height of Scholasticism.[45] This abiding Christian anxiety to recompose the world was focused on the question of the origin of what is evil in the world. If God is omnipotent and if his creation, including matter, is indeed good, where does all that is evil in the world come from? Gnostics found in their separation of the creator god from the god of salvation an easy solution to this Christian dilemma. They propose an anti-cosmic dualism. According to Marcion, the creator God of the Old Testament is himself an evil tyrant who laid down a law impossible to fulfill, created a natural order hostile and oppressive to the human spirit, and plunged the soul into a body subject to suffering, sickness, and death. Thus the creator God himself would become the principle and source of all evil in the world. The God of the New Testament, on the other hand, is an "alien god," the transcendent God of salvation, whose purpose is no longer the redemption of the world but rather redemption from the world, from all that is evil. "Gnosticism," writes Blumenberg,

---

43. Blumenberg, *The Legitimacy of the Modern Age*, 126.
44. Williams, *Why Study the Past?*
45. Blumenberg, *The Legitimacy of the Modern Age*, 130.

has no need of theodicy since the good God has never had anything to do with the world. Even the bringer of salvation, sent by the good God to deliver the lost *pneuma* through *gnosis*, can only appear to assume a human body in order to deceive the demiurge's watchmen. The downfall of the world becomes the critical process of final salvation, the dissolution of the demiurge's illegitimate creation.[46]

The price Marcion had to pay for this resolution of the dilemma that confronted early Christianity was of course the dignity of the ancient cosmos and the harmonious place of human persons within it. In the classical tradition the cosmos was considered to be both beautiful and rational, the perfect exemplar of divine order. "Born to contemplate the cosmos and to imitate it," Cicero wrote, "he is far from being perfect, but he is a little part of the perfect" (*De Natura Deorum* 2.11–14). Here, the Greek notion of the cosmos gives a profound sense of belonging to the world.

The gnostic revaluation of the classical cosmos on the other hand is motivated by an equally profound sense of human alienation from the world. The gnostics retained the notion of cosmos as "order," but with a vengeance. The attribute of order and lawfulness, which in the classical tradition had secured the attunement of human reason and action to the cosmological order, was now viewed as radically opposed to the inner essence and aspirations of humankind. The cosmic order was no longer understood to be in harmony with human reason, but was experienced now as an alien force acting only to thwart human freedom. All meaning and goodness were located outside of this order, outside of this world. This negative valuation of the cosmos is in turn balanced by a positive conception of a strictly "otherworldly" deity. The true God is an alien God, totally Other, not merely supra-mundane but fundamentally contra-mundane. With this, as Hans Jonas writes, "the sublime unity of the cosmos and God is broken up, the two are torn apart, and a gulf never completely to be closed is opened: God and the world, God and nature, spirit and nature, become divorced, alien from each other, even contraries."[47] But if these two are alien to each other, then human persons and the world, nature, and the body are also alien to each other. The gnostic solution to the problem of the origin of what is bad or evil

---

46. Blumenberg, *The Legitimacy of the Modern Age*, 128–29, cited in Brient, *The Immanence of the Infinite*, 45.

47. Jonas, *The Gnostic Religion*, 251, cited by Brient, *The Immanence of the Infinite*, 47.

CHAPTER 4: THE REFORM OF THE WORLD AND THE MAKING OF A SECULAR AGE

in this world was bought at the price of an irreducible alienation from the world and from ourselves as worldly, embodied beings.

Augustine's Christian response to this problem of theodicy was as radical as the difficulty that confronted it. Evil simply does not exist. The act of creation is good by definition and produces nothing but good. Evil is nothingness, *privatio*, lack of what ought to be. Augustine learnt from the books of the Platonists that it has no ontological foundation. Whatever is, is good, since being is entirely from God. Having no ontological foundation, evil is a matter of evil will. The fallen self-centered will is recalcitrant. Human suffering may then be understood as God's just punishment for human disobedience. The concept of human freedom together with the doctrine of original sin steps in to bear the burden of what is evil in the world.

But Blumenberg contends that Gnosticism was not overcome by Augustine's solution to the problem of evil but "only transposed [and] returns in the form of the 'hidden God' and His inconceivable absolute sovereignty" in late medieval Nominalism.[48] Augustine's doctrine of predestination restricted grace to a small number of the elect and thus left the continuing guilt of the all too many to explain the lasting corruption of the world. But is not God once again responsible for the evil of the world if he is responsible for arbitrarily withholding his grace from the sinner?

Blumenberg fails to explain why it took centuries for the tensions in Augustinian power to emerge with such destructive power in the "theological absolutism" of late medieval Nominalism. But one answer would surely be that they only did so when the equilibrium of Augustinian ideas was lost. Sacramental ontology balanced an emphasis on divine transcendence with a corresponding emphasis on divine immanence in an exemplification of Chesterton's "experiment of an irregular equilibrium." In complete contrast with Gnosticism, it was a systematically central concern of the Platonist-Christian tradition to provide a theoretical framework for understanding the simultaneous transcendence and immanence of the divine in the world. Both gnostics and Nominalists rejected the ancient and Scholastic conception of a beautiful and intelligible cosmos, hierarchically and teleologically ordered, in which human nature finds its natural place. Both reject the ancient and Scholastic view of humankind as "born to contemplate the universe" in harmony with the ruling principle of the universe through the highest part of the soul, the intellect. For both, human good and meaning ultimately lie outside this world order altogether, dependent on the

---

48. Blumenberg, *The Legitimacy of the Modern Age*, 135.

transcendent God of salvation. Blumenberg's assertion that Nominalism exhibits the resurgence of at least certain elements of ancient Gnosticism is thus not without some warrant, at least superficially.[49]

But if he points in the right direction, he does not appreciate the way in which modernity takes form within the metaphysical and theological structures of Christian tradition.[50] He correctly perceives that modernity arose not in opposition to or as a continuation of the medieval world but out of its rubble. However, superior or more powerful ideas did not drive out or overcome medieval ideas; rather they pushed over the remnants of the medieval world after the internecine struggles between Scholasticism and Nominalism had reduced it to rubble. Modern "reason" was able to overcome medieval "superstition" and "dogma" only because that "dogma" was fatally weakened by the great theological crisis that brought the world in which it made sense to an end.[51]

This revolution in thought was itself a reflection of a deeper transformation in the way people experienced the world. Scholastics in the High Middle Ages were ontological realists, that is to say, they believed in the real existence of universals. To put it another way, they experienced the world as the instantiation of the categories of divine reason. They experienced, believed in, and asserted the ultimate reality not of particular things but of universals: in a red balloon the color red is a universal, for example. They articulated this experience in a syllogistic logic that was perceived to correspond to or reflect divine reason. Creation itself was the embodiment of this reason, and the human person, as a rational animal and *imago dei*, stood at the pinnacle of this creation, guided by a natural *telos* and a divinely revealed supernatural goal.

Nominalism brought this world to an end. For the Nominalists, all real being was individual or particular and universals were thus mere fictions. Words did not point to real universal entities but were merely signs useful for human understanding. Creation was radically particular and thus not teleological. As a result, God could not be understood by human reason but only by biblical revelation or mystical experience. Human beings thus have no natural or supernatural end or *telos*. In this way the Nominalist revolution against Scholasticism destroyed the medieval

---

49. Hubener, "Das 'gnostische Rezidiv,'" cited in Brient, *The Immanence of the Infinite*, 52n82.

50. Gillespie, *The Theological Origins of Modernity*, 12.

51. Gillespie, *The Theological Origins of Modernity*, 14.

world and brought to an end the effort to salvage the dignity of the ancient cosmos for its role in the Christian system and to reconcile it with the Christian notion of an omnipotent creator.

The God that Aquinas describes was omnipotent in the glory of his works and the certainty of his goodness was manifest in the world. The nominalist God, by contrast, was fearful in his omnipotence, utterly beyond human understanding, and a threat to human well-being. This God cannot be captured in words and can be experienced as a titanic question that evoked awe and dread. This is the question the "ID" story presents as standing at the beginning of modernity.[52] And at the end of modernity this dark god of nominalism appears enthroned within the bastion of reason as the grim lord of Stalin's universal terror.[53]

The new vision of God that rose to prominence in the fourteenth century emphasized divine power and unpredictability rather than divine love and reason, but this new God made sense of tremendous changes in the world itself, changes which made the Nominalist vision believable. Peter Sloterdijk calls the period of the Black Death (1347–1349) the "date of all dates" in European intellectual history and Boccaccio's *Decameron*, a collection of tales told by a small group trying to escape the plague, the "charter of foundation" of modernity.[54] Fifty million people died in Europe. It was an event comparable to a nuclear war. Survivors faced the question of theodicy; the difficulty of continuing to believe in a loving, benevolent God, a God whose goodness is manifest in the world.

Blumenberg assumed that worldliness in some obvious sense is the fundamental characteristic of the modern age, in contrast with medieval

---

52. "Modern rationality, best exemplified by the development of science, is antimetaphysical [to] avoid any speculation on the infinite and the absolute so as not to reawaken the Gnostic spectre of incontrollable power. *Pace* Voegelin, who criticizes modernity as an epoch bursting with triumphant hubris, Blumenberg notices its deeply protected secret of fragility: self-assertion, which started with the Cartesian rebellion against *deus fallax*, was and remains a decisionistic *gesture* which has nothing to do with self-deification. It does not rely on the *fundamentum inconcussum* of indubitable absolute knowledge. It is an act of finite will against infinite voluntarism; an act in which the finite human mind, no longer capable of trusting in God, decides to trust in itself. It is precisely this fragile decisionistic core, hidden under the surface of triumphant rational rhetoric, which opens a completely new perspective on 'interrogating modernity' ..." Bielik-Robson and Whistler, *Interrogating Modernity*, 198–99.

53. Gillespie, *Nihilism before Nietzsche*, 173.

54. Sloterdijk, "Man muss sich von allem freimachen," 35–36, cited by Vanheeswicjk, "The End of Secularization?," 17n31.

otherworldliness. But for Hannah Arendt it is not worldliness that characterizes the modern age but an "unequalled *worldlessness*." "Modern man when he lost the certainty of the world to come, was thrown back upon himself and not upon this world."[55] Blumenberg invokes Arendt at the very beginning of *The Legitimacy of the Modern Age* but fails to use her analysis as an impetus to question his assumption.[56] She identifies the paradox of the "unworldly worldliness" of the modern age. An inner-worldly asceticism has become the inner-worldly alienation of the new capitalist mentality.

The greatness of Max Weber's discovery about the origins of capitalism lay precisely in his demonstration that an enormous, strictly mundane activity is possible without any care for or enjoyment of the world whatever, an activity whose deepest motivation, on the contrary, is worry and care about the self. World alienation, and not self-alienation as Marx thought, has been the hallmark of the modern age.

Man has "removed himself from the earth to a much more distant point than any Christian otherworldliness had ever removed him."[57] An ontic dualism posits mind over against a mechanistic, meaning-shorn universe, without internal purposes such as the older cosmos had before Nominalism. This stance contributes to a turn inward as a base for a triumphant and destructive grasp of the world, intellectually and practically.

> Whatever the word "secular" is meant to signify in current usage, historically it cannot possibly be equated with worldliness; modern man at any rate did not gain this world when he lost the other world, and he did not gain life, strictly speaking either; he was thrust back upon it . . .[58]

Thus an age that has defined itself by the very intensity of its "this-worldly" orientation is at the same time haunted by an ever growing sense of world loss, of the "*Unheimlichkeit*," the uncanniness or unhomeliness of modern reality.[59] On the one hand the modern turning away from the transcendent and contemplative ideals and values of antiquity and the Middle Ages is evidenced by a profoundly new, active, and constructive approach to the world. Modern science is predicated on an objective stance that demystifies the cosmos and allows for a technological mastery of nature.

---

55. Arendt, *The Human Condition*, chap. 35, "World Alienation."
56. Blumenberg, *The Legitimacy of the Modern Age*, 8–9.
57. Blumenberg, *The Legitimacy of the Modern Age*, 8.
58. Blumenberg, *The Legitimacy of the Modern Age*, 9.
59. Brient, "Hans Blumenberg and Hannah Arendt."

CHAPTER 4: THE REFORM OF THE WORLD AND THE MAKING OF A SECULAR AGE

The modern conception of the self is grounded in a new conception of the autonomy and dignity of the individual, and modern political theory begins with the notion that society is an artifact to be constructed in the service of the very individuals who constitute the body politic. Yet, we are made uneasy by the nagging suspicion that the life in this world that we have remade for ourselves is somehow hollow, an artificial construction without depth or solidity, a merely superficial order, which threatens to dissolve into meaninglessness, beyond the screens of our addiction to virtual reality. The technological advances made possible by modern self-assertion and modern science have also brought man-made mass death and environmental catastrophe. Power over nature has led to the power to destroy nature. The modern world has seen an unprecedented rise in individual freedom, and yet the autonomy of the individual has all too often resulted in the anomie of the individual. Loss of community advances alongside emancipation. Paradoxically, then, modern worldliness is attended by an uneasy sense of world alienation.

Contra Blumenberg, it seems that this worldlessness shows that secular modernity was unable to recompose the world. A gulf had opened that was never completely closed. Secular modernity did not recover a deep sense of belonging to the world as a cosmos, or of loving the world, for all its vaunted worldliness. To adapt an image used by Georg Lukacs in *The Destruction of Reason*, we have taken up residence in the "Grand Hotel Abyss . . . a beautiful hotel, equipped with every comfort, on the edge of an abyss, of nothingness, of absurdity."[60] Worldlessness and not worldliness is our condition in a secular age.

---

60. Lukacs, *The Destruction of Reason*, 242–43.

Chapter 5: Ambivalence and the Critique of Modernity

Amor mundi: Hannah Arendt and Hans Jonas

IT HAS BEEN CLAIMED that the only possible form that philosophy can take today is the critique of modernity.[1] If world loss is an inherent danger of the modern project of self-assertion, that does not imply that the fundamental orientation of the modern age is altogether bankrupt: modern world-alienation is not the inevitable consequence of a "wrong turning" in the past. The course of the development of the modern age is just as contingent, dynamic, and dialogical as its Christian past. Its history is the history not only of the development of modern self-assertion but also of the rich, varied, and continuing history of modern attempts to arrive at solutions to its malaise. Yet the form these attempts have taken has often been that of critiques of the modern world—for the love of the world.

The work of two of Martin Heidegger's conflicted Jewish "children,"[2] Hannah Arendt and Hans Jonas, can be understood in this way as responses to modern wordlessness and as critiques of a modernity that was characterized by Jonas as a revival of Gnosticism.[3] Both wrote student dis-

---

1. Spaemann, *Philosophische Essays*, 6.
2. Wolin, *Heidegger's Children*.
3. Jacob Taubes once characterized his own apocalyptic and nihilistic attitude, in a reflection on Carl Schmitt: "Let it all go down. *I have no spiritual investment in the world as it is.*" (Cited in Kopp-Oberstebrink and Treml, eds., *Apokalypse und Politik*, 305.) Establishing Taubes at the nexus of the debate, Willem Styfhals has traced the context of Jonas's characterization of modernity as gnostic and how such figures as Eric Voegelin, Odo Marquard, and Gershom Scholem, as well as Hans Blumenberg and Hans Jonas, contended with Gnosticism and its tenets on evil and divine absence as metaphorical detours to address issues of cultural crisis, nihilism, and the legitimacy of the modern world. Styfhals argues that these concerns centered on the difficulty of spiritual

sertations on Augustine.⁴ Arendt remained in intimate critical dialogue with Augustine for the rest of her life. They attempted to overcome modern Gnosticism, and Jonas's work represents the first and most crucial victory against Gnosticism in the (modern) West.⁵ It is not easy to distinguish between what is Jewish and what is Christian in their philosophy; they are so interpenetrated, so codependent, that they cannot be separated without excessive loss. Their thinking remains a school of resistance to modern Gnosticism that has a profound affinity with Christian attempts to love and to recompose the world.⁶

Arendt discerns this gnosis as the foundation of the modern technoscientific project: to "free" men and women from their worldly prison, that is, to break their ties to the earth, to render life artificial. Arendt originally wanted to give her masterwork, *The Human Condition*, another title: *Amor Mundi*. Its prologue relates how the launch of a satellite in 1957 was hailed by an American reporter as the first "step toward escape from men's imprisonment on earth." This strange statement echoed another line carved on the funeral obelisk of a Russian scientist: "Mankind will not remain bound to the earth forever." The emancipation and secularization of the modern age ends with a repudiation of the earth as a prison for human bodies. Science is directed towards making life "artificial," towards cutting the last tie through which men and women even still belong to nature. It is the same desire to escape from imprisonment on earth that is manifest in the attempt to create life in a test tube and in the eagerness to journey to the moon: the wish to escape the human condition, and from nature.

At the core of Jonas's thinking was a plea for a determined "revolt against escapism," a *Revolte gegen die Weltflucht*: against any tendency to withdraw from the problems of the present, particularly against any ethical indifference with regard to the realistic threat of a total annihilation of humankind and the entire natural world.⁷ And as a philosopher of life—a

---

engagement in a world from which the divine has withdrawn, after what Anson Rabinbach called the "non-redemptive apocalypse" of the Holocaust. Styfhals, *No Spiritual Investment in the World*.

4. Coyne, *Heidegger's Confessions*. Coyne reveals Heidegger's hidden debt to Augustine and how Augustinian concepts inform some of Heidegger's most fundamental themes.

5. Vatter, *The Republic of the Living*, 131.

6. Cacciari, *Europe and Empire*, 50.

7. Brumlik, "Revolte wider die Weltflucht," 8, cited in Wiese, *The Life and Thought of Hans Jonas*, 102.

sharp critic of the nihilistic cultures of modernity that had proved capable of producing the Holocaust, a founding father of environmental thought, and a pioneer in biological and medical ethics—Jonas strove for the rights of nature. "After Auschwitz, Earth."[8] He sought to revalue the world in the face of an absent God and to partially reinsert men and women into the continuum of biological life by connecting their freedom back to worldliness and bodily life. He argues that life—not only human life, but also all organic life—makes a claim to freedom and subjectivity. Insofar as the organism differentiates itself metabolically from the surrounding physical world and constantly reasserts its self-maintaining identity within that world, it possesses "selfhood." And insofar as it struggles to maintain this precarious distinction in the face of the constant possibility of its disappearance into the non-being that will engulf it in the end, it possesses "subjectivity," which is to say, the desire and capacity for freedom. "It is in the dark stirrings of primeval organic substance," he writes in the first words of his *The Phenomenon of Life*, "that a principle of freedom shines forth for the first time within the vast necessity of the physical universe—a principle foreign to suns, planets, and atoms."[9]

In his essay "Gnosticism, Existentialism, and Nihilism," Jonas suggested that the alienation of the ancient gnostic from the created world he had studied was similar to that of the modern nihilist: "after a long sojourn in those distant lands returning to my own, the contemporary philosophical scene, I found that what I learnt out there made me now better understand the shore from which I had set out."[10] Both gnostics and modern existentialists share a central experience of exile, homelessness, and estrangement in the world, to which the self responds with feelings of dread or anxiety over its captivity in an alien realm. The absence of the gnostics' alien God, who has no connection with the fallen world is comparable to the "death" of God in modernity. Whether absent or dead, the vacuum left behind by a *deus absconditus* implies the loss of absolute reference points, not only for

---

8. Lazier, *God Interrupted*, 60.

9. Nirenberg, "Choosing Life."

10. Jonas, *The Phenomenon of Life*, 211–35; O'Regan, *Gnostic Return in Modernity*; and Lapidot, "The Legitimacy of Nihilism." Lapidot describes the difference between Hans Blumenberg and Hans Jonas in their formulation of the relation between modernity and Gnosticism. Whereas Jonas read modernity as super-gnostic, Blumenberg asserted modernity as the overcoming of gnosis. Against the reading of this difference as a disagreement between two diverging anti-gnostic positions, Lapidot contends that, in contrast to Jonas, Blumenberg's position is not anti-gnostic, but in fact post-gnostic.

CHAPTER 5: AMBIVALENCE AND THE CRITIQUE OF MODERNITY

understanding the meaning of human life in the world, but also for guiding human values and conduct. But whereas the gnostic creation had at least a negative transcendence, the modern one is completely indifferent, utterly wanting in the possibility of any and all transcendence, and therefore more terrifying. Already in the seventeenth century, with God not yet dead but increasingly noninterventionist in his creation, Pascal was getting scared: "Cast into the infinite immensity of spaces of which I am ignorant, and which know me not, I am frightened."[11] But the terror of scientific modernity, entirely stripped of any teleological view of nature, is much worse. "That nature does not care, one way or the other, is the true abyss," Jonas declared. "That only man cares, in his finitude facing nothing but death, alone with his contingency and the objective meaninglessness of his projecting meanings, is a truly unprecedented situation."[12]

The essay recapitulates the grand themes of Jonas's work. From his early studies of ancient dualisms to his later studies of modern ones, the goal of all his thinking was to help humanity deal with the "truly unprecedented situation" of its modern alienation from nature. He clearly believed that, without a philosophy capable of teaching us how to live in this state of crisis, humanity would end by destroying the very possibility of life on earth.

> My main fear relates to the apocalypse threatening from the unintended dynamics of technical civilization as such, inherent in its structure, whereto it drifts willy-nilly and with exponential acceleration: the apocalypse of the "too much," with the exhaustion, pollution and desolation of the planet... Darkest of all is the possibility... that in the global mass misery of a failing biosphere ... "everyone for himself" becomes the common battle cry, [and] one or the other desperate side will, in the fight for dwindling resources, resort to the *ultima ratio* of atomic war.[13]

Jonas had a clear sense of which philosophies had already shown themselves inadequate to the urgent task of preventing this future. Chief among them was the existentialism of his teacher Heidegger, which had failed so spectacularly to help Heidegger make an ethical choice when confronted with the triumphant power of Nazi nihilism in 1933. As far as Jonas was concerned,

---

11. Pascal, *Pensees*, 26.
12. Jonas, *The Phenomenon of Life*, 214.
13. Jonas, *The Imperative of Responsibility*, 202, cited by Morris, *Hans Jonas's Ethic of Responsibility*, 157.

it was precisely this refusal to take responsibility for life that was the fatal flaw in Heidegger's teachings. For Jonas, Heidegger's ethical indifference toward the inhumanity of the Nazis is causally related to his existential world feeling, which is a secularizing resumption of the ancient gnostic sensibility of *weltflucht*. The categories of Heideggerian existentialism do not describe human existence as such but only one particular type, which is characterized by a sense of estrangement from the cosmos and a tendency to ethical nihilism. In *Being and Time*, Heidegger speaks of "thrownness" into the voidness of the world, "fallenness," "abandonment," and a "fundamental disposition to dread." These concepts had allowed Jonas to recognize Gnosticism as an understanding of existence, an *Entweltlichungstendenz*, a tendency toward "de-worldification" or a making absent from the world.[14] They also give his gnostic reading of modern philosophy its explosive force. In condemning modern Gnosticism he is condemning his teacher, who refused to apologize for or even to mention his association with the Nazis who had killed Jonas's own mother in Auschwitz.

Jonas did not content himself with exposing the inability of previous philosophies to reconcile Being with nature. Instead, he set out to show that "Being, in the testimony it gives of itself, informs us not only about what it is but also about what we owe it." By this he meant that, through its constant struggle to maintain its Being in the face of the non-Being that always threatens it, every organic metabolism reveals to humanity its "binding obligation to the guarding of being."[15]

The extraordinary point was that organic life itself contains the ethics that we need to learn.

Following Kant, Jonas articulated that ethics as an imperative. Kant's categorical imperative had been "Act so that you can will that the maxim of your action be made the principle of a universal law."[16] Jonas's imperative—first articulated in his essay "Technology and Responsibility: Reflections on the New Tasks of Ethics"—was more biological and less individual: "Act so that the effects of your actions are compatible with the permanence of genuine human life."[17] In *The Imperative of Responsibility*:

---

14. "Heidegger, more than anything else, epitomized for Jonas, the connection between Gnosis and modernity." Gur-Ze'ev, *Diasporic Philosophy and Counter-Education*, 12; and see Hotam, "Overcoming the mentor."

15. Jonas, *Mortality and Morality*, 101.

16. Kant, *Groundwork*, 30.

17. Jonas, "Technology and Responsibility," 11.

CHAPTER 5: AMBIVALENCE AND THE CRITIQUE OF MODERNITY

In Search of an Ethics for the Technological Age, Jonas argued that ontology teaches an ethics of obligation and that the way we live reveals how well we have learned it.

Late in life, Jonas acknowledged his belief in a God whom he described with a term drawn from his liturgy: *rotseh ba-hayyim*, he who wills life. Jonas was steeped in a particular sensibility: *ahavat yisrael*, the love of Israel, of the Jewish people, and the commitment to it as a community of fate. But he was able to move from love of Israel to love of the world without leaving the former, to attend to the universal without abandoning the particular. He perceived a link between defending Judaism and defending life. He was the student of the long history of thought—Christian, gnostic, and philosophical—that turned the Jew into a figure for the flesh. This history taught him that the defense of Judaism was therefore a defense of life itself. For Jonas, the Jews and the organic life of the world were bound together in one common love, in one destiny. His Jewishness was not a constraint for him, but a great release into the most universal ethic of all. "He put Judaism and the organism side by side at the gates of freedom, fighting for existence against extermination."[18]

If Jonas's critique of modernity deals with technological evil then that of his friend Hannah Arendt deals with political evil. His work helps put her political thought in a wider cosmological and theological frame, albeit one that her suspicion of metaphysics may have led her to refuse.[19] Her response to modern and Heideggerian "de-worldification" is concerned with the man-made world as distinct from nature or the earth. It encompasses both the private realm, "the houses and gardens of citizens,"[20] and the "common world," that part of the world that is shared and accessible to all, what "we have in common without owning."[21] This common world is the focus of most of Arendt's attention and includes a variety of phenomena: the built environment of cities and towns, monuments and parks, roads and bridges, cultural artifacts such as works of art and literature; and more intangible but no less enduring frameworks such as constitutions and laws. Most important for Arendt's purposes, the common world houses the "public realm," which she identifies as the location for political action,

---

18. Nirenberg, "Choosing Life."
19. Vogel, "The Responsibility of Thinking in Dark Times."
20. Arendt, *The Human Condition*, 72.
21. Kiess, *Hannah Arendt and Theology*, 99.

the "space for appearing" where citizens gather and everything "can be seen and heard by everybody."[22]

In distinguishing the man-made world from nature more generally, Arendt does not mean to imply that the two exist independently of one another. But she finds the distinction helpful for what it helps to reveal about some of the distinctive ways that human beings experience life. Most basically, life in the world offers a shelter against the elements of nature and helps to ease the burden of meeting the necessities of life. More deeply, the world offers an enduring context that outlasts the lifespan of those who inhabit it and has the potential to be shared across generations. This is the case in a limited sense with our homes and possessions, but all the more so with the common world: the common world is what we enter when we are born and what we leave behind when we die. It transcends our lifespan into past and future alike; it was there before we came and will outlast our brief sojourn in it. It is what we have in common not only with those who live with us but also with those who were here before and with those who will come after us.[23]

The world endures not through the durability of the objects alone, but through the willingness of citizens to care for them: to repair those that have been broken and to replace those that have been worn out. Such care also entails knowing which objects to remove from the realm of use altogether. This is where culture plays an important role. As "the only things without any function in the life process of society," works of art are the most worldly objects, "fabricated not for men, but for the world which is meant to outlast the lifespan of mortals, the coming and going of generations."[24] Arendt suggests that the world only becomes a home when citizens can recognize certain objects as valuable and beautiful enough to preserve as the shared backdrop against which all other activity takes place. It endures "only insomuch as it transcends the sheer functionalism of things produced for consumption and the sheer utility of objects produced for use."[25]

The birth and death of human beings are not simple natural occurrences, but are related to a world into which single individuals—unique,

---

22. Arendt, *The Human Condition*, 50.

23. Arendt, *The Human Condition*, 55.

24. Arendt, *Between Past and Future*, 209, cited by Kiess, *Hannah Arendt and Theology*, 101.

25. Arendt, *The Human Condition*, 173.

CHAPTER 5: AMBIVALENCE AND THE CRITIQUE OF MODERNITY

unexchangeable, and unrepeatable entities—appear and from which they depart.

> Birth and death presuppose a world which is not in constant movement, but whose durability and relative permanence makes appearance and disappearance possible, which existed before any one individual appeared into it and will survive his eventual departure. Without a world into which men are born and from which they die, there would be nothing but changeless eternal recurrence, the deathless everlastingness of the human as well as all other animal species.[26]

Without a world in which to appear, the discrete character of a human life blends in with the rest of nature. In the background are lessons Arendt took away from her analysis of the concentration camps. By removing Jews and other groups from the world, administrators were effectively cutting them off from any space in which their discrete identities could become perceptible. From this Arendt learnt that human plurality demands a space to appear, if the basic features of each individual life are to be recognized and affirmed. The objective quality of the world not only helps to mediate our relationships with others, but also to stabilize our identities in time. Through the transformation of our thoughts, words, and deeds into worldly artifacts, what goes on in the world becomes a part of the world, and the world itself lives on as a space for human activity.

All of this is contingent upon the notion that the world endures. Arendt observes that we live in a consumer society that approaches all things as potential goods to be consumed. She describes the economic imperative of limitless growth whose engine is not conservation but destruction. The durability of conserved objects is the greatest impediment to the turnover of production and consumption. These attitudes carry over into the realm of culture. Culture becomes entertainment, to be consumed or quickly abandoned; or it comes to be regarded as a useful tool for realizing various external goods, such as self-improvement or social status: "The point is that a consumers' society cannot possibly know how to take care of a world and the things that belong exclusively to the space of worldly appearances, because its central attitude toward all objects, the attitude of consumption, spells ruin for everything it touches."[27]

---

26. Arendt, *The Human Condition*, 96–97.
27. Arendt, *Between Past and Future*, 21.

The result for Arendt is that we have little left of that worldly in-between that mediates our relations with one another.

> What makes mass society so difficult to bear is not the number of people involved, or at least, not primarily, but the fact that the world between them has lost its power to gather them together, to relate and to separate them. The weirdness of this situation resembles a spiritualistic séance where a number of people gathered round a table might suddenly, through some magic trick, see the table vanish from their midst, so that the two persons sitting opposite each other were no longer separated but also would be entirely unrelated to each other by anything tangible.[28]

Deprived of a place of our own and a space in which to appear, we are pressed in upon one another. This leads not to more connections but to more loneliness, the feeling of being abandoned not only by others but by the world of things as well. Without objects to connect us to our past, we also feel abandoned by our predecessors. Our loneliness is compounded by our amnesia and our world alienation is intensified. And without a public realm of active, creative persons taking responsibility for the integrity and continuation of a form of talking and understanding, we are condemned either to the animal pointlessness of the mere effort to subsist, or to the more typically modern unfreedom of "mass society," in which financial achievement and reward or security replaces glory and repute; the notion of worthiness to be remembered, and the quality of public action as creative, as formative of a "conversation" extending beyond individual death, is undermined. Society becomes increasingly enslaved to idolatrous objectifications, fetishes, and slogans. For Arendt, we live in "dark times."

Arendt's account of *amor mundi* is born from her recognition of the world's fragility and need for ongoing care if it is to remain a place fit for human habitation. The world only endures if each new generation takes up the civic virtue of *amor mundi* as its own. This Arendtian love of the world can be defined as a grateful emotional response to the fact that meaningful life has been given unto us. We know we were born into a world that preceded our arrival and will endure our departure. This "spring of remembrance" gives rise to loving gratitude to the world for having bestowed our lives with meaning. This world is always threatened by time and not just consumerism like an ever-encroaching desert. "The time is out of joint," always, and

---

28. Arendt, *The Human Condition*, 52–53.

CHAPTER 5: AMBIVALENCE AND THE CRITIQUE OF MODERNITY

those graced with *amor mundi* are called, ceaselessly, "to set it right."[29] This involves an important element of conservation: tending our homes and gardens, replacing worn-out use-objects with new ones, preserving cultural treasures, repairing civic institutions and infrastructure, and also passing the world on to the young through education.

In "The Crisis of Education," published in *Between Past and Future*, Arendt writes, "Education is the point at which we decide whether we love the world enough to assume responsibility for it and by the same token save it from that ruin which, except for renewal, except for the coming of the new and young, would be inevitable."[30] The fact that we are born into the world—the fact of natality—is the essence of education. She means that every newborn baby comes into the world both free and yet also constrained. Newcomers are free insofar as there is no way of knowing in advance what a young person will become or who she will be. The newcomer is constrained, however, because he is always born into an already-existing world, one with particular customs, limitations, and opportunities. To educate that newcomer is to respond both to the freedom and constraint into which he is thrown. As free, the child must be taught to act courageously in new and surprising ways. As constrained, the newcomer must accept the responsibility as a member of an already existing world, one he must somehow make his own.[31]

To educate means to lead into or draw out, from the Latin *educare*. Education is the activity of leading a child into the world, of drawing her into the world. Parents educate their children by drawing them out of their private selves and into the world of the family, their community, and their society.

Schools educate, in turn, by drawing students out of the confines of their families and into the wider political and social world. Education is always an entry into an old world. And yet, it is always a new experience with infinite possibilities for every new initiate.

Education, for Arendt, is about the love for the world. To have children is to bring new young people into an old and existing world. To make that choice is to "assume responsibility" for that world, to love it enough—in spite of all of the evil and ugliness—to welcome the innocent. Only when we

---

29. Arendt, *Between Past and Future*, 192.
30. Arendt, *Between Past and Future*.
31. Berkowitz, "'The Love of the World.'"

decide to assume such a solemn responsibility for the world as it is and to love that world, can we begin the activity of education.

Education is also a process of saving the world from ruin—a ruin that is inevitable for all mortal and human endeavors. Made by humans acting together, the world will disappear if we do not care for it and refresh it. The world is not a physical entity but is the "in-between" that connects us all. Like a "table that is located between those who sit around it," the world is the world of things, actions, stories, and events that connect and divide all persons living together in a common world. Without newcomers who are introduced into the world and taught to love it as their own, the world will die out.

To love the world enough to lead students into it means also that we love our children enough to both bring them into the world and leave to them the chance of changing it. Arendt writes:

> And education, too, is where we decide whether we love our children enough not to expel them from our world and leave them to their own devices, nor to strike from their hands their chance of undertaking something new, something unforeseen by us, but to prepare them in advance for the task of renewing the common world.[32]

The role of newcomers is not limited to conservation. The world's endurance is also contingent upon their resolve "to intervene, to alter, to create what is new."[33] For Arendt, the opportunity to undertake something new is what we conserve the world for, and it is this capacity for new beginnings, the action that takes place within the world, that contributes to the world's renewal:

> The miracle that saves the world, the realm of human affairs, from its normal, "natural" ruin is ultimately the fact of natality, in which the faculty of action is ontologically rooted. It is, in other words, the birth of new men and the new beginning, the action they are capable of by virtue of being born.[34]

Arendt's *amor mundi* is a civic virtue that seeks the good of the common world. It is a non-possessive love that wills its ongoing existence independent of our personal participation in it and restrains the self-love that sees the world as another object to be consumed. Among contemporary

---

32. Arendt, *Between Past and Future*, 196.
33. Arendt, *Between Past and Future*, 192.
34. Arendt, *The Human Condition*, 247.

democratic theorists there is a striking parallel to this account of *amor mundi* in Sheldon Wolin's notion of "tending." For Wolin, to tend "is to be concerned about something that exists, something that requires being taken care of if it is to perdure."[35] "The idea of tending is one that centers politics around practices, that is, around the habits of competence and skill that are routinely required if things are to be taken care of." This politics is attuned to the historicity of things, one that emerges organically from the "biography of a place" as opposed to the politics of "intending," which attempts to escape the vulnerabilities of temporal existence through top-down organization and planning. The power of the politics of tending "lies in the multiplicity of modest sites dispersed among local governments and institutions under local control." This echoes Arendt's own focus on ordinary practices at the level of education, work, and culture, which unceremoniously carry out the task of repairing and conserving the world so that it serves as a space for citizens from one generation to the next, sustaining remembrance and the gift of recollection.[36]

In her doctoral dissertation on Augustine, Arendt observes that he wrote, "this world is for the faithful ... what the desert was for the people of Israel—they live not in houses but in tents." For Augustine it is our loves—*cupiditas* or *caritas*—that determine our home, our ultimate place of belonging, either this world or the world to come. So Arendt asks, "Would it not then be better to love the world in *cupiditas* and be at home? Why should we make a desert out of this world?"[37]

She was fiercely critical of Christianity for its legacy of worldlessness, and her criticism focused on Augustine. The early church subverted the public realm. In classical thought this public realm is the sphere of true freedom. Rule, coercive power, and even violence belong to the household since they are means of mastering necessity, and organizing the threatening incipient chaos of daily life. Without the patterns of dominance securely fixed in the domestic order, no one would be able to go out into the *polis* among equals, freed from private need so as to engage in the creative, intelligible work of establishing shared meanings and shared futures in action worthy of remembrance. The early church was a community of people who were more or less marginalized by their refusal of Roman imperial authority and their

---

35. Wolin, *The Presence of the Past*, 90.

36. Wolin, *The Presence of the Past*, 90, and *Politics and Vision*, 603, cited by Kiess, *Hannah Arendt and Theology*, 122.

37. Arendt, *Love and Saint Augustine*, 19.

anticipation of the end of the world. What can replace the common world of the public realm as a bond between such persons? The sense of belonging to a community that is in important respects more like a kindred, a family, than a *polis*, a community in which achievement, excellence, or creativity are irrelevant to membership, even damaging. It is a body held together by love, *caritas*: "the bond of charity between people, while it is incapable of founding a public realm of its own . . . is admirably fit to carry a group of essentially worldless people through the world."[38] *Caritas* is, in the Augustinian system, a love that is indifferent to merit and achievement: it sees the bonds between persons as resting simply on their common createdness and equal sinfulness, and thus operates impartially and, in a sense, impersonally. In her dissertation Arendt had argued that *caritas* means "loving the eternal" in ourselves and others, and that this is the essence of Christian "neighborly love": we see in one another tokens of both the creative and redemptive work of God. As creatures, we love at still at a distance, we "coexist"; but as sinful objects of the saving work of Christ, we are brought together in communion. A non-worldly society is thus created, the "city of God." By the time she came to write *The Human Condition* Arendt was far more openly hostile to the idea of non-worldly community but the analysis of Augustine and the principle of "worldless" love remains the same. The *civitas Dei* is a substitute for the public realm, and thus its enemy. She remarks that Augustine knew "at least what it once meant to be a citizen" but concludes that it is Augustine who makes it more or less impossible for a Christian to be a citizen.[39]

Rowan Williams and Eric Gregory have responded to this claim and questioned Arendt's philosophy. Williams argues that Augustine did not intend to shift the locus of citizenship for the *polis* to the church, but was instead "engaged in a *redefinition* of the public itself," showing that it is the classical conception of the public realm "which fails to be truly public, authentically political."[40] For Williams, "The opposition is not between public and private, church and world, but between political virtue and political vice."[41]

Augustine's redefinition of the public refuses to accept the classical assumption that political community is best sustained through the striving for

---

38. Arendt, *Love and Saint Augustine*, 129.

39. Arendt, *The Human Condition*, 14.

40. Williams, "Politics and the Soul," 107–130, cited by Kiess, *Hannah Arendt and Theology*, 113–14.

41. Williams, *On Augustine*, 111.

CHAPTER 5: AMBIVALENCE AND THE CRITIQUE OF MODERNITY

secular immortality of those who act in the public realm to be acclaimed and remembered. Striving for immortality may restrain certain vices and prevent tyranny: it may even unite a society negatively against a foreign enemy, but it can hardly be said to create a genuine interest in a common world. On the contrary, Augustine unmasks this struggle for immortality as an expression of *libido dominandi*, the lust to dominate others. It is fixated on the self's own interests and leads to an agonistic and elitist conception of politics. It produces enmity and discord, as Rome's civil wars attest.

Williams argues that in appealing to such striving it is Arendt rather than the "worldless" Augustine who is trying to escape from the limits of the mortal human condition. "The guarantee of a place in the human story, gained by active participation in the public realm, seeks to assuage the fundamental restlessness that is constitutive of our human creaturehood by offering us the glamour of an assured historical future." Arendt is trying to confer upon the world a "final security and 'finishedness.'" For Augustine no such security is possible. Real temporality is more vulnerable. It is "the endlessly revisable character (morally speaking) of our social and political relationships, that, in the Augustinian world keep us faithful to the insight of humility—that we are timebound in everything here below, that our love is an unceasing search."[42]

By reconceiving all human relationships on the basis of charity, Augustine does not seek to replace the world with love or go into hiding, but to reimagine the terms by which the ancient world understood the relation between body and soul, household and *polis*. In this way he provides resources for questioning the instrumental way in which it conceived these spheres, and for going beyond these dichotomies in Arendt's own thought. The household, "far from being the sphere of bondage and necessity," becomes "a 'laboratory of the spirit,' a place for the maturation of souls" while the city is reimagined as "a creative and pastoral community," which shares power and accepts limits. Instead of opposing these spheres to one another, Augustine unites them under a broader purpose: "both the small and large-scale community are essentially purposive, existing so as to nurture a particular kind of human life."[43]

Gregory extends William's critique by questioning Arendt's specific claims about the world-alienating effects of Augustine's *caritas*. "Augustine's God does not compete with the neighbor for the self's attention, as if God

---

42. Williams, "Politics and the Soul," 126.
43. Williams, "Politics and the Soul," 120.

were simply the biggest of those rival objects considered worthy of love." Rather, "the Augustinian self loves the neighbor in God."[44]

> Augustine's God is a worldly God ... recognized in the intersubjectivity accomplished through the revelation of God as the divine neighbor. To love God is to love the whole of creation existing in God. The love of God is expressed in an ordered love that loves God in loving God's world, a world that bears "his footprints." (*civ.* 11.28).
>
> To love an eternal and incomprehensible God, for Augustine, stretches the soul to allow for a qualitatively different kind of love which can now include all that is not God ... In his God, "our love will know no check."[45]

As Nietzsche, Blumenberg, and Arendt all failed to understand, loving God and the world is not necessarily a zero-sum game. Christian ambivalence makes a sacrament as well as a desert of the world.

Gregory also shows that Augustine allows Christians to love the world in a way that Arendt denies them. For Arendt, a human passion such as love, given its intimate and potential capriciousness, should not be welcomed into the political sphere. Passions of the heart, rather, should be "transformed, deprivatized [and] deindividualized" to prepare them for this sphere.[46] The true polis is one in which decisions are made by words or persuasion, not through force or the violence to which the passions can lead. For Arendt the suggestion that Christian love ought to "go public"—to seek a political expression of compassion—would subvert and ultimately destroy the necessarily more limited scope of political action.

Gregory responds that to refuse to allow love into politics is to ignore the fact that love is constitutive of being human. We cannot not love. The challenge rather is for human loves to be rightly ordered. Disordered loves must be healed. The loves of a society form its character. Liberal societies depend on the prudential recognition of principles and procedures. But such societies will only flourish if their citizens have developed the habits and dispositions to care for others.

If what Augustine says about the proper spiritual formation of the ruler can be adapted to the formation of the citizen in the modern context, there

---

44. Gregory, *Politics and the Order of Love*, 240.

45. Gregory, *Politics and the Order of Love*, 40, cited by Kiess, *Hannah Arendt and Theology*, 114–16.

46. Arendt, *The Human Condition*, 50.

is much that is material for a contemporary ethic of public life and public service. It remains true that what Augustine is really interested in is how the body of Christ lives—not because he is interested in "the church" more than "the state" or because he has any notion of a schism between public and private virtue—but because he would argue that only a theology of reconciliation with God's act and a participation in that act can deliver real justice. Christ-centered justice in society is related to the habits of penitence and self-scrutiny that are enjoined by life in the body of Christ. "In effect, he argues that the just society is penitential. True justice requires believers to seek from God the forgiveness of their sins and the grace to perform good works."[47] Thus, for Augustine, there must be a comprehensive reworking of classical ideals of virtue or piety, a new model of the "statesman"; the public man, the ruler or administrator, will exercise the proper kind of virtue in the uniting of personal humility and repentance with a compassionate concern—born from Christianly educated emotion—to maintain those conditions that will allow others to attain spiritual maturity. The themes of proper appeal to feeling, the proper formation of desire and delight, the entire pedagogy of the church's preaching and liturgy, the focal significance of Christ as the source of justice because he is the embodiment of truth, of true relation to the Father, and of self-forgetting compassion and humble acceptance of the constraints of fleshly life, all come together in a vision of a fully reconciled social existence.

Williams and Gregory show that Arendt's concerns about the unworldly character of Augustine's account of the love of God and neighbor were largely unfounded. Instead of coming at the expense of commitment to the world, *caritas* can help deepen it. Arendt blames Augustine for a worldlessness whose real causes are to be found in later developments according to the "Reform Master Narrative" and the "Intellectual Deviation story." But her engagement with Augustine is not simply an opposition to his ideas that allows her to define her own *amor mundi*. Their thought displays a profound affinity and she builds upon insights that they share in her attempt to show modern persons how to love the world. "Augustine recurs in almost every one of her important works, and many of her journal essays and newspaper articles—either speaking directly or offstage, whispering from the wings."[48]

---

47. Dodaro, *Christ and the Just Society*, 112, cited by Williams, "Politics and the Soul," 129.

48. Scott, "What St. Augustine Taught Hannah Arendt."

In a chapter added to the second edition of *The Origins of Totalitarianism*, Arendt concludes her account of the debacle of European civilization on a surprisingly hopeful note. She writes, "Beginning is the supreme capacity of man ... *initium ut esset homo creatus est*" 'that a beginning be made man was created,' said Augustine. This beginning is guaranteed by each new birth; it is indeed every man."[49] Arendt's quotation from Augustine's *City of God* (book XII, ch. 20) is taken out of context. In that section Augustine was not talking about any "capacity of man." He was refuting the Platonic theory of souls eternally coming in and going out of the world. But if this specific passage does not support her exegetical claims in quite the way she thinks, the claim that human beings are an ontological beginning and have the capacity to make new beginnings are recognizably Augustinian commitments. Eternal recurrence trivializes both God's capacity to do new things and our own, and this is why Augustine so adamantly rejects it.[50] Jonas and Arendt turned to Augustine in their effort to resist modern Gnosticism. Augustine inspired Arendt to challenge the ostensibly Catholic Heidegger's preoccupation with death by making natality rather than mortality the central category of political thought.[51]

Arendt also turns to Augustine's overcoming of Gnosticism for the conception of the banality of evil she presents in her account of the trial of Adolf Eichmann in Jerusalem. Arendt was at work on a revision of her doctoral dissertation on Augustine for publication when she left for Jerusalem. She tested the Augustinian conceptual scheme in her coverage of the trial of one of the major organizers of the Holocaust for *The New Yorker* and found it both theoretically viable and practically applicable. Arendt suggests that Eichmann lacked "any diabolical or demonic profundity" and that his evil could not be traced to any deeper level of roots.[52]

---

49. Arendt, *The Origins of Totalitarianism*, 479.

50. Kiess, *Hannah Arendt and Theology*, 157.

51. Bielik-Robson, "Love Strong as Death." Bielik-Robson argues that, seen from the perspective of its beginning, the finite human life is immediately dialogic—while seen from the perspective of its end it sinks into the soliloquy of death. This is Arendt's major *piece de resistance* against Heidegger's influence, a new affirmation of finite life, which takes roots in an anti-Heideggerian impulse which manages to mobilize latent reserves of alternative vitalistic traditions, among which is the Jewish heritage with its imperative "choose life!" Bielik-Robson, "Being-Towards-Birth"; and Arendt, *The Human Condition*, 9.

52. Arendt, *Eichmann in Jerusalem*, 288.

CHAPTER 5: AMBIVALENCE AND THE CRITIQUE OF MODERNITY

> Despite all the efforts of the prosecution, everybody could see that this man was not a "monster," but it was difficult indeed not to suspect that he was a clown. And since this suspicion would have been fatal to the entire enterprise [his trial], and was also rather hard to sustain in view of the sufferings he and his like had caused to millions of people, his worst clowneries were hardly noticed and almost never reported.[53]

Augustine had tried to deny Manichaeanism of its mythological power and avoidance of responsibility. Both Arendt and Augustine share the same basic ontological framework, one which prioritizes the goodness of the created order for Augustine or the man-made world for Arendt over evil; this in turn leads both to theorize evil in terms of its effect upon that which exists, rather than as something that has existence itself. Just as, for Augustine, goodness is a matter of participation in God's creation through the intelligible Word, and evil is a measure of nonparticipation in the Word—a lack of reality and mute unintelligibility—so for Arendt evil is ontologically describable only negatively, in terms of what it destroys, what it lacks. Evil is empty, shallow, banal; it destroys the possibility of real human community, community manifest through action in speech and creative of a common world in terms of which we find our meaning and our flourishing.[54]

Arendt also shared Augustine's sense of the precariousness of human temporality in the *saeculum*. From her earliest studies of the concentration camps to her account of the worldlessness of modern citizens, Arendt consistently attends to the fragility of the conditions that allow individuals to exercise their basic human capacities. Hers is a world that remains ever subject to the ruin of time, one that is always "passing away" and that for this very reason demands our love. And she never abandoned another essential Augustinian insight—that the world is a product of our loves. She envisages citizenship in terms of the everyday task of making a common world, a task sustained by the *amor mundi* of each citizen. She remained indebted to Augustine's understanding of the world's fragility and the importance of love for ensuring its continuing existence.

Arendt also came to see that Christian unworldliness could mean promise and danger and not just calamity for the world. This is evident in her reflections on Pope Pius XII and Pope John XXIII. Her reaction to Rolf

---

53. Arendt, *Eichmann in Jerusalem*, 55.
54. Matthews, *Evil in the Augustinian Tradition*, 195, cited by Kiess, *Hannah Arendt and Theology*, 77.

Hochhuth's drama about Pope Pius XII, *The Deputy*, is an indictment of his alleged unworldliness and the disastrous failure of judgment to which it leads. He is accused of failing to understand what was taking place around him and of "a rigid adherence to a normality that no longer existed in view of the collapse of the whole moral and spiritual structure of Europe."[55] This loss of feeling for reality was exhibited in the "flowery loquacity" of Church statements, which attempted to hide its overwhelming silence, its failure to speak publicly against the fate that was engulfing European Jews. If the Church's conduct during World War II demonstrated to Arendt the calamity that can result from an unworldly life lived in the world, Pope John XXIII manifested to her both the promise and the danger of a true Christian's appearance in the public realm. His "astounding faith" liberated him from all utilitarian attitudes and gave him a confidence that enabled him to treat all as his equals and present himself to the world exactly as he was. In response, the world attended to his words and his actions and made his existence and permanent reality in the countless stories about him passed on for future generations. Despite her deep admiration for his virtues, however, Pope John also represented for her the danger of Christian life, its capacity to shake the world. She cites Luther's words that the "most permanent fate of God's word is that for its sake the world is put into uproar. For the sermon of God comes to change and revive the whole earth to the extent that it reaches it."[56] She testifies that in "dark times" an unworldly Christian kindled light.[57]

Contemptus mundi: Adorno

Jonas and Arendt present a school of resistance to modern Gnosticism that has a profound affinity with Christian attempts to love and to recompose the world. Arendt learns from as well as criticizes Augustine in her attempt to show modern persons how to love the world. By contrast with her *amor mundi*, Theodor Adorno resists the same "dark times" by adopting a radically secularized version of *contemptus mundi*. Both aspects of Christian ambivalence about the world, *amor* and *contemptus*, can be used to kindle light. Both are parts of a repertoire of resistance to the "world" of modernity.

55. Arendt, "*The Deputy*, Guilt by Silence?," 52.
56. Bernauer, ed., *Amor Mundi*, 21.
57. Arendt, *Men in Dark Times*, 57–70.

CHAPTER 5: AMBIVALENCE AND THE CRITIQUE OF MODERNITY

In their *Dialectic of Enlightenment*, Max Horkheimer and Theodor Adorno carry out a critique from within of the "disenchanted" world.[58] The theme of "disenchantment" is taken up in the very first paragraph: "the Enlightenment has always aimed at liberating men from fear and establishing their sovereignty ... The program of the Enlightenment was the disenchantment of the world."[59] But far from liberating humanity, "the fully enlightened earth radiates with disaster triumphant," and humankind "instead of entering into a truly human condition, is sinking into a new kind of barbarism." In several books and many articles, Adorno sought to understand the tragic consequences of the "dialectic of enlightenment." Enlightenment had professed to improve the condition of men and women by banishing myth and installing reason in its place, and by the conquest of nature. But its strategy was broken-backed: the domination and manipulation of external nature required a domination of the individual's internal nature; that is, our physic constitution had to be modified so that men and women would be able to forsake the fulfillment of their psychic needs in order to master outer nature: "The subjective spirit which cancels the animation of nature can master a despiritualized nature only by imitating its rigidity and despiritualizing itself in turn ... Everything—even the human individual, not to speak of the animal—is converted into the repeatable, replaceable process..."[60]

By the twentieth century, the material conditions for a free and economically productive society had been created. The creation of such a society had of course been the goal of the Enlightenment. But the existence of these material preconditions had not resulted in a more humane social order. The very attempt to create a free and more humane society had resulted in one that was oppressive and dehumanizing: the presence of the material preconditions for the existence of a liberated society seemed somehow to generate the nonexistence of the subjective conditions necessary for the realization of such a society. To account for the failure of the project of enlightenment, Adorno proposed the thesis of the reification of the human subject: the all-pervasive forces of rational administration translate the potentially repressive features of the Enlightenment into a concrete technocratic praxis. A "culture industry" is mobilized by

---

58. Horkheimer and Adorno, *Dialectic of Enlightenment*; and Surin, "*Contemptus mundi* and the disenchanted world."
59. Horkheimer and Adorno, *Dialectic of Enlightenment*, 1.
60. Horkheimer and Adorno, *Dialectic of Enlightenment*, 57–84.

dominant social institutions and powerful commercial interests to ensure the "cretinization of the masses," *Volksverblodung*, and to produce a helpless conformity, *Anpassung*, guaranteed to perpetuate the subliminal authoritarianism of late capitalist society. Modern society is thus administered to provide a context of unremitting delusion, *Verblendzusammenhang*, in which individuals accept without protest the oppressive "reality" of their society, which they feel obliged to perpetuate.[61]

According to Adorno, the relations of production of late capitalist society create a "socially necessary mirage" that blinds men and women to the real nature of a society that consigns them to be "cogs in their own machines." The subjective conditions for the realization of free and humane social order do not exist because the existing psychological constitution of men and women prevents them from imagining the world to be different, to be otherwise than it now appears. Human consciousness, instead of revealing to individuals the true nature of the objective social configurations that surround them, had been mutilated by these very conditions. As a result, distorted personal and social relationships, which could have been changed by the actions of men and women, were accepted as natural and unchangeable relations between objects. The possibility of an emancipatory praxis is extinguished as the autonomy of the subject, the ego, is eclipsed by the overpowering superiority of the object. Lacking anything else to love, the prisoner loves his cell.

A critique of culture in a "disenchanted" world will therefore seek to "demystify" social reality, and thus reveal it to be not an absolute and immutable nature, but "second nature," that is, the illusion of something natural that camouflages actual historical conditions, an illusion that is the congealed product of human praxis—and therefore capable of being removed by a countervailing practice. Human beings have only to break the spell of this seemingly objective "second nature," and in so doing unfetter the potential for liberation that lies in this objectivity, a potential that is "close enough to touch." No matter how unbreakable this spell is, it remains what it is—a spell. Hence, those persons who do not fall victim to it may have the chance of surviving long enough to hope for the day when the spell will be broken. But to do this they will have to adopt what Jürgen Habermas called Adorno's "strategy of hibernation," which Kenneth Surin has described as his radically secularized version of *contemptus mundi*.[62]

---

61. Horkheimer and Adorno, *Dialectic of Enlightenment*, 120–67.
62. Habermas, "Consciousness Raising of Rescuing Critique"; and Surin, "*Contemptus*

CHAPTER 5: AMBIVALENCE AND THE CRITIQUE OF MODERNITY

The effective critic of culture, Adorno maintains, can engage in potentially liberating criticism only if he or she is sufficiently detached from the domain of social interests. Exclusion from this domain will serve to immunize the critic against the reifying logic of the principle that everything and anything in late bourgeois society is to be experienced as a commodity, a logic that makes subjects into objects. This commodity principle has become so deep-rooted that even the "committed" individual is a potential victim of the forces of reification: "The feigning of true politics here and now, the freezing of historical relations which nowhere seem ready to melt, oblige the mind to go where it need not degrade itself."[63]

The philosophical foundations of this critical task are developed in Adorno's *Negative Dialectics*. The *Dialectic of Enlightenment* had argued that, in its attempt to grasp and understand nature in its entirety, Enlightenment reason forces its object into a rigid schema, and so ultimately fails to comprehend what it seeks to know. Because it is driven by fear of nature and myth, rationality continues to be shaped by nature and thus continuously dominates its object of inquiry rather than successfully understanding it.

The "dialectic" contained within the Enlightenment, then, is that it continuously transforms into its opposite. Reason turns itself into a self-generating myth, believing that it possesses perfect knowledge and pure objectivity.[64]

Adorno's conception of the dialectic of Enlightenment is related to his commitment to what he calls "negative dialectics." If reason does indeed impose a false structure upon objects in the world, so that it is unable to grasp what does not comply with its artificial ordering, Adorno argues that a more adequate form of thought must become aware of its own dominating nature, and ruthlessly criticize itself. He calls the manner of reasoning that is blind to its own dominating impulse a form of "identity thinking." Negative dialectics strives to achieve a form of nonidentity thinking. Although all thought, to even conceptualize something, must identify it in some way, nonidentical thought remains conscious of this dilemma, and refuses to imagine that its present representation of an object is adequate to its reality. Adorno contrasts his approach with that of Hegel and Marx, for whom dialectical thought involved the weighing of opposing positions

---

mundi and the disenchanted world," 195.

63. Adorno, "Commitment," 194.
64. Brittain, *Adorno and Theology*, 4.

and contradictions with the goal of achieving a progressively progressive conceptualization of truth. Adorno is distrustful of the notion of inevitable progress. He insists that thought is never adequate to its object, and so can only be approached negatively—through the act of ongoing immanent self-criticism.

The truth is thus to be found in all that is estranged, unusual, marginalized, and injured by the conformist ideologies of the totally administered society. Freedom can survive in a setting of violence and hopelessness only if it takes the form of negation. The unbroken cohesion of rationalized "immanence" that is the enemy of hope can be countered only by a "transcendence," a historical "transcendence," attentive to the fragmentary, the insignificant, the vanquished, and the irrelevant. In a society where common sense and reason only serve to reinforce the prevailing universal blindness, every attempt to initiate an emancipatory practice comes to be regarded as foolishness and insanity. Paradoxically, therefore, it is only the person deemed to be eccentric or even insane who can resist the process of psychic petrification. The use of reason to motivate an emancipatory praxis is viewed by institutionalized instrumental reason as a form of madness; just as, conversely, the inability of instrumental reason to sustain and shape patterns of redeemed existence creates a more dangerously insane world. The insanity of instrumental reason must therefore be countered by a "reasonable insanity." But this "reasonable insanity" cannot be systematically pursued: the (insane) technocratically rational world will not sanction the positive pursuit of a more humane way of living. Moreover, the programmatic implementation of a "reasonably insane" mode of existence will have to be undertaken with reference to notions like "justice" and "truth," the very substance of which has been withered by the reified world. Adorno therefore advocates a way of responding negatively to the reified world, a strategy of enhancing and exaggerating the merest traces of negativity and idiosyncrasy that manage somehow to resist being integrated into the prevailing mass irrationality: "there is no longer beauty or consolation except in the gaze falling on horror, withstanding it, and in unalleviated consciousness of negativity holding fast to the possibility of what is better."[65]

The adoption of an adversarial stance to the reified fabric of social life, focusing as it does on the ruins and detritus of late bourgeois society,

---

65. Adorno, *Minima Moralia*, 25, cited by Surin, "*Contemptus mundi* and the disenchanted world," 197.

CHAPTER 5: AMBIVALENCE AND THE CRITIQUE OF MODERNITY

is Adorno's radically secularized version of *contemptus mundi*.[66] The secular practitioner of *contemptus mundi*, because he or she refuses to become an accomplice of the reifying powers at work in society, is able to confront society's comfortable and comforting (and therefore static) vision of itself with its true nature, which is the unrelenting barbarism of the always-the-same. By holding up a prism to that which is degraded as seemingly unreal—thereby showing the difference between society's false image and its true nature—the critic is able to throw a faint light on the almost vanishing traces of redeemed or reconciled life, traces that are forms and sites of resistance, which the disenchanted world seeks to administer out of existence.

A strategy of self-conscious inner-worldly withdrawal, the stance of a "reasonable insanity," is able to decline late bourgeois society's offer of false happiness. Only in this way can critique avoid being colonized by the apparatus of mass culture.[67] But a price has to be paid. Critique saves the most minute of spaces for the redeemed life by seeming to fall into absurdity. In the fourth century, Antony renounced the world in favor of an *imitatio Christi* in the desert, with an "ironic sanity." He said, "A time is coming when men will go mad, and when they see someone who is not mad, they will attack him saying, 'You are mad, you are not like us.'"[68] His statement testifies to the "intractable oddity of monasticism."[69] Adorno would say that the time feared by Antony has indeed arrived, and that in today's totally administered society its arrival is indicated by a somnolent mass indifference to any attempted critique of a reified society. The critic who wants to rouse men and women from their sleep risks being marginalized and even attacked, as Adorno himself experienced.

Critics frequently accuse Adorno's work of collapsing into mere negativity, trapping his philosophy in nihilism at its bleakest. They argue that Adorno, traumatized by the horrors of the Nazi era, refused to allow any real possibility for hope or new life. He is accused of the gnostic world alienation that Jonas and Arendt sought to overcome, which associates all of human history with the forces of evil: his work has no recourse but to invoke a longing for some otherworldly deliverance that might arrive from outside history.[70]

66. Surin, "*Contemptus mundi* and the disenchanted world," 197.
67. Frank, *Commodify Your Dissent*.
68. Ward, trans., *The Sayings of the Desert Fathers*, 5.
69. Williams, *The Wound of Knowledge*, 103.
70. Brittain, *Adorno and Theology*, 7.

However, critics of modernity do have to confront the ancient Christian tension between loving and hating the world and the problem of how to live *in the world but not of it*—the "world" here denoting not the created world but the fallen, human world characterized by pride and greed. The history of Christianity can be understood in terms of the preservation or loss of equilibrium between understanding the world as the good creation of God and understanding the world as alienated from God, *amor* and *contemptus*. Neither understanding could be denied. To live *in the world but not of it* is a life lived according to the original intention of creation and not according to its current, fallen state. A similar structure—especially between authentic freedom and alienation—is to be found in any political philosophy that has an idea of a radically transformed world somehow being possible. The history of Christian thought displays the difficulty of maintaining the appropriate equilibrium between *amor* and *contemptus*.

This dilemma is repeated in critiques of modernity, for example, in the question of the relationship between the world of oppression and the emancipated world in the work of Slavoj Žižek and Terry Eagleton. One Christian temptation has been to emphasize the alienation of this world on behalf of another, coming world; the disadvantage of this strategy has been the goodness of creation here and now runs the risk of being denied in the name of this other world. The extreme limit case is Gnosticism, with its version of salvation as liberation from a world of oppression. Despite his general criticisms of Gnosticism, Žižek comes close to this alternative.[71] To the opposite Christian approach, the world is indeed affirmed as the good creation of God. Here the temptation is to complacency rather than despair; to diminish the impact of sin on the current state of affairs—and to fail to distinguish the "world" as creation from our modern world. This approach might perhaps be illustrated by one of the theological jokes of Stanley Hauerwas, made at the expense of Anglicans, whom he claims should no longer be allowed to say "incarnation" because they generally mean by that, "God became human and said, 'Say, this is not too bad.'"[72] In this approach, there is far more continuity between the world as it is and as it should be. Redemption is redemption of this world. The trouble with this strategy is that there is a constant threat of concealing the very real oppression and suffering of the world, and of falling prey to ideology.

71. Bielik-Robson, "A Matter of Faith."
72. Hauerwas, *In Good Company*, 169.

CHAPTER 5: AMBIVALENCE AND THE CRITIQUE OF MODERNITY

Žižek accuses Eagleton of denying how fallen the world is, and its need for radical change.[73]

Adorno is certainly closer to Žižek in terms of the unstable Christian equilibrium between loving the world and hating what it has become. But far from representing a resigned pessimism, some dark version of Gnosticism, or a desperate longing for otherworldly salvation, his philosophy is motivated by a deep and sustained commitment to confront the realities of human suffering. His criticism of the traditions of the Enlightenment is not motivated by a rejection of the ideals of the Enlightenment, but instead intends to rejuvenate it and defend its ideals. Behind his relentless criticism and negative dialectics is a utopian vision that is attentive to possibilities for society that remain unrealized, and is deployed to criticize existing life on that basis. It is in the struggle to transcend the domination of our subjectivities, and discover the causes of our suffering, that we find traces of freedom and of truth. His theology helps to prevent the conventions of the *status quo* from silencing those who cry out against oppression and who work for a more just and rational society.[74]

Moreover, in Adorno's "strategy of hibernation," as Habermas terms his implicit moral strategy, hibernation can be a covert preparation for a more overt action.[75] Habermas dismisses this strategy of a certain with-

---

73. Sigurdson, *Theology and Marxism in Eagleton and Žižek*, 163–64.

74. Brittain, *Adorno and Theology*, 14.

75. Sawicki, "Towards a Politics of Apathy," 86–101; Rowan Williams, in "The Benedict Option: A New Monasticism for the 21st Century," has described the Benedict Option of Rod Dreher as strategy of hibernation. Dreher has repeatedly defended the withdrawal that characterizes the Benedict Option from accusations of defeatism by emphasizing that it is strategic. Its purpose is to sustain communities of formation and so to prepare for reengagement. See Dreher, *The Benedict Option*. Balthasar uses the metaphor of the beating of the heart to describe this relation of the church to the world. Systole and diastole are two phases of the cardiac cycle. They occur as the heart beats, pumping blood through a system of blood vessels that carry blood to every part of the body. Systole occurs when the heart contracts to pump blood out, and diastole occurs when the heart relaxes after contraction. For Balthasar systole stands for the progressive, transforming assimilation of the world into the realm of the church, and diastole stands for the constantly recurring self-transcendence by which the church goes to meet the world outside it. What is assimilated from the world into the church must, as church, pass into the self-transcendent mission of the inner realm to the outer one. On the other hand the church cannot be considered in terms of self-transcendence alone or there would be no subject to take the self-transcending step. If the church only concerns itself with the needs and necessities of the world outside, it risks having nothing to bring to the world that the world could not acquire for itself. There is no light without a luminary even if that luminary always sheds its light away from itself. The more radical the systole

drawal for its "obvious weakness" and its "defensive character." But at the close of *Notes from Underground*, Dostoevsky's man from underground offers what could be conceived as Adorno's rejoinder to Habermas:

> As far as I am concerned, I have merely carried to an extreme in my life what you have not even dared to carry halfway, and, what's more, you've taken your cowardice for good sense, and found comfort in deceiving yourselves. So that I, perhaps, come out even more "living" than you. Take a closer look![76]

This can be compared with Adorno's association in his *Minima Moralia* of withdrawal or hibernation with a paradoxical augmentation of living or "life": "The sense of life radiated by Goethe's women was bought with withdrawal, evasion; and there is more in this than mere resignation before the victorious order."[77] The moment of awakening need not occur at some undefined, temporal distance from the moment of hibernation but may occur, paradoxically—or dialectically—within the moment of hibernation itself. "Nothing less is asked of a thinker today than that he should be at every moment both within things and outside them."[78] This is to say, that for Adorno, anything we might want to call "life" is not possible without removing ourselves from the purview of the culture industry, and the "obvious weakness" is not in withdrawal from, but in capitulation to mass culture. Adorno's hibernation does not have to be a form of abject retreatism that pines for the day "genuine" political action will be possible. It is a contemporaneous resistance to the culture industry and ideology. For Habermas, the *Minima Moralia* may be construed without irony as a doctrine concerning the right way to live. The book was written in exile, "in conditions enforcing contemplation."[79] It may thus be compared with the pessimism of Ecclesiastes as it was understood from Jerome's commentary up until that of Luther: they are both books about detachment from the "world."

---

was and is the more efficacious will be the diastole. "For this reason, lest everything in the Church become superficial and insipid, the true, undiminished program for the Church today must read: the greatest possible radiance in the world by virtue of the closest possible following of Christ." Balthasar, *The Christian State of Life*, II.III.4; see also Balthasar, *My Work in Retrospect*, 58.

76. Dostoevsky, *Notes from the Underground*, 95, cited by Sawicki, "Towards a Politics of Apathy," 88.

77. Adorno, *Minima Moralia*, 90.

78. Adorno, *Minima Moralia*, 74.

79. Adorno, *Minima Moralia*, 18.

CHAPTER 5: AMBIVALENCE AND THE CRITIQUE OF MODERNITY

The exception to the distance and withdrawal that constitute Adorno's "strategy" is suffering. For Adorno, one must not, under any circumstances, become indifferent to suffering, whoever or whatever its cause. His is a hibernation without sleep.

It may also be not quite so radically secular as Surin assumes. Adorno writes, "Ascetic ideals constitute today a more solid bulwark against the madness of the profit economy than did the hedonistic life sixty years ago against liberal repression."[80] Adorno's hibernation could be understood as a subversive form of "new monasticism," an innerworldly asceticism of resistance.[81]

The work of Giorgio Agamben suggests that such innerworldly asceticism can be freed from its association with the "Protestant ethic" of innerworldly alienation and capitalist domination described by Weber, and returned to its original Pauline association with messianic life. Weber described how, in the Puritan conception of secular callings, "[Christian asceticism] strode into the marketplace of life, slammed the door of the monastery behind it, and undertook to penetrate just that daily routine of life with its methodicalness, to fashion it into a life in the world, but neither of nor for this world."[82] Agamben reclaims calling as the language of messianic transformation. Paul speaks of his calling as *doulos,* the slave of the Messiah (Romans 1:1; Galatians 1:10). Agamben contends that the "most rigorous definition of messianic life," is the passage in the First Letter to the Corinthians 7:29–31 (NRSV):

> I mean, brothers and sisters, the appointed time has grown short; from now on, let even those who have wives be as though (*hos me*) they had none, and those who mourn as though they were not mourning, and those who rejoice as though (*hos me*) they were not rejoicing, and those who buy as though (*hos me*) they had no possession, and those who deal with the world as though (*hos me*) they had no dealings with it. For the present form of this world is passing away.

There is a particular kind of "making use" of the world that treats it in a manner appropriate to its ontology of "passing away"—a using that is not proprietary, not related to human sovereignty or judicial ownership yet still dwells in the world; Paul writes, "remain in the calling in which

80. Adorno, *Minima Moralia,* 97.
81. The Rutba House, *School(s) for Conversion.*
82. Weber, *The Protestant Ethic,* 154.

you have been called" (7:17, NRSV) in a manner that opens it up to being made new, to being "known by God" (8:3, NRSV). The messianic is not a new identity with a new set of rights. "The messianic vocation is the revocation of all vocations."[83] The professional character of every worldly status and activity is interrupted and revoked. Christians are commanded to turn over all the things with which we busy ourselves to a free and common use like the *usus facti* of the early Franciscans, who allowed themselves to use things but not to possess them.

Yet this nullification of secular vocation is not abandoning it for somewhere else but dwelling within it as in exile, in dispossession. This dispossession allows the power of God to transform it in keeping with its true condition or figure, its "passing away." This transforming power is a kind of messianic use of the world that stands in opposition to possessive juridical and technological control. Secular vocations are not replaced by something new, but there is rather a making new that occurs within them that transfigures and opens them up to their true use. This is a messianic slavery liberated from juridical bondage to worldly possession for free creaturely action that glorifies God in the earthly body.[84]

---

83. Agamben, *The Time That Remains*, 23.
84. Kroeker, "Messianic Ethics and Diaspora Communities," 128.

Chapter 6: Ambivalence and Discipleship

Kneeling before the world

THE SECULARIZATION OF THE 1960s was the focal point of a relatively sudden and shocking collapse of Christian culture and practice in Europe.[1] "In the religious history of the West, these years [the "long sixties" from 1958 to 1974] may come to be seen as marking a rupture as profound as that brought about by the Reformation."[2] Western Christians reacted by dividing into liberals and conservatives in ways that were to become increasingly militant.

Some theologians sought to reinterpret Christianity in secular terms and to construct a "secular theology" or "religionless Christianity." This theology was given practical expression by "English Bonhoefferism," a kind of clergy-led Anglican anti-clericalism that idealized the "secular city" and non-churched laity as the place where Christ was to be met and that risked neglecting and alienating churchgoers, many of whom were understood to be immature and somehow clinging on to an outmoded supernaturalism and religious world view.[3]

The collapse of the British Student Christian Movement in the "long 1960s" can be ascribed to the adoption by its leadership of this "English Bonhoefferism."[4] "[C]ontextualizing limited religious decline as part of God's plan to abolish organized religion," their understanding of secularization demanded a deliberate transposition of Christian ideas into secular forms. The SCM embarked on an early, original, and influential journey into political activism—alienating and losing its Christian membership.

1. Brown, "What was the Religious Crisis of the 1960s?"
2. Mcleod, *The Religious Crisis of the 1960s*.
3. Chapman, "Theology in the Public Arena," 101.
4. Brewitt-Taylor, "From Religion to Revolution."

"Theologies of secularization were important agents of the very religious decline that they sought to describe."[5] Defensive, conservative forms of Christianity survived—evangelicalism and fundamentalism—not least in the student world.

"English Bonhoefferians" had argued for a new "worldly holiness" that does not seek to separate itself from the world but to live in it with a radical commitment to others.[6]

Jacques Maritain responded to the crisis and division of the 1960s after the Second Vatican Council in *The Peasant of the Garonne*, to offer a comprehensive explanation of Christian ambivalence about the "world."[7]

At the end of his life, he adopted the blunt persona of "an old layman" who questions himself about the present time.[8] "The peasant of the Garonne" put his foot in his mouth and called a spade a spade in his most controversial book, published in 1968. He presented a theological interpretation of "the religious crisis of the 1960s" and a sardonic response to those whom he declared too ready to "kneel before the world."

For Maritain, the deepest source of this crisis of secularization is spiritual. He describes what can be understood as an aspect of the "Reform Master Narrative" with the metaphor of a pendulum, which has swung from a "masked Manichaeism" characteristic of the Church prior to the Second Vatican Council to the postconciliar mistake of "kneeling before the world." The one called forth the other. Both extremes rest upon a fundamental error concerning the value of the world and temporal affairs. It turns on "a long misunderstanding with a bitter fruit" concerning the distinction between the "mystical" and the "ontosophic" meaning of the "world."[9] The mystical truth concerning the world is a practical truth, lived out by the saints. The ontosophic truth concerning the world is a speculative truth, affirmed by both theologians and philosophers.

The practical truth lived by the saints is a contempt for the world deriving from their boundless love for God. St. Paul refers to the world as a dung hill (Phil 3:8, NRSV) in comparison with Christ and the knowledge of God. The world is seen as an obstacle to God insofar as the world is in sin and refuses God. The world hates God; it persecutes Christ and his

---

5. Brewitt-Taylor, "From Religion to Revolution," 811.
6. Robinson, *Honest to God*, chap. 5.
7. Maritain, *The Peasant of the Garonne*, 28.
8. Maritain, *The Peasant of the Garonne*.
9. Maritain, *The Peasant of the Garonne*, 44.

followers. The saints, overwhelmed by their love of God, struggle against the world, exercise self-denial, and show contempt for the world. This is the mystical truth of contempt for the world.

The ontosophic truth, a truth of theology and philosophy, reason and revelation, affirms the goodness of the world.[10] The world has natural structures that are intelligible and natural ends that are good. This is the speculative truth. Grace builds upon and perfects nature. Grace does not destroy nature.

The dangerous misunderstanding lies in making the practical truth a speculative one, or vice versa. Centuries prior to the Council, the church came to misunderstand the mystical truth. The "dung hill" was extended to the world itself and "a masked Manichaeism was thus superimposed on the Christian faith without ruining it."[11] It was a pastoral failure and not a doctrinal one, by which a practical Manichaeism was "spread inwardly, in the form of purely moralistic prohibitions, injunctions to flight, habits of fear, and disciplines of denial in which love has no part, and which led the soul to starvation and sickliness, and to a torturing sense of impotence."[12] The moral took precedence over the theological, while flight from sin took precedence over charity. Human initiative, and refusal to sin, obscured the divine initiative to love and grace.

In addition to this mistaken contempt for the world, Christians prior to the Council were well aware of the growing hostility of modern civilization to Christianity, and thus formed a defensive reaction and inferiority complex. Furthermore, there was generally poor doctrinal formation. Thus at the time of the Council there was an "enormous weight of frustration and disillusionment and resentment, which burst out into the open on the occasion of *aggiornamento*," or "updating." The pendulum swung from quasi-Manichaeism to frenzied modernism.[13] For the theologians, it was to mean a love for the latest trends and a love for the ephemeral. Their spiritual teaching affirmed the goodness of the world, but failed to mention the other world, the cross, and the demands of sanctity. The temporal mission of the layman was mistaken for the mission of the Church as a whole.

---

10. Maritain, *The Peasant of the Garonne* 38.
11. Maritain, *The Peasant of the Garonne*, 46.
12. Maritain, *The Peasant of the Garonne*, 48.
13. Maritain, *The Peasant of the Garonne*, 50.

This "insane mistake" of kneeling before the world amounted to a complete temporalization of Christianity.[14] The world in its natural and temporal structures absorbs into itself the kingdom of God. "But if the other world is done away with, and if, by the same token, God loses his infinite transcendence, then there is no longer any Heavenly Father, there is only the Emperor of this world, before whom everyone should kneel."[15]

If there is no other world, God has lost his transcendence, Christians are on their knees before the world, and the world has lost the saints.

Maritain tries to imagine what takes place in the soul of a saint at the crucial moment when he or she makes their first irrevocable decision.[16] He pictures Francis of Assisi when he throws away his clothing and appears naked before his bishop, or Benedict Labre when he decides to become a lice-infested beggar. At the root of such an act, Maritain contends that there was something so profound in the soul that he himself does not know how to express it—a simple refusal, a total, stable, supremely active refusal to accept things as they are. This is not a question of not knowing that the world is good in its essence. The act has to do with an existential sense that things as they are are intolerable. In the reality of its existence the world is infected with lying, injustice, wickedness, distress, and misery: creation has been corrupted by sin to such an extent that the saint refuses to accept it as it is. Evil—the power of sin, and the universal suffering it brings—is such that the only thing the saint has immediately at hand is to oppose it totally, and that intoxicates the saint with liberty, exultation, and love. The saint's response is to give everything, to abandon everything—the sweetness of the world, and what is so good, and more than anything, himself—in order to be free to be with God. To do this is to be totally stripped and given over in order to seize the power of the cross; it is to die for those he or she loves.

> Once the soul of a man has been touched in flight by this burning wing it becomes a stranger everywhere. It can fall in love with things, never take repose in them. The saint is alone in treading the wine press, and among the peoples there is no one with him (Isa 63:3, NRSV).[17]

For Maritain, the great vision of a Christian renewal of temporal structures, the true activation of the temporal mission of the lay Christian, requires "a

---

14. Maritain, *The Peasant of the Garonne*, 56.
15. Maritain, *The Peasant of the Garonne*, 60.
16. Maritain, *The Peasant of the Garonne*, 58.
17. Maritain, *The Peasant of the Garonne*, 59.

CHAPTER 6: AMBIVALENCE AND DISCIPLESHIP

great and patient work of revitalizing in the order of intelligence and the order of spirituality."[18] He interprets the Council as a call to inwardness, to the spiritual life, and to contemplation. In the last section of *The Peasant of the Garonne*, "The True New Fire—The Affairs of God's Kingdom," he returns to the themes of *Liturgy and Contemplation*, which he had written with his wife Raïssa before her death in 1960, to insist that contemplation is the common vocation of all Christians.

He recalls that Raïssa had wanted to write a book called *Contemplation on the Roads*, which was addressed to those persons—much less rare than is realized—who, while living the ordinary life of a good Christian in the world, "are ready to go further, and whose hearts are burning to go further, but who find themselves prevented by many fears and obstacles, more or less illusory..."[19] For Raïssa, "The great need of our age, in what concerns the spiritual life, is to put contemplation on the roads."[20] She wrote,

> Saint Thérèse of Lisieux [in her *petite voie*] has shown that the soul can tend to the perfection of charity by a way in which the great signs that Saint John of the Cross and Saint Teresa of Avila have described do not appear... Saint Therese in her Carmel prepared in an eminent way that diffusion wider than ever, of the life of union with God which the world requires if it is not to perish.[21]

Maritain suggests that:

> [A]t this moment many souls are dying of thirst, and receive hardly any help except from the few hidden but radiant centres that, in consecrated or lay persons, contemplation has reserved for itself on this poor earth, and through which the Spirit of God comes to touch them... the titanism of human effort is the great idol of our times. And consequently it is clear that an invisible galaxy of souls dedicated to the contemplative life—in the world itself, I mean, in the very heart of the world—is our ultimate reason for hoping.[22]

When Maritain wrote *The Peasant of the Garonne* he was living as a member of the community of the Little Brothers of Jesus in Toulouse. The charism of the Little Brothers and Sisters was discovered and lived by Charles de Foucauld in the early twentieth century. Like Luther, he

18. Maritain, *The Peasant of the Garonne*, 53.
19. Maritain, *The Peasant of the Garonne*, 233.
20. Maritain, *The Peasant of the Garonne*, 235.
21. Maritain, *The Peasant of the Garonne*, 235.
22. Maritain, *The Peasant of the Garonne*, 234.

also left his monastery to live in the world—but to live a contemplative life in the world. His followers live and work among the poor and marginalized in imitation of the hidden life of Jesus in Nazareth. They have ordinary jobs and an open house, in which there is always a tabernacle of the Blessed Sacrament. They live as missionaries with silence as a means of influence, presence as a means of communication, and poverty and friendship as their witness to *agape*. They seek to obey the charge of Jesus heard by Charles de Foucauld: "To souls in silence, I say go and set up your devotional retreats in the midst of those who do not know me; carrying the Gospel by the persuasive force of example, not by speaking but by living: sanctify the world, carry me into the world . . ."[23]

Ressourcement

Like Maritain, Henri de Lubac also responded with dismay to theologies of secularization. He argued that, while in the past the theocratic temptation may have threatened the church, today, because of a similar confusion, the secularist temptation is strong. Ironically, he believed that both temptations base themselves on the same separation of grace and nature. Both fail to return to the sacramental ontology that had been integral to the theology of the fathers and most of the medieval Church. A postconciliar decline of a sacramental ontology coincided, he believed, with a utilitarian and technological society devoted to secular progress. Such a de-sacramentalized society offered no "way out" to our desire: refusing to know God, insensible to revelation, it imprisons us in a closed world without love and without hope—and we are in danger of dying there, suffocated.[24] He rejected the secularism, or "immanentism" as he termed it, which separated the natural order and the supernatural order, the order of grace, in order to exalt the former while compromising or dismissing the latter.

In *A Brief Catechesis on Nature and Grace*, de Lubac repudiates on the one hand the extreme of radically opposing nature and grace, as if grace were entirely alien to nature, and on the other hand, the extreme

---

23. de Foucauld, "The Visitation," cited as an epigraph by Thurston, *Hidden in God*. See also Kaspar, "Charles de Foucauld"; Daiker, *Beyond Borders*; and Merton, *The Inner Experience*, chaps. 14 and 15.

24. de Lubac, *The Motherhood of the Church*, 149, cited in Boersma, *Nouvelle Theologie*, 262.

of radically confusing them.[25] He emphasizes the distinct character of divine transcendence and the supernatural and is sharply critical of Edward Schillebeeckx's conception of the Church as sacrament of the world. In the first chapter of its document on the Church, *Lumen Gentium*, the Council fathers had stated that in Christ the Church was "like a sacrament, or as a sign and instrument both of the very closely knit union with God and the unity of the whole human race." Schillibeeckx had interpreted this formulation to mean that the Council had declared Christ to be the "sacrament of the world." But in de Lubac's sacramental ontology the Church is *sacramentum Christi* not just *mundi*. The eucharistically constituted body of Christ signifies Christ and makes him present in the world. The unity of the Church as the truth of the Eucharist was the embodiment of the eschatological unity of the whole Christ *totus Christus*. To Schillibeeckx it seemed that the Church was merely the visible embodiment of a prior unity of the human race, while for de Lubac the unity of the human race existed only through the Church.

For de Lubac, Schillibeeckx's account of Christ as the sacrament of the world betrays a foundational error in ecclesiology, and his abandonment of a sacramental ontology. This error is consistent with his acceptance of "desacralizing secularization," his rejection of a "theophanic world" and a "sacralising religion," in order to return the "world" fully to its "worldly state." But for de Lubac, the Christian mission is to bring the *lumen Christi* into a world that does not know Christ, and thus to illuminate the darkness of the age with the splendor of him who abides, mysteriously, obscurely, yet really in his body the Church. This instrumental, mediatory role of the Church is intrinsic to what the Council meant when it described the Church as sacrament: the Church is a sign that effects what it signifies.

De Lubac feared that Schillibeeckx's notion of the Church as a sacrament of the world compromised the sacramental nature of the relationship by collapsing the natural into a purely natural realm. He warned of the danger of confusing progress with the coming of a new creation and of supposing that the latter is the outcome of the former. He believed that Schillibeeckx had accepted nature as an isolated entity, and that the consequence of his position would be an immanentist and secularist mentality that would leave the Church with nothing to say to the world. De Lubac feared that, by describing the Church as the sacrament of the world rather than of Christ, Schillibeeckx would end up naturalizing and secularizing

---

25. de Lubac, *A Brief Catechesis on Nature and Grace*.

the Church. He thus saw him as undermining the sacramental ontology, which he sought to restore.[26]

Charles Péguy coined the term *ressourcement* to describe a movement "from a less perfect tradition to a more perfect tradition, a call from a shallower tradition to a deeper tradition, a backing up of tradition, an overtaking of depth, an investigation into deeper sources; a return to the source in the literal sense of the word."[27] For the Catholic theologians associated with *ressourcement* or *nouvelle théologie*—Henri de Lubac, Jean Daniélou, Yves Congar, and Hans Urs von Balthasar, among others—the preeminent source for theological reflection is the word of God interpreted within the Church. In a secondary sense, the theologians of the tradition, especially the Fathers of the Church, represent abiding sources for the renewal of Christian theology.

Along with other theologians of *ressourcement*, de Lubac recognized in the Platonist-Christian synthesis a sacramental ontology that they believed had been lost through the modern separation between nature and the supernatural. As a result, *ressourcement* theology set out to reintegrate the two by pointing to the sacramental participation of nature in the heavenly reality of Christ. The *ressourcement* theologians were convinced that the vision of sacramental participation was the only viable answer to the secularism of the modern age.[28] Their answer can also be recognized as the most significant Christian response to the modern worldlessness and Gnosticism identified and addressed by Blumenberg, Jonas, and Arendt. It is a return to the Great Tradition of Christian *amor mundi*.

This answer has been developed by the concept at the heart of Radical Orthodoxy: the metaphysics of *methexis*, participation. John Milbank and Catherine Pickstock focus on Duns Scotus's notion of the "univocity of being," which, according to them, treated God and creation as encompassed by the larger, common reality of "being." In the Scotist view, God's being was different from created being only in degree. God and man are, as a result, contestants in the same space, competitors in a relation of power. Following Aquinas, Milbank and Pickstock reassert the claim that the substantial entities of creation only exist insofar as they participate in the gratuity of God's gift of being. God bestows upon creation a finite participation in his

---

26. de Lubac, *A Brief Catechesis on Nature and Grace*, Appendix B; and see Boersma, *Nouvelle Theologie*, 265.

27. Péguy, cited by Healy Jr., "Evangelical *Ressourcement*," 56.

28. Boersma, *Heavenly Participation*, 16.

CHAPTER 6: AMBIVALENCE AND DISCIPLESHIP

own substantiality: creation does not have an existence by virtue of itself but only and always because of the gratuity of God.

The radical implication of this view of participation is that creation has no autonomous existence. Creation does not stand alongside God as another focus of being or existence, neither does it lie "outside" God. When God creates the universe, there is not one "thing" (God) and then, suddenly two "things" (God and creation). And in this participatory doctrine of creation there is no autonomous secular space—no area devoid of reference to the divine.[29]

The work of the *ressourcement* theologians is also taken forward by the theology of Sarah Coakley. She explores what it means to for Christians after the "sexual revolution" of the religious crisis of the 1960s to re-inhabit the Platonist-Christian synthesis.[30]

In the first volume of her systematic theology, *God, Sexuality and the Self*, she observes that when people talk about "sex" and "sexuality" today, they often presume that the first and obvious point of reference is sexual intercourse or other genital acts.[31] The presumption is that *physiological* desires and urges are basic and fundamental in the sexual realm, and to this is often added a second presumption: that unsatisfied (physical) sexual desire is a necessarily harmful and "unnatural" state. From such a perspective, priestly or monastic celibacy is monstrous—a veritable charade, necessarily masking subterfuge and illicit sexual activity. A popularized form of Freudianism is often invoked in support of this latter view about the "impossibility" of celibacy.

Early Christianity—at least those strands of it heavily influenced by forms of Platonism—was enormously drawn to the vision of "desire" in Plato's *Symposium*, and from the second and third century onward it began to discuss this matter intensively. Although it could find little or nothing in Jesus' teaching about *eros* as such, it did not read his views on love as *agape* in any way disjunctive from the Platonic tradition of *eros*. And what it did inherit from Jewish Scripture, and then from the earliest rabbinic exegesis of Jewish Scripture, was a fascination with the symbol of sexual union as a "type"—indeed, in the Song of Songs the highest type—of God's relation to Israel or church.

---

29. Oliver, "Introducing Radical Orthodoxy."

30. Mcleod, *The Religious Crisis of the 1960s*, chap. 8.

31. Coakley, *God, Sexuality and the Self*, 7–11; Coakley, *The New Asceticism*; and Laird, *Into the Silent Land*.

The entanglement of this Platonic tradition of "desire" with the emergence of ascetic forms of Christian life enjoining celibacy on its members has made this strand of thinking particularly problematic, especially for contemporary feminism. If desire is really about desire for God, and involves some sort of "purification" of physical expression, how can Plato's program not involve a kicking away, at some point in the ascent, of the ladder that connects the divine to everything classically associated with the "woman": materiality, physical desire, marriage, childbirth? Is not this tradition of ascetic Platonist Christianity arguably one of the most inimical to feminist concerns? And is it not equally—if not more—problematic for the contentious contemporary issue of homoeroticism, which the Platonic text both assumes and then rises "above"?

Coakley declares that the central project of her systematic theology as a whole will nevertheless be to give new coinage to this tradition of Christian Platonism, but also to reevaluate it and reexpress it in ways that meet and answer some of the most difficult challenges that contemporary culture presents to the churches. She recognizes that among these challenges is the need to demonstrate the way in which the wisdom of this tradition is as applicable to those who are sexually active as to those who are not. Such a reexpression of this tradition is required even as it raises its own implicit critique of a contemporary erotic malaise.

For Coakley that means that first, Freud must be—as it were—turned on his head. It is not that physical "sex" is basic and "God" ephemeral; rather, it is God who is basic and "desire" the precious clue that ever tugs at the heart, reminding the human soul—however dimly—of its created source. Hence, in a sense that will be parsed more precisely as the book unfolds, *desire is more fundamental than "sex."* It is more fundamental, ultimately, because desire is an ontological category belonging primarily to God, and only secondarily to humans as a token of their createdness "in the image." But in God, "desire" signifies no *lack*—as it manifestly does in humans. Rather, it connotes that plenitude of longing love that God has for God's own creation and for its full and ecstatic participation in the divine, trinitarian life.

The immense cultural anxiety that for Coakley, in a secular society, is now accorded to "sex" and "gender" and to their contested relations, can here be negotiated in a different, theological light. Not that "sex" and "gender" do not matter; on the contrary, she argues that the profound difference that incarnation makes to Christian Platonism will prove that

CHAPTER 6: AMBIVALENCE AND DISCIPLESHIP

they do indeed so "matter," and deeply so. But it is not in the way that contemporary secular gender theory would almost obsessively have it. Such an obsession, she suggests, resides in the lack of *God* as a final point of reference. As for sexual "orientation," too: what orientation could be more important than the orientation to God, to divine desire? Her book lacks a detailed discussion of the "problem" of "homosexuality" because it is concerned with what for her is a deeper, and more primary, question: that of putting desire for God above all other desires, and with judging human desires only in that light. Ascetic transformation, ascetic fidelity: these are the goals that she argues fatally escape the notice of a culture bent either on pleasure or on moral condemnation. And to move beyond this false choice is necessarily a spiritual and bodily task, involving great patience and commitment. Coakley argues that the road from "sexuality" and the "self" to participation in the trinitarian God is a long haul of erotic purgation, but its goal is one of infinite delight.[32]

The foundation of her "unsystematic systematics" is contemplative prayer as the place of the transformative encounter of human desire with the ecstatic yearning of divine love. She shares with Raissa Maritain a sense of the promise of contemplative vocations in the world: in her definition, mission is "the contagiously visible life of prayer in a place."[33]

Sarah Coakley's commitment to a "new asceticism" offers a "lived theology."[34] It renews the question of how contemporary Christian discipleship is to be conceived of in relation to its history of ambivalence about the "world." I want to try to supplement her theology by turning to the work of Dietrich Bonhoeffer and Thomas Merton, before returning to Charles Taylor to consider his own response to his account of the making of a secular age.

If the reality of Christian identity is discipleship, then this identity is more pilgrimage than possession, a lived reality rather than a set of propositions or a means of interpreting experience.[35] But one of the marks of Christian discipleship must surely be the need to continue to live with ambivalence about the "world." I want to examine how Bonhoeffer and Merton were faithful to this ancient ambivalence, rather than presenting them as simply moving from a world-denying to a world-affirming ethos; and so to

---

32. Coakley, *God, Sexuality and the Self*, 11.
33. Coakley and Martin, eds., *For God's Sake*.
34. The Project on Lived Theology, "Overview."
35. Volpe, *Rethinking Christian Identity*, 34.

show how they conceive of the balance between presence to the world and detachment from the world that all disciples must find.

I also want to try to discern what it is that the church has to say to the world. This text was written in the British Library in London. A former head of learning there wrote an essay about her experience of home schooling her eleven-year-old daughter after she said no to her secondary school.[36] To explain her refusal, her daughter gave her a drawing of a narrowing tunnel of time, beyond which stood skyscrapers and riot police: the world is going to get more modern and violent, she said, and the tunnel of school "would not protect her, but crush her identity and stop her from doing anything to make the world better." Would the church protect her?

A faith more open, munificent, and sensuous: Dietrich Bonhoeffer

Bonhoeffer's biographer Eberhard Bethge records that Bonhoeffer read all of the works of Nietzsche when he was young and that his plea for the earth and loyalty to its creatures never left his mind.[37] Throughout Bonhoeffer's writings the theme of "belonging wholly to the earth" constantly recurs. In 1928 he preached that,

> The profound old saga tells of the giant Antaeus, who was stronger than any man on earth; no one could overcome him until once in a fight someone lifted him from the ground; then the giant lost all his strength which had flowed into him through his contact with the earth. The man who would leave the earth, who would depart from the present distress, loses the power, which still holds him by eternal, mysterious forces. The earth remains our mother, just as God remains our Father, and our mother will only lay in our Father's arms him who remains true to her. That is the Christian's song of the earth and her distress.[38]

If this commitment to "belonging wholly to the earth" led Bonhoeffer to interpret the metaphysics and inwardness of Platonist Christianity as *ressentiment* and a betrayal of the earth, he is still faithful to the Christian ambivalence about the world. A Nietzschean *amor mundi* coexists in his thought with a Kierkegaardian *contemptus mundi*. His thought has

36. McKenzie, "Turning for Home."
37. Bethge, "The Challenge of Dietrich Bonhoeffer's Life and Theology," 27.
38. Bonhoeffer, *No Rusty Swords*, 37; and see Fraser, *Redeeming Nietzsche*, 5–8.

CHAPTER 6: AMBIVALENCE AND DISCIPLESHIP

affinities with both Arendt's love of the world and Adorno's "strategy of hibernation."[39]

Kierkegaard's response to the present age has a family resemblance to that of Nietzsche but Kierkegaard wrote to counter the effect of mass society on modern Christians by seeking to convert the mass into single individuals.[40] His attack on Christendom is an attempt to subvert the alliance of church, state, and market.[41] To that end he declares that Christianity's first and foremost duty is to return to the monastery from which Luther broke away.[42] For Kierkegaard, Luther's "affirmation of ordinary life" and denial of a special status to the monk produced a leveling down, not a leveling up. Luther failed to see the enormous danger. For, as Kierkegaard put it, "Place Number 1 has fallen out and Place Number 2 has become the highest place."[43] The place of the saint, the martyr, even the monk has fallen out and the highest thing left, even as an ideal, is the average Christian practice in Christendom. This was the gist of Kierkegaard's attack on such "Christendom." All he demanded was that the church should admit that the Christianity commonly inculcated was only a mild accommodation to human weakness. With this admission, he thought, a little honesty would be introduced into the situation, and by holding high the ideal, men and women would be taught by their weakness to take refuge in grace.[44]

In his *Journals*, Kierkegaard describes the monastery as an essential dialectical element in Christianity that we need to have out there, like a buoy at sea in order to see where we are. But in his *Concluding Unscientific Postscript* he defines his ideal of hidden inwardness by rejecting the external witness of monasticism. He also interprets monasticism as a false solution to the problem of relating to the infinite while inescapably existing in the finite, in the world. The movement of renunciation must be accompanied by a return to the finite, allowing the absolute relation to the absolute *telos* to permeate every aspect of finite existence. In the face of a clamorous mass culture, a person can become an individual through the custody of a secret

---

39. Bernauer, "Bonhoeffer and Arendt at One Hundred."

40. Tuttle, *The Crowd is Untruth*; and Westphal, *Kierkegaard's Critique*, chap. 4.

41. Malesic, *Secret Faith in the Public Square*, chaps. 3 and 4; and Walsh, *Kierkegaard: Thinking Christianly*, chap. 7.

42. Kierkegaard, *Journals*, 240.

43. Kierkegaard, *Journals*, cited by Swenson, "Soren Kierkegaard—a Danish Socrates," 65.

44. Lowrie, *A Short Life of Kierkegaard*, 221.

grave and spacious enough to guard the soul against dispersal. The monk betrays the incognito of such a "knight of faith."

Bonhoeffer wrote, "Already one hundred years ago Kierkegaard said that Luther today would say the opposite of what he said back then. I think that is true—*cum grano salis*."[45] He develops this Protestant reengagement with monasticism in the face of the disintegration of the churches in Germany in the Nazi era. He interprets this disintegration as the inevitable consequence of grace acquired too cheaply. There is strong evidence that Bonhoeffer's expression "cheap grace" came from Kierkegaard.[46] Kierkegaard's *The Individual and the Church: Concerning Luther and Protestantism* served as a direct source for Bonhoeffer's *Discipleship*. Bonhoeffer's copy of the Kierkegaard work is heavily underlined in several places where Kierkegaard's influence seems most obvious. In *Discipleship*, Bonhoeffer offers an account of Luther's return from the cloister to the world as a frontal assault, the worst blow the world had suffered since the days of the early Christianity: hitherto the Christian life had been the achievement of a few under the favorable conditions of monasticism; now it was a duty laid on every Christian living in the world. It was a hand-to-hand conflict between the Christian and the world, which had the potential to re-evangelize the secular.[47] His *Discipleship* is also directly inspired by the *Imitatio Christi* of Thomas à Kempis, whose first chapter is headed "The Imitation of Christ and Contempt for the Vanities of the World."[48]

In a letter written from prison after his arrest by the Gestapo to Erwin Sutz on Reformation Day, October 31, 1943, Bonhoeffer wrote, "The entire training of budding theologians today belongs in church, monastery-like schools in which the pure doctrine, the Sermon on the Mount, and worship can be taken seriously—which is not the case with all three things at the university and in present day circumstances is impossible."[49] He adds that the church ought to lose its fear and stand up for the victims of state-sponsored oppression.

Bonhoeffer hoped that such monastic schools might give this fearlessness to those who trained at them. Perhaps his experiment at Finkenwalde, the small illegal seminary for the Confessing Church, reported in *Life*

---

45. Bonhoeffer, *Letters and Papers from Prison*, 173.
46. Kelly, "Kierkegaard as 'Antidote,'" 5; and Kirkpatrick, *Attacks on Christendom*.
47. Bonhoeffer, *The Cost of Discipleship*, 8.
48. Frick, "The *Imitatio Christi* of Thomas à Kempis and Dietrich Bonhoeffer."
49. Bonhoeffer, *A Testament to Freedom*, 412.

CHAPTER 6: AMBIVALENCE AND DISCIPLESHIP

Together, provided a partial answer, a training for martyrdom.[50] In a letter of January 14, 1935, to his brother Karl-Freidrick, he wrote:

> The restoration of the church must surely come from a new kind of monasticism, which will have only one thing in common with the old, a life lived without compromise according to the Sermon on the Mount in the following of Jesus. I believe the time has come to gather people together for this.[51]

Bonhoeffer imagines this theological formation would be sustained against the danger of conformity to the world by the contemplative practice of an *Arkandiziplin*, a space where the church protects her life from the corruption of the world so as to be able to truly become, once again, the church, and which preserves for the disciple the *incognito* of Kierkegaard's knight of faith.[52] Unlike the "English Bonhoefferians," Bonhoeffer himself did not present a choice between the traditional spiritual disciplines and responsible action in the world. Rather the "discipline of the secret" would preserve Christians from merging their identity in Jesus Christ with their actions in the world or its prevailing ideologies and untruths.[53]

> In his account of the intrinsic relation between self and society, prayer and action, spirituality and justice, he recalls the Augustinian claim that the pursuit of holiness, the education of desire, the quest to love what is truly loveable, involve *paideia* through those moral and spiritual practices that distinguish the City of God from the earthly city.[54]

Bonhoeffer states his version of the ancient Christian ambivalence about the world in the letter he wrote to Eberhard Bethge on July 21, 1944, the day after the plot to kill Hitler failed.

> During the last year or so I've come to know and understand more and more the profound this-worldliness of Christianity. The Christian is not a *homo religiosus*, but simply a human being, as Jesus was human—in contrast, shall we say, to John the Baptist. I don't mean the shallow and banal this-worldliness of the enlightened, the busy, the comfortable, or the lascivious, but

---

50. Slane, *Bonhoeffer as Martyr*, chap. 12.
51. Cited by Bethge, *Dietrich Bonhoeffer*, 462.
52. Malesic, *Secret Faith in the Public Square*, chap. 5 and 6.
53. Kelly, "Prayer and Action for Justice."
54. Northcott, "'Who am I?,'" 24.

> the profound this-worldliness, characterized by discipline and the constant knowledge of death and resurrection.[55]

Bonhoeffer understood that the profound this-worldliness of Christianity was founded in the apocalyptic witness of the New Testament to the uniting of the reality of God with the reality of the world in Jesus Christ. Jesus reveals that the love of God and the love of creation are not incompatible; in fact, they are united. As Alexander Schmemann explains, the decisive content and term of reference for apocalyptic is not the world but the kingdom of God, and thus rather than being "anti-world" it is "pro-kingdom."[56] The eschatological reign of the God of Israel announced, inaugurated, and given in and by Christ, determines the church's relationship with the world. This world has condemned itself to die, to be the world whose form passes away. In the prayer of the tenth chapter of the Didache, "Let grace come and let this world pass away."[57] This is the Christian no to the world and it always has been required of those who want to enter the kingdom that they die with Christ and that their true lives are hidden with Christ in God. At the same time, this creation in rebellion is redeemed and recreated in Christ, in whom all things find their *telos*. This means that for those who believe in Christ and are united to him, this very world, its time and matter, its life, and even death, have become the means of communion with the kingdom of God, the sacrament of its coming among men and women.

Schmemann can thus reject the opposition between nature and the supernatural and attempt to reintegrate the two with a "sacramental this worldliness."[58]

> Christ came not to replace "natural' matter with some "supernatural" and sacred matter, but to restore it and to fulfill it as the means of communion with God. The holy water in Baptism, the bread and wine in the Eucharist, stand for, i.e. represent the whole of creation, but creation as it will be at the end, when it will be consummated in God, when He will fill all things with Himself.[59]

---

55. Bonhoeffer, *Letters and Papers from Prison*, 369.

56. Schmemann, *Church, World, Mission*, 29–30, cited by Harvey, *Taking Hold of the Real*, 45.

57. Staniforth, trans., *Early Christian Writings*, 232.

58. Harvey, *Taking Hold of the Real*, chap. 1.

59. Schmemann, *Of Water and the Spirit*, 49, cited by Boersma, *Heavenly Participation*, 9; and see Schmemann, *For the Life of the World*.

CHAPTER 6: AMBIVALENCE AND DISCIPLESHIP

The church's sacraments are the beginning of a cosmic restoration. The entire cosmos is meant to serve as a sacrament: the material gift of God in and through which we enter into the joy of his heavenly presence.

This Orthodox understanding informs a dramatic moment of *amor mundi* in Dostoevsky's *The Brothers Karamazov*. Alyosha Karamazov leaves a monastery to "return to the world." Dostoevsky describes how it is just as he emerges from his darkest despair that "the silence of the earth seemed to merge with the silence of the heavens, the mystery of the earth touched the mystery of the stars."[60] It is when it is on earth as it is in heaven, in the words of the Lord's Prayer that Dostoevsky specifically uses, that Alyosha throws himself onto the earth, embraces it, and, weeping, kisses it, just as his elder Zossima had enjoined him to do. It is, then, not the earth as such, nor even less, the earth as a kind of pagan deity, but the earth as it is in heaven, the earth upon which God's will be done *on earth as it is in heaven*—the earth now revealed as infused with divine energies—that is honored, celebrated, and venerated. It is the earth revealed as a nexus of divine *logoi*, the earth seen in its iconicity that is venerated by Alyosha just as Orthodox believers venerate icons through bowing before them and kissing them, and loving not merely the icons but infinitely more what they reveal.[61] Bonhoeffer wrote:

> So long as Christ and the world are conceived as two opposing and mutually repellent spheres, man will be left in the following dilemma: he abandons reality as a whole, and places himself in one or other of the two spheres. He seeks Christ without the world or the world without Christ ... There are not two realities but one reality, and that is the reality of God, which has become manifest in Christ in the reality of the world. Sharing in Christ we stand at once in the reality of God and the reality of the world.[62]
>
> ... [W]hen I encounter the reality of the world it is always already sustained, accepted and reconciled by the reality of God.[63]

This understanding of the worldliness of Christianity brought Bonhoeffer to a faith that was "more open, munificent, and sensuous."[64] In the context of the Nazi state and the war, it was a faith that allowed him to enjoy human

---

60. Dostoevsky, *The Brothers Karamazov*, 456.
61. Foltz, *The Noetics of Nature*, 202.
62. Bonhoeffer, *Ethics*, 195.
63. Bonhoeffer, *Ethics*, 197.
64. Balmer, "Between God and the Führer," citing Marsh, *Strange Glory*, chap. 14.

relationships, and "the full this-worldliness of life." This was what was disappearing, or rather being forcibly taken, from Europe—"all that is human," "personal life secure with . . . loved ones and . . . possessions," the joy and tenderness of friendship, marriage, and family. Christians must preserve and hallow these things, rather than only preaching a strenuous austerity.[65]

Bonhoeffer was engaged but imprisoned. He was "restless and longing and sick, like a bird in a cage . . . yearning for colors, for flowers, for the voices of birds, thirsting for words of kindness . . ."[66] Bethge was married with a new baby and afraid of wartime separation. Bonhoeffer uses the metaphor of polyphony in a letter to his friend:

> There's always a danger in all strong, erotic love that one may lose what I might call the polyphony of life. What I mean is that God wants us to love him eternally with our whole hearts—not in such a way as to injure or weaken our earthly love, but to provide a kind of *cantus firmus* to which the other melodies of life provide the counterpoint. One of these contrapuntal themes (which have their own complete independence but are yet related to the *cantus firmus*) is earthly affection. Even in the Bible we have the Song of Songs; and really one can imagine no more ardent, passionate, sensual love than is portrayed there (see 7:6). It's a good thing that the book is in the Bible, in face of all those who believe that the restraint of passion is Christian (where is there such restraint in the Old Testament?). Where the *cantus firmus* is clear and plain, the counterpoint can be developed to its limits. The two are "undivided and yet distinct," in the words of the Chalcedonian Definition, like Christ in his divine and human natures. May not the attraction and importance of polyphony in music consist in its being a musical reflection of this Christological fact and therefore of our *vita christiana*? . . . Only a polyphony of this kind can give life a wholeness and at the same time assure us that nothing calamitous can happen as long as the *cantus firmus* is kept going.[67]

For Bonhoeffer, Christians are called to participate in this profound worldliness that breaks into the world in the action of Jesus Christ, a form of life that requires discipline and an understanding of death and resurrection. The disciple of Christ is set apart from the world in order to be for the world. True discipleship is a demonstration of true worldliness that follows a God

---

65. Hill, "The Full This-Worldliness of Life."
66. Bonhoeffer, *Letters and Papers from Prison*, 535–36.
67. Bonhoeffer, *Letters and Papers from Prison*, 393–94.

who entered into the suffering of the world, "allowing oneself to be caught up into the way of Jesus Christ, into the messianic event."[68]

When Bonhoeffer spoke of a "world come of age" after Christendom, it was an ironic commentary on an adolescent world's belief in the maturity of its own technological and ideological achievements, achievements that Bonhoeffer understood to be destructive illusions. In *Creation and Fall*, he writes, "Humankind is a prisoner, a slave of the world, and its dominion is an illusion. Technology is the power with which the earth seizes hold of humankind and masters it."[69] Bonhoeffer's concern in presenting the idea of "a world come of age" is with how best to confront the technological organization and management of life in the modern world with the uniting of God and world in Christ. He shows Christians the kind of worldliness necessary to deal with the worldliness of a secular age.[70]

The "discipline of the secret" must complete itself in worldliness, not by becoming profane, or merely nonreligious, but by taking the place of Christ in the world: discipleship is participation in Christ's suffering for others, in communion with the Crucified One. It is only by exposing ourselves to the world in this suffering way that we can transcend the world in the way that Christ transcended it.[71] Like Adorno, Bonhoeffer rethinks the doctrine of *contemptus mundi* for a secular age. The world is condemned for the sake of the world.[72]

Where do you go from the top of a thirty-foot pole?
Thomas Merton

Like Bonhoeffer, Thomas Merton did not simply move from a world-denying to a world-affirming ethos. He too was faithful to the ancient ambivalence of Christians about the world.

In his bellicose autobiography *The Seven Storey Mountain*, which was first published in 1948, he wrote,

> If any man love the world, the charity of the Father is not in him. For all that is in the world, is the concupiscence of the flesh, and

---

68. Bonhoeffer, *Letters and Papers from Prison*, 535–36.
69. Bonhoeffer, *Creation and Fall*, 67.
70. Harvey, *Taking Hold of the Real*, chap. 1–3.
71. Anderson, *Historical Transcendence and the Reality of God*, 97–98, cited by Surin, "*Contemptus mundi* and the disenchanted world," 187–88.
72. Surin, "*Contemptus mundi* and the disenchanted world," 188.

the concupiscence of the eyes, and the pride of life. All men who live only according to their five senses, and seek nothing beyond the gratification of their natural appetites for pleasure and reputation and power, cut themselves off from that charity which is the principle of all spiritual vitality and happiness because it alone saves us from the barren wilderness of our own abominable selfishness. It is true that the materialistic society, the so-called culture that has evolved under the tender mercies of capitalism, has produced what seems to be the ultimate limit of this worldliness. And nowhere, except perhaps in the analogous society of pagan Rome, has there ever been such a flowering of cheap and petty and disgusting lusts and vanities as in the world of capitalism, where there is no evil that is not fostered and encouraged for the sake of making money. We live in a society whose whole policy is to excite every nerve in the human body and keep it at the highest pitch of artificial tension, to strain every human desire to the limit and to create as many new desires and synthetic passions as possible, in order to cater to them with the products of our factories and printing presses and movie studios and all the rest.[73]

Merton is often interpreted as abandoning such *contemptus mundi* for the *amor mundi* of his vision in 1958:

In Louisville, at the corner of Fourth and Walnut, in the center of the shopping district, I was suddenly overwhelmed with the realization that I loved all those people, that they were mine and I theirs, that we could not be alien to one another even though we were total strangers. It was like waking from a dream of separateness, of spurious self-isolation in a special world, the world of renunciation and supposed holiness ... This sense of liberation from an illusory difference was such a relief and such a joy to me that I almost laughed out loud ... I have the immense joy of being man, a member of a race in which God Himself became incarnate. As if the sorrows and stupidities of the human condition could overwhelm me, now I realize what we all are. And if only everybody could realize this! But it cannot be explained. There is no way of telling people that they are all walking around shining like the sun.[74]

But *contemptus mundi* continues to balance *amor mundi* in his thought, even in his "turning toward the world." The prophetic edge of his critique of the modern world is increasingly the way he understands the traditional

---

73. Merton, *The Seven Storey Mountain*, 147.
74. Merton, *Conjectures of a Guilty Bystander*, 156–58.

CHAPTER 6: AMBIVALENCE AND DISCIPLESHIP

notion of *contemptus mundi*.[75] It is a movement of *approfondissement* rather than abandonment.

In his talk in Bangkok on the day that he died, Merton used one of his favorite Zen koans: "Where do you go from the top of a thirty-foot pole?" Twenty years earlier as a young Trappist he had been faced with a similar sort of riddle: "Where do you go from the top of a seven storey mountain?" The task of his life would be to discover how the conversion he had shouted from his "mountain top" in Kentucky could continue to deepen and become effective in compassion, humility, and maturity.[76]

Merton came to see his earlier view as insufficiently attentive to the good of the created world, to his solidarity with others, and to his own humanity. He recognized that his attitude could lead to what Maritain called "angelism": hatred of the human and of embodiment, for the sake of higher gnostic perfection. In his maturity Merton realized that monastic separation was a paradoxical invitation to be close to the world in a new way through his increasing sense of compassion. Compassion in a Buddhist sense means reaching out in love to all that exists in order to bring about enlightenment. The *Bodhisattva*, enlightened though he or she may be, delays nirvana in order to bring others to enlightenment. Merton came to see such compassion as a way to understand the meaning of *agape*.[77]

Merton argues in *Conjectures of a Guilty Bystander* that true *contemptus mundi* is essential for understanding a third way, neither conservative nor liberal, in which he proposes how the church should respond to the modern world. The equilibrium of *contemptus mundi* and *amor mundi* in his later thought is evident in his responses to Bonhoeffer and to John Robinson.

He asserts that the anguish, ambiguity, and even absurdity of the problem of the church in the modern world is rooted in the unadmitted assumption that the kingdom of God can be promoted on earth by direct means. For conservatives this takes the form of a belief that the restoration of Christendom with the church as the kingdom of God on earth with a divine mandate to dominate culture, politics, and society. For liberals and radicals it takes the form of an admission that the progressives and revolutionaries of "the world" have unconsciously hit upon the right answers and are building the kingdom of God where the church has failed to do

---

75. Cunningham, *Thomas Merton and the Monastic Vision*, 78.
76. Malits, *The Solitary Explorer*, 141.
77. Cunningham, *Thomas Merton and the Monastic Vision*, 192–93.

so. Hence the Christian must join the revolution—and thus guarantee that Christianity will survive.[78]

For Merton such adaptations to "the world" can be the expression of fear and shame at having failed to "hold" the modern world. To be dominated by this fear is implicitly to confront the world in abject shame at the name and power of Christ. The last thing that should concern a Christian or the church is survival in a temporal or worldly sense: to be concerned with this is an implicit denial of the victory of Christ and of the resurrection.[79] "The vocation of the monk in the modern world . . . is not survival but prophecy."[80]

Merton contends that the tradition of *contemptus mundi* in Christianity and in Buddhism needs to be reexamined and understood. Originally *contemptus mundi* was intended to give the believer a certain freedom of action, a distance, a detachment, a liberation from care without which any question of love for the people in the world would be completely irrelevant. Before Christians can properly estimate their place in the world they have to get back to the fundamental Christian respect for the transiency of both the world and the institutional structure of the church. True *contemptus mundi* is a compassion for the transient world and a humility that refuses arrogantly to set up the church as an "eternal" institution in the world. But if we despise the transient world of secularism in terms that suggest an ecclesiastical world that is not itself transient, there is no way to avoid disaster and absurdity.[81]

Merton praises Bonhoeffer for reacting against Barthian radicalism in his *Ethics* by emphasizing the rights and dignity of nature in a very Catholic, humanistic way. He cites with approval a line from Bonhoeffer's *Ethics*: "The life of the body assumes its full significance only with the fulfillment of its inherent claim to joy."[82] And he quotes lines from one of Bonhoeffer's prison letters where he writes,

> I am sure we honour God more, if we gratefully accept the life he gives us with all its blessings, loving it and drinking it to the full, grieving deeply and sincerely when we have belittled or thrown

---

78. Merton, *Conjectures of a Guilty Bystander*, 53.
79. Merton, *Conjectures of a Guilty Bystander*, 126.
80. Merton, *Survival or Prophecy*, 129.
81. Merton, *Conjectures of a Guilty Bystander*, 53.
82. Merton, *Conjectures of a Guilty Bystander*, 201, citing Bonhoeffer, *Ethics*, 157.

CHAPTER 6: AMBIVALENCE AND DISCIPLESHIP

away any of the precious things of life ... than we do if we are insensitive toward life.[83]

Merton responds "Worldliness, Yes, of course. The right kind, which sees the world redeemed in Christ." He continues,

> But one must not conclude from this that a materialistic, technocratic worldliness is equally blessed. The "good things" offered in such profusion by the affluent society are not self-evidently gifts and blessings from God. Technology can degrade men and women, despoil the world, ravage life and lead to ruin. What if these "good things" corrupt and destroy life, or pervert it by ruining its true sensitivity and capacity for love, peace, fruitfulness and joy?[84]

Merton argues that some of Bonhoeffer's disciples make this mistake. John Robinson is cited, arguing that, "to live for others means to accept life on their terms." For Merton the great question is: Precisely what is meant by, "accepting life on their terms"? What are "their terms"? He observes that Bonhoeffer was far from accepting Nazism "on its own terms."[85] He died resisting it. The question for Merton is: To what extent are we to take the affluent society of the West on its own terms?

Bonhoeffer's worldliness does not consist, like that of some of his disciples, in absolving the world from all guilt. It begins, on the contrary, with a very clear recognition of the modern world as guilty and fallen—but also, therefore, as having the greatest claim on Christian mercy, all the more so as Christians themselves are deeply implicated in the same guilt. This is surely quite a different optimism from the free-wheeling and breezy propensity of some Christians to affirm the torn and anguished world of the twentieth century as the flowering of Christian humanism and happiness. For Merton this affirmation shows not only the most pitiable lack of imagination and understanding, but is also a cruel and scandalous failure of Christian compassion. It is a humanism which, appealing to man and to Christ, actually derides both—but more out of stupidity than malice.[86]

Merton writes that his own thought is increasingly informed by that of Bonhoeffer, which strikes him as a more mature Christianity than either

---

83. Cited in Merton, *Conjectures of a Guilty Bystander*, 289.
84. Merton, *Conjectures of a Guilty Bystander*, 316.
85. Merton, *Conjectures of a Guilty Bystander*, 323.
86. Merton, *Conjectures of a Guilty Bystander*, 253–54.

the old triumphalism or the new optimism and naturalism.[87] After a stay in hospital Merton reflected:

> In the hospital life is covered over with a kind of organized ugliness for which no one is responsible: it is in large part the ugliness of sickness and suffering which the hospital attempts to alleviate. But under this drab and routine front, there is a great deal of human goodness and beauty, a deep fund of richness and generosity in the richness and generosity in the nurses, the doctors, the nuns and all the people who work here. I think the question of "turning to the world" is in fact a question of being patient with the unprepossessing surface of it, in order to break through to the deep goodness that is underneath. But to my way of thinking "the world" is precisely the dehumanized surface. What is under the surface and often stifled and destroyed is more than "the world": it is the spirit and likeness of God in men. Much of the ambiguity in talk about the world—especially mine—is that everyone tends to be quite selective about the elements he admits into his concept of "the world." My particular concept focuses on the sham, the unreality, the alienation, the forced systematization of life, and not on the human reality that is alienated and suppressed.[88]

This *approfondissement* of the *contemptus mundi* of *The Seven Storey Mountain* is an expression of a discovery that was to bring him close to the Buddhist tradition: a discovery of the illusory self. Flight from the world is not achieved simply by a change of place. Merton had been badly traumatized by a world of violence, disorder, irrationality, hopelessness, and evil. He tried to shut it out behind the walls of a monastery. But the world, he came to realize, entered with him. He discovered the "enemy" and it was he himself. Contemplation took him from behind his own back and stood him before his face and made him look at himself.[89] The "real" world is not what is outside a person, but has to do with his or her inner life: "For that is where the world is first of all, in my deepest self."[90] When it looked as if he would be overwhelmed by what he called a "submarine earthquake"—he experienced a breakthrough and a resurrection: "the sign of Jonas."

It is the discovery of the true self that allows the monk, the Christian to be in the world but not of it. This is the basis of the Christian mission to

---

87. Tardif, ed., *At Home in the World*, 5.
88. Merton, *Conjectures of a Guilty Bystander*, 256–57.
89. Hinson, "Contemptus Mundi—Amor Mundi."
90. Merton, *Contemplation in a World of Action*, 154–55.

CHAPTER 6: AMBIVALENCE AND DISCIPLESHIP

the world.[91] He or she can speak the truth because the ego of self-oriented desire that seeks to dominate and organize the world is absent and no longer an obstruction to reality.[92] As in Buddhist teaching, far from implying lack of concern for the welfare of others, detachment is essential for true compassion because it is liberation from the ego. *Mahaakarunaa*, "great compassion," is opposed to the elementary compassion, which the novice on the path attempts to radiate and practice before self-orientated desire has been replaced with outward-moving energy. Mahaakassapa, a disciple of the Buddha, is praised because "he teaches the doctrine to others out of pity, out of caring for them, because of his compassion for them."[93] Likewise, Merton would take responsibility for the world in a new way.

Merton's whole spirituality came to turn on the question of ultimate human identity.[94] His message is that we are one with God. Our own deepest self is not so much our own self as it is the self that is one with the "Risen and Deathless Christ in Whom all are fulfilled in One."[95] Merton's writing take its readers on a journey to God in which the self that begins the journey is not the self that arrives. The self that begins is the self that we thought ourselves to be. It is this self that dies along the way until in the end "no one" is left. This "no one" is our true self. It is the self that stands prior to all that is this or that. It is the self in God, it is the self bigger than death yet born of death. It is the self the Father loves forever.

This true self in God is opposed to the false self of egocentric desires. The task Merton sets before us is a prayerful asking of Who Am I, not relative to this or that aspect of my being, but rather who am I ultimately before God? The question is, in other words, who am I absolutely? It is obvious that, based on my experience, I know who I am by virtue of my relationships with others in each of the relationships that has gone into the making of what I call my personality. The identity given to me by those relationships is certainly real enough, but none of these relationships either individually or collectively constitutes the totality of my being. None of these relationships gave me my very existence, but rather, found me as already existing and from there helped to form, for better or worse, my empirical

---

91. Merton, *Conjectures of a Guilty Bystander*, 325.
92. Williams, *A Silent Action*, 17.
93. Harris, "Detachment and Compassion in Early Buddhism."
94. Finley, *Merton's Palace of Nowhere*, 21.
95. Merton, *Mystics and Zen Masters*, 42, cited by Finley, *Merton's Palace of Nowhere*, 21.

identity. Even my parents, though the causes of my biological existence, did not create the unique essence of my being but rather discovered me as a newly unfolding mystery in their midst.

Merton makes no attempt to question the reality and importance of the empirical self that we call our personality. Indeed, he teaches that in the spiritual life a deep respect must be given to our whole person, including the day-to-day realities of life and the self that is formed by them. What Merton does say, however, is that when the relative identity of the ego is taken to be my deepest and only identity, when I am thought to be nothing but the sum total of all my relationships, when I cling to the self and make it the center around which and for which I live, then I make my empirical identity into the false self. My own self then becomes the obstacle to realizing my true self. The false self is

> the man I want myself to be but who cannot exist, because God does not know anything about him ... The one who wants to exist outside the reach of God's will and God's love—outside of reality and outside of life ... [is] an illusion. For most people in the world there is no greater subjective reality than this false self of theirs, which cannot exist. A life devoted to the cult of this shadow is what is called a life of sin.[96]

The true self is not some obscure and hidden identity that we must pull forth from the darkness like a rabbit from a hat. Nor is it some evasive entity running lost in the labyrinths of our minds. The true self is rather our whole self before God. It is the self the Father created us to become. It is the self in Christ. It is the self that breathes, that stands and sits. It is the self that is. The true self, being simple like God, can be realized only in the mode of simple awareness proper to it. This mode of awareness is learnt in the practice of contemplative prayer. The two elements of contemplative awareness and the search for the true self are inseparable. An exploration of the true self will bring us to an understanding of prayer and a prayerful attentiveness will bring us to an understanding of the true self. For the self that prays truly is the true self. It is in prayer that we discover our own deepest reality and cease to be strangers to ourselves.

Merton's discovered his illusory self—"this patchwork, this bundle of questions and doubts and obsessions ... This incoherence!!!" But this discovery was not his last word. "Somehow out of all this comes the miracle, the "unbearable lightness of being," the recognition that my reality rests

---

96. Merton, *New Seeds of Contemplation*, 34.

CHAPTER 6: AMBIVALENCE AND DISCIPLESHIP

"like a feather on the breath of God." In myself I may be a "patchwork," an "incoherence," a "nothing"; yet in God I have eternal and inexhaustible meaning. "I am because of the love of God."[97]

Merton described his vision in Louisville as a realization that this discovery was true of every person.

> At the center of our being is a point of nothingness [*le point vierge*] which is untouched by sin and by illusion, a point of pure truth, a point or spark which belongs entirely to God, which is never at our disposal, from which God disposes of our lives, which is inaccessible to the fantasies of our own mind or the brutalities of our own will. This little point of nothingness and of absolute poverty is the pure glory of God in us. It is so to speak His name written in us, as our poverty, as our indigence, as our dependence, as our sonship. It is like a pure diamond, blazing with the invisible light of heaven. It is in everybody, and if we could see it we would see these billions of points of light coming together in the face and blaze of a sun that would make all the darkness and cruelty of life vanish completely . . . I have no program for this seeing. It is only given. But the gate of heaven is everywhere.[98]

Merton came to realize, like Bonhoeffer, that the question of choosing the world or choosing Christ is completely misguided. It is rather a question of dying to our false self to discover our true self:

> Do we really choose between the world and Christ as between two conflicting realities absolutely opposed? Or do we choose Christ *by choosing the world as it really is in Him, that is to say created and redeemed by Him, and encountered in the ground of our own personal freedom and of our love?* Do we really renounce ourselves and the world in order to find Christ, or do we renounce our alienated and false selves in order to choose our own deepest truth in choosing both the world and Christ at the same time? If the deepest ground of my being is love, then in that very love itself and nowhere else will I find myself, *and* the world, *and* my brother *and* Christ. It is not a question of either/or but of all-in-one . . . which finds the same ground of love in everything.[99]

---

97. Ware, "Afterword," 89.

98. Merton, *New Seeds of Contemplation*, 157.

99. Merton, *Contemplation in a World of Action*, 155–56, cited by Finley, *Merton's Palace of Nowhere*, 60.

Merton came to conceive of *contemptus mundi* as a rejection of those aspects of the world that are the communal expressions of the false self.[100] Worldliness is "involvement in the massive and absurd mythology of technological culture and in all the contrived and obsessive gyrations of its empty mind."[101] It is servitude to care and illusion. One of its symptoms in Christians is an anxious concern with adaptation and relevance. Merton interprets this concern as a tacit expression of the false self's assumption that we are nothing but what the world makes us to be, and so that irrelevance according to the criterion of the world is tantamount to nonexistence.[102] Detachment is liberation from such cares.

Through humility, the monk, the contemplative, the Christian can come to know others more profoundly than those others know themselves. This does not make them superior to other people: just less distracted, and therefore more real. Merton believed that the monk had a duty not just to survive in the modern world but to dissent from it, calmly accepting its incomprehension and indifference because what he is living was the night of our technological barbarism; "monks must be as trees which exist silently in the dark and by their vital presence purify the air."[103]

And he came to understand their vocation to include a responsibility to show others the way—by example—back to essential life.[104] In 1960 he read Hannah Arendt's *The Human Condition* and found the work profoundly unsettling. In his response to the book he begins to formulate an implicit conception that Rowan Williams was to take up in his defense of Augustine against Arendt's criticism: that of the contemplative community as a true polis, "the only real city." The monastery does not just repudiate the world to maintain a space of its own that offers no hope of transformation. Monasticism should offer a space for the cultivation of the human, for what Kierkegaard called "aesthetic existence," art, education, friendship, and play as Bonhoeffer describes the church doing, in a way that for Merton brings him close to the humanism of Irenaeus for whom man lives the glory of God.[105] Merton's vision is of the monastery and the church after Christen-

---

100. Merton, *Conjectures of a Guilty Bystander*, 256–57.

101. Merton, *Conjectures of a Guilty Bystander*, 259–60; and see Weiss, *The Environmental Vision of Thomas Merton*.

102. Finley, *Merton's Palace of Nowhere*, 50.

103. Merton, *Basic Principles of Monastic Spirituality*, 61.

104. Inchausti, *Thomas Merton's American Prophecy*, 72.

105. Merton, *Conjectures of a Guilty Bystander*, 315, 334.

CHAPTER 6: AMBIVALENCE AND DISCIPLESHIP

dom "is not of the possibility of a secure enclave, an Indian reservation in the modern world, but of a genuinely civic and political life open to all, and a vision of the material world itself as sacramental; it is a reclaiming of the present, the prosaic and the human."[106]

In the early sixties Merton adopts the role of a "guilty bystander." He moves towards open intervention in public life as "the conscience of the peace movement" to confront what he calls "the Unspeakable."

> The goodness of the world, stricken or not, is incontestable and definitive. If it is stricken, it is also healed in Christ. But nevertheless one of the awful facts of our age is the evidence that it is stricken indeed, stricken to the very core of its being by the presence of the Unspeakable. Those who are at present so eager to be reconciled with the world at any price must take care not to be reconciled with it under this particular aspect: as the nest of The Unspeakable. This is what too few are willing to see . . . You are not big enough to accuse the whole age effectively, but let us say you are in dissent. You are in no position to issue commands, but you can speak words of hope. Shall this be the substance of your message? Be human in this most inhuman of ages; guard the image of man for it is the image of God.[107]

His final lecture in Bangkok presents the discovery of the illusory self as the means by which the monk identifies himself in the world of revolution.

> The monk is essentially someone who takes up a critical attitude towards the world and its structures. . . . If one is to call himself in one way or another a monk, he must have in some way or other reached some kind of critical conclusion about the validity of certain claims made by secular society and its structures with regard to the end of man's existence. In other words, the monk is somebody who says, in one way or another, that the claims of the world are fraudulent. The difference between the monk and the Marxist is fundamental insofar as the Marxist view of change is oriented to the change of substructures, and the monk is seeking to change man's consciousness.[108]

Buddhist and Christian monasticism start from the problem inside man himself. Instead of dealing with the external structures of society, they start with man's own consciousness. Both Christianity and Buddhism

---

106. Williams, "'The Only Real City,'" 64.
107. Merton, *Raids on the Unspeakable*, 7.
108. Merton, "Marxism and Monastic Perspectives," 330.

agree that the root of man's problems is that his consciousness is all fouled up and he does not apprehend reality as it fully and really is; that the moment he looks at something, he begins to interpret it in ways that are prejudiced and predetermined to fit a certain wrong picture of the world, in which he exists as an individual ego in the center of things. This is called by Buddhism *avidya*, or ignorance.

> Instead of starting with matter itself and then moving up to a new structure, in which man will automatically develop a new consciousness, the traditional religions begin with the consciousness of the individual, seek to transform and liberate the truth in each person, with the idea that it will then communicate itself to others. ... The monk is a man who has attained, or is about to attain, or seeks to attain, full realization. He dwells in the center of society as one who has attained realization—he knows the score. Not that he has acquired unusual or esoteric information, but he has come to experience the ground of his own being in such a way that he knows the secret of liberation and can somehow or other communicate this to others.[109]

What is essential to monastic and Christian life can survive the loss of the structures of Christendom, for it goes deeper. "Its concern is with this business of total inner transformation."[110]

Moral responsibility requires an engagement with spiritual disciplines that were traditionally reserved for the cloister. Just as in Bonhoeffer's account of the personal *askesis* of the "discipline of the secret," a certain depth of disciplined existence is a necessary ground for fruitful action.[111]

> [Contemplation] is very far from being just one kind of thing that Christians do ... it is ... the key to the essence of a renewed humanity that is capable of seeing the world and other subjects in the world with freedom—freedom from self-oriented, acquisitive habits and the distorted understanding that comes from them ... contemplation is the only ultimate answer to the unreal and insane world that our financial systems and our advertising culture and our chaotic and unexamined emotions encourage us to inhabit. To learn contemplative practice is to learn what we need so as to live truthfully and honestly and lovingly. It is a deeply revolutionary matter.[112]

109. Merton, "Marxism and Monastic Perspectives," 333.
110. Merton, "Marxism and Monastic Perspectives," 340.
111. Northcott, "'Who am I?,'" 27.
112. Williams, "The New Evangelisation."

CHAPTER 6: AMBIVALENCE AND DISCIPLESHIP

The dilemma of mutilation: Charles Taylor

Charles Taylor responds to the religious crisis of the 1960s and to the story he tells of the reform of the world and the making of a secular age by reimagining contemporary Christianity.

In *A Secular Age*, Taylor describes the religious crisis of the 1960s as a profound alteration of the conditions of belief in Western society.[113] A new age of authenticity is characterized by a culture of expressive individualism, which owes a considerable debt to Romanticism. The revolts of the sixties were against the disciplined and disengaged "buffered self" and the culture of the fifties, which seemed to many conformist and crushing. Their aim was to break down all the barriers that society had erected to self-realization and flourishing, particularly those between reason and sensuality. Taylor argues that the effect of these changes on religion have been highly complex. On the one hand, people are increasingly looking for a life of greater immediacy, spontaneity, and spiritual depth than can be provided for them in an immanent order of unbelief that precludes transcendence, while on the other hand many do not find the authenticity and wholeness that they desire in the established forms of religion. This has created an important tension between the new forms of spiritual quest and the old patterns of authority, which seek to foreclose them. Alongside this is the phenomenon of diffusive Christianity, in which people distance themselves from established forms of religion yet at the same time are unwilling to entirely break with them. Taylor concludes his account of religion today by suggesting that its future is likely to be determined by the tension between spiritual quest and foreclosing authority and the important cross-pressure that this produces.

He suggests the salient feature of today's Western society is not so much the retreat of religious belief but the "mutual fragilization" of competing religious and nonreligious, believing and nonbelieving options: rival stories are always at hand offering a very different account of the world. In particular he argues that the debate between belief and unbelief centers not on issues of metaphysics, theology, or even science, but rather on the ethical presuppositions that underlie these different stances.

Crucial, therefore, is the question of what fullness or flourishing consists in. From this perspective, Taylor turns to the two major dilemmas that he sees as confronting both faith and unbelief that are a legacy of Christian

---

113. Taylor, *A Secular Age*, chaps. 13–14.

love and hatred of the world. The first is the question of how to define moral and spiritual aspirations for human beings while showing a path to transformation that does not crush, mutilate, or deny what is essential to our humanity. For while the religious desire to transcend humanity might threaten the affirmation of human values, the unbelieving assertion of human values risks equally cutting off all pathways to transcendence.

The second dilemma concerns the problem of violence. While this is often seen as a religious problem, Taylor instead points to the deep metaphysical roots of violence in human nature. As he puts it, the dilemma facing both religious and nonreligious positions is that the struggle against evil can itself generate evil, so that the goodness of the final goal is itself undone in the process of trying to reach it.

Taylor responds to the religious crisis of the 1960s and to the story he tells of the reform of the world and the making of a secular age with a wager on the complementarity between the modern quest for authentic individuality and the deeply felt need for community.[114] His vision of such a complementarity culminates in *A Secular Age* with the proposal of "a communion of disparate itineraries toward God, linked by an ever-expanding network of agape." For Taylor this network of agape is the gospel idea of the church before it was deformed by its historical entry into the power field of the world. This conception the kingdom is neither excarnate nor hegemonic. It is an order of human flourishing whose primary image is the Communion of Saints.[115]

He calls attention to the specifically Christian contribution to the general shift of ancient religions in the Axial Age away from "embedded" religion. Embedded religion conceived of society as prior to its individual members and sacralized existing social orders, reinforcing loyalty to family and clan. Christianity, in contrast, calls persons out of the existing social order into personal relationships with God and into forms of flourishing that transcend the natural and ordinary. The New Testament "is full of calls to leave or relativize solidarities of family, clan, society, and be part of the Kingdom ... This in turn helped to give force to a conception of society as founded on covenant, and hence as ultimately constituted by the decision of free individuals."[116]

---

114. Herdt, "The Authentic Individual in the Network of Agape."
115. Taylor, *A Secular Age*, 754.
116. Taylor, *A Secular Age*, 155.

CHAPTER 6: AMBIVALENCE AND DISCIPLESHIP

This characterization of the kingdom as a "network of agape" is indebted to Ivan Illich, who saw that "If the Good Samaritan had followed the demands of sacred social boundaries, he would never have stopped to help the wounded Jew. It is plain that the Kingdom involves another kind of solidarity altogether, one which would bring us into a network of agape."[117] "The enfleshment of God extends outward, through such new links as the Samaritan makes with the Jew, into a network, which we call the church . . . a skein of relations which link particular, unique, enfleshed people to each other."[118] The coming of Christ made true community possible, a community of love capable of being initiated only by divine love.[119] This is a community made up of personal relationships; human community is not thought of here as prior to its members as in embedded religion.

Christianity's particular contribution to dis-embedding religion, then, should have resulted in a network of agape, which questions the established order of things for the sake of a new, personal relationship with God and with one another. Instead, something went wrong. Perhaps the contradiction lay in the very idea of a disciplined attempt to impose the kingdom of God, and the temptation of power. The network of agape grows by invitation not imposition; persons are freely if irresistibly attracted to it. The drive to transform the existing social order was a good one. The failure was to think that this could be done through a program of reform, discipline, and hegemony. "What we got was not a network of agape but rather a disciplined society in which categorical relations have priority and therefore norms."[120] What emerged were "categorical societies." These are conceived as made up of similar units (individuals/citizens) bound together not by personal relationships, but by impersonal rules.[121]

The corruption of this new network comes when it falls back into something more "normal" in worldly terms. Sometimes a church community becomes a tribe (or takes over an existing tribal society) and treats outsiders as Jews treated Samaritans (Belfast). But the really terrible corruption is a kind of falling forward, in which the church develops into something unprecedented. The network of agape involves a kind of fidelity to the new relations; and because we can all to easily fall away from

---

117. Taylor refers to Cayley, *The Rivers North of the Future*; Taylor, *A Secular Age*, 158.
118. Taylor, *A Secular Age*, 739.
119. Taylor, *A Secular Age*, 282.
120. Taylor, *A Secular Age*, 158.
121. Taylor, *A Secular Age*, 282.

this (it is this falling away we call "sin"), we are led to shore up these relations; we institutionalize them, introduce rules, divide responsibilities. In this way we keep the hungry fed, the homeless housed, the naked clothed; but we are now living caricatures of the network life. We have lost some of the communion, the *conspiratio*, which is at the heart of the Eucharist. The spirit is quenched.

Something new emerges out of all this: modern bureaucracies, based on rationality and rules. Rules prescribe treatments for categories of people, so a tremendously important feature of our lives is that we fit into categories; our rights, entitlements, and burdens depend on these. These shape our lives, make us see ourselves in new ways, in which category belonging bulks large, and the idiosyncratically enfleshed individual becomes less relevant, not to speak of the ways in which this enfleshed person flourishes through his or her network of friendships. For Illich, there is something monstrous, something alienating about this way of life. The monstrous comes from a corruption of the highest, the agape network. *Corruptio optimi pessima*. Corrupted Christianity gives rise to the modern, which is the object of Illich's *contemptus mundi*.

Illich sees how this process was taken furthest in Latin Christendom. Rules, oughts, and punishments take over more and more. But he also sees it in things like the growth of an objectifying standpoint on everything, including human life, which steadily becomes more and more dominant in modernity. He follows the development of this decentered outside view through a series of often startling analyses—the development of our gaze, our eventual capture by a view of ourselves as we show up in media images, or in X-ray imaging, or in various ways of representing underlying processes visually on graphs. We are in the process alienated from our anchoring in the world, in real fleshly reality; which we can only recover through the lived body, whose testimony is being distorted or even denied by "virtual" reality.

Similarly, in his tracing of our self-conception as users of tools, as separable instruments, and then into our sense of ourselves as part of systems, we move even further away from the lived body in a process of "excarnation."

This takes us further away from the network of *agape*. This can only be created in enfleshment. *Agape* moves outward from the guts; the New Testament word for "taking pity," *splangnizesthai*, places the response in the bowels. We cease being able to make sense of this the more we go along with

CHAPTER 6: AMBIVALENCE AND DISCIPLESHIP

these alienating self-images. Resurrection only makes sense when we take enfleshment seriously and so overcome excarnation.

Illich's story is not just about Christianity, but also about modern civilization as the historical creation of "corrupted" Christianity. Thus it comes close to the story Taylor tries to tell: how the modern secular world emerged out of the more and more rule-bound and norm-governed Reform of Latin Christendom in its institutionalization and therefore corruption of *agape*.

For Taylor, Illich warns us that legal and moral codes can become idolatrous traps, which tempt us to complicity with violence. We should not become totally invested in the code, even the best code of a peace-loving egalitarian liberalism. We should find the center of our lives beyond the code, deeper than the code, in networks of living concern, which are not to be sacrificed to the code and which must from time to time subvert it to keep it responsive to the just claims and needs of real people, especially those who are least visible and least powerful.

Illich's suspicion of bureaucracy and technology, systems and codes, can only be understood in relation to his analysis of the myriad barriers to friendship that exist in modern life. The kinds of asceticism, silence, and withdrawal that he encouraged were practices that are a necessary condition for friendship to flower in modern deserts.[122] "The only chance now lies in our taking this vocation as that of the friend. This is the way in which hope for a new society can spread. And the practice of it is not really through words but through little acts of foolish renunciation."[123]

Taylor argues that there was a long-standing tendency in the West to slide towards an identification of Christian faith with civilizational order. This not only makes us lose sight of the full transformation that Christians are called to, but it also made Christians lose a crucial distance from the hegemonic order identified as Christendom, and their vocation to be modern civilization's "loyal opposition." Taylor credits Maritain in *Humanisme Integral* with a reimagination of Christian civilization, not as a return to Christendom but as a dispersed network of Christian lay institutions and centers of intellectual and spiritual life: "Instead of a fortified castle erected in the middle of the land we must think of an army of stars thrown in the

---

122. Burkart, "From Economy to Friendship," 160; Illich, "Philosophy ... Artifacts ... Friendship"; Illich, "Health as One's Own Responsibility—No Thank You!"

123. Illich, quoted in Cayley, *The Rivers North of the Future*, 170; and see Vernon, "Freedom—by giving stuff up," chap. 7 in *The Good Life*.

sky." The central feature of this new culture will be "the spiritual advent, not of the self-centered ego, but of creative subjectivity."[124]

Taylor's reimagination of Christianity in a secular age takes place in dialogue with Nietzsche, the great champion of the "world" and enemy of excarnating forms of Christianity that denigrate embodiment. His account of Christian *amor mundi* must overcome the "dilemma of mutilation." At the close of *Sources of the Self* he returns to the crucial conflict explored in rather different ways by both Nietzsche and Dostoyevsky: the demands of benevolence can exact a high cost in self-love and self-fulfillment, which may in the end require payment in self-destruction or even in violence. Rebellion against the ascetic demands of religion in the name of paganism could be motivated by the recognition that a terribly high cost was being demanded. Michel Foucault articulated the way in which high ethical and spiritual ideals are often interwoven with exclusions and relations of domination. Feminists have contributed to this understanding by showing how certain conceptions of the life of the spirit exclude women, accord them a lesser place, or assume their subordination.

From all these examples, the general truth emerges that the highest spiritual ideals and aspirations also threaten to lay the most crushing burdens on humankind. The great spiritual visions of human history have also been poisoned chalices, the causes of untold misery and even savagery. Religion has always been associated with sacrifice, even mutilation, as though something has to be torn away or immolated if we are to please the gods. The sad story doesn't end with religion. The Kharkov famine and the Killing Fields were perpetrated by atheists in an attempt to realize the highest ideals of human perfection. "Naturalist" neo-Lucretian or Nietzschean views, which affirm immanence and exclude transcendence, take the self-destructive consequences of a spiritual aspiration as a refutation of this aspiration. For Taylor, they make the mistake of believing that a good must be invalid if it leads to suffering or destruction. Thus Enlightenment naturalism thought it was refuting Christianity in showing the cost of asceticism; Nietzsche often gives a picture of "morality" that shows it to be merely envy, or a device of the weak, or *ressentiment*, and that thus deprives it of all claim on our allegiance. But Taylor argues that this line of reasoning is deeply mistaken. Not only can some potentially destructive ideals be directed to genuine goods; some of them undoubtedly are. Even nonbelievers can feel the powerful appeal of the

---

124. Taylor, *A Secular Age*, 739–44, citing Maritain's words in Barre, *Jacques et Raissa Maritain*, 396, 398.

CHAPTER 6: AMBIVALENCE AND DISCIPLESHIP

gospel, just as Christians will recognize the appalling destruction wrought in history in the name of the faith.

That is why, for Taylor, a stripped down secular outlook, without any religious dimension or radical hope in history, is not a way of avoiding the dilemma, although it may be a good way to live with it. It doesn't avoid it because this too involves its "mutilation." It involves stifling the response in us to some of the deepest and most powerful spiritual aspirations that humans have conceived. This, too, is a heavy price to pay.

Taylor asks, is this the last word? Does something have to be denied? Do we have to choose between various kinds of spiritual lobotomy and self-inflicted wounds? He admits that most of the outlooks that promise that we will be spared these choices are based on selective blindness. Is this dilemma inescapable, that the highest spiritual aspirations must lead to mutilation or destruction? He concludes by asserting that he does not accept the dilemma of mutilation as our inevitable lot. It is our greatest spiritual challenge, not an iron fate. There is a large element of hope implicit in Judeo-Christian theism (however terrible the record of its adherents in history), and in its central promise of a divine affirmation of the human, more total than humans can ever attain unaided.[125]

At the close of *Sources of the Self*, Taylor declines to go on to articulate a transcendent basis for the ethical that could overcome the dilemma of mutilation. He appeals instead to Dostoevsky, "who has framed this perspective better than I ever could here,"[126] and who is a source not just of concrete illustrations for Taylor's concepts, but also of new cognitive insight, which he draws upon in his dialogue with Nietzsche. Dostoevsky's articulation of this perspective lies in his development of "a poetics of agapic love."[127] This poetics, at least in its negative dimension, is reflected in Taylor's analysis of the paradox of modernity:

> Before the reality of human shortcomings, philanthropy—the love of the human—can gradually come to be invested with contempt, hatred, aggression ... The history of despotic socialism, i.e., twentieth century communism, is replete with this tragic turn, brilliantly foreseen by Dostoevsky over 100 years ago ... and then repeated again and again with a fatal regularity, through the one party regimes on a macro level, to a host of "helping"

---

125. Taylor, *A Secular Age*, 518–21.
126. Taylor, *Sources of the Self*, 518.
127. Ward, "Transcendence and Immanence in a Subtler Language," 274.

institutions on the micro level from orphanages to boarding schools for aboriginals.[128]

Taylor's identification and analysis of this paradox draws heavily on a close reading of Dostoevsky's presentation of the psycho-spiritual dynamics of the strange dialectic whereby philanthropy slides into misanthropy. This dialectic culminates in *The Brothers Karamazov* with the compassion of Ivan Karamazov as a representative of exclusive atheist humanism. Ivan affirms compassion for suffering humanity to the point of rejecting God and immortality in its name. In the words of "Rebellion": "I don't want harmony, for love of humankind I don't want it ... And therefore I hasten to return my ticket."[129] Ivan claims his compassion is more compassionate than that of Christianity—and of Christ himself. He represents modern humanism in its claim that its compassion is more comprehensive and more efficacious than Christian compassion. To this claim, Dostoevsky responds which a question that might be formulated as: "You reject God in the name of compassion, but can compassion be formulated or even understood without the idea of God?" True to his dialogic approach, respectful of the freedom even of his fictional characters, Dostoevsky shows how the insight into the unsustainability of compassion within a purely immanent humanism gradually becomes accessible to Ivan's own consciousness. Not only the reader, but Ivan himself, becomes aware of an ineluctable slide from compassion into contempt for suffering human beings, a slide most dramatically evident in the Grand Inquisitor's argument (of which Ivan is the ostensible author) for a "compassionate" tyranny over the weak.

Taylor claims that only the "unconditional love of the recipients of compassion" flowing from "grace" can overcome this ugly dialectic of philanthropy/misanthropy. In cutting ourselves off from the world, we also cut ourselves off from the grace that flows like a current through the world: Dostoevsky's own term for grace is "living life," *zhivaya zhizn*.[130] Paradoxically, one can close oneself to this grace for the highest reasons as Ivan Karamazov does, because, "the more noble and sensitive and morally insightful one is, the likely one is to feel this loathing ... for ourselves and for this world."[131]

---

128. Taylor, *A Secular Age*, 697.
129. Dostoevsky, *The Brothers Karamazov*, 307–8.
130. Ward, "Transcendence and Immanence in a Subtler Language," 277.
131. Taylor, *Sources of the Self*, 451.

CHAPTER 6: AMBIVALENCE AND DISCIPLESHIP

But does the unconditional love that can overcome the world actually exist? And if it does, how can it be experienced in life and shown convincingly in art? These are the questions that preoccupied Dostoevsky. As an artist at the center of whose aesthetic is the image of Christ, his whole concern was to show the transcendent ideal as incarnate in reality and transformative of reality, without falsifying reality, which is radically resistant to the ideal. The outcome of this testing of agapic love against the cycle of power and violence inherent in unredeemed reality is never certain, never equally persuasive for all readers. It is drawn in its starkest terms in the confrontation between the silent Christ and the Grand Inquisitor. The silence of Christ is broken elsewhere in *The Brothers Karamazov* by two characters who can be taken to embody agapic love in theory and in practice.

In regard to theory, there is the monk Zossima's advice to the woman who finds herself unable to believe in God, advice strikingly precise in the manner in which it reverses the connection between God and compassion presupposed in the formulations of Nietzsche and Ivan Karamazov: "Try to love your neighbors actively and tirelessly. The more you succeed in loving, the more convinced you'll be of the existence of God."[132] Zossima's words only make sense if it is possible to love the other one sees without the support of a consciously acknowledged divine command; that is, such a love must have a real presence in the world already, not reducible, as it is to Nietzsche, to lower egotistic drives or psychic forces. This independent reality of compassionate love is guaranteed by it rootedness in the higher reality of divine love. Dostoevsky, through Zossima, expresses the notion that compassion is neither exclusively this-worldly, nor otherworldly. It is enacted in this world, directed toward living, suffering human beings. Transcendence and immanence are held together.

In regard to the practice of what Zossima calls "active love," there is Alyosha Karamazov's founding of a tiny community of twelve children in the last pages of the novel. This is a concrete showing of a community held together in agapic love; a community characterized by a unity that does not diminish but enlarge the unique personhood of each child, a merging in which particular names—Ilyushecka, Kolya, Kartashov—voices, and faces are all retained. It is an icon in words of Taylor's "network of agape."[133]

---

132. Dostoevsky, *The Brothers Karamazov*, 256, cited by Ward, "Transcendence and Immanence in a Subtler Language," 277.

133. Ward, "Transcendence and Immanence in a Subtler Language," 278.

Taylor uses the insights of Dostoevsky in his dialogue with Nietzsche. In *Sources of the Self* he begins to articulate "a doctrine of affirming power" as transfiguration.[134] This makes use of a late Romantic and Nietzschean insight into the power of imagination, but takes its cue from the book of Genesis in a theistic affirmation of being. The goodness of the world is not something quite independent from God's seeing it as good. His seeing it as good and loving it can be conceived not simply as a response to what it is, but as what makes it such.[135] Human affirmation of the goodness of creation is analogous to God's "seeing as good," which means "a seeing which also helps effect what it sees." Transfiguration is an effective seeing-as. To reject the world, like Ivan Karamazov, is to be cut off from grace. This is pride, since we refuse to understand ourselves as part of the problem.

> What will transform us is an ability to love the world and ourselves, to see it as good in spite of the wrong. But this will only come to us if we can accept being part of it, and that means accepting responsibility ... Loving the world and ourselves is in a sense a miracle in the face of all the evil and degradation that it and we contain. But the miracle comes on us if we accept being part of it. Involved in this is our acceptance of love from others. We become capable of love through being loved ... We are able to love our fellow creatures when we enter into the stream of God's love for creation and his affirmation of creation. Our affirmation of the world participates through grace—Dostoevsky's "living life"—in God's love, which sees the world as good and as such effects its goodness.[136]

Taylor uses an insight that Nietzsche would be open to—the creative power of the imagination to show him a way to affirm the world without rejecting benevolence. Affirmation is possible with *agape*, the love of God which grace allows us to love.

In *A Secular Age* Taylor responds to the dilemma of mutilation not only with a reimagination of Christianity beyond excarnation and hegemony but also with an account of "God's pedagogy."[137]

---

134. Shearn, "Charles Taylor, Nietzsche and Theology"; and Taylor, *Sources of the Self*, 455.

135. Taylor, *Sources of the Self*, 449.

136. Taylor, *Sources of the Self*, 452, 516.

137. Taylor, *A Secular Age*, 669.

CHAPTER 6: AMBIVALENCE AND DISCIPLESHIP

> Humans are born out of the animal kingdom, to be guided by God; and the males (at least the males) with a powerful sex-drive and lots of aggression. . . . being guided by God means some kind of transformation of these drives; not just their repression or suppression but some real turning of them from within, conversion so that all the energy now goes along with God; the love powers agape, the aggression turns into energy, straining to bring things back to God, the energy to combat evil.[138]

In the biblical narrative, humanity exhibits just this mix of violence and redirection of violence toward God's ends: from generalized violence to ritualized human sacrifice, as ordered violence turned back toward divinity in the "scapegoat mechanism" described by Rene Girard. Then from human sacrifice to the rejection of human sacrifice as the practice of the pagan "other," to whom Israel still responds with holy war. Each revelation "comes with a gift of power," which can be misused.[139]

As Girard argues, in Christ, God as the victim provides a new paradigm for the connection between violence and divinity. In Christendom this achievement is reversed by sanctioned violence against those outside of the community of the faith. But violence was also redirected toward the overcoming of sinful acts and attitudes.[140] "We might see God as the supreme tennis player, who responds to our bad moves with new ways of countering them."[141] God's pedagogy is an immanent dialectical process and struggle between the use and misuse of divine power by the human creature, a struggle in which it is possible to discern the divine call upon human lives and a spiritual direction. It is "a perspective of transformation."[142]

Taylor acknowledges there are only "intimations" of how to move past the dilemma of mutilation and that these "are not of a kind that could be decanted into a general code or program.[143] There should be no Christian triumphalism, only anticipatory confidence. Taylor wants to rehabilitate Christianity as an attractive option but he acknowledges that "religious faith can be dangerous."[144] Taylor is open to possibility that, as Nietzsche saw, we may

---

138. Taylor, *A Secular Age*, 668.
139. Taylor, *A Secular Age*, 669.
140. Taylor, *A Secular Age*, 669–70.
141. Taylor, *A Secular Age*, 671.
142. Taylor, *A Secular Age*, 673.
143. Taylor, *A Secular Age*, 674–75.
144. Taylor, *A Secular Age*, 769.

not be able to entirely separate our virtues from our vices. This is not a facile critique. Only communities of true agape— whose verbal icon is Alyosha Karamazov's community of twelve children—could be the refutation of Nietzsche's genealogy. To be a Christian is to have faith, an anticipatory confidence that one is "standing among others in the stream of love which is that facet of God's life we try to grasp, very inadequately, in speaking about the Trinity."[145] Being inspired by such love in community is "the path towards a much more powerful and effective healing action in history."[146] Attempts to overcome the Nietzschean critique can "only point to the exemplary lives of certain trail-blazing people and communities."[147]

Taylor's response to Nietzsche and "the dilemma of mutilation" has been compared to the father's response to the prodigal son.[148] Nietzsche is the lost son—even if he does not return. He found his Lutheran milieu oppressive to the point of spiritual sickness and went abroad, at least metaphorically, in the hope of escaping his home. Taylor lets him voice concerns and insights while suggesting paths back home through a hermeneutic of violence and perspective of transformation, and an invitation to join communities envisioned by divine affirmation. When the prodigal is welcomed back, the father's house will not remain the same. But perhaps these communities are like an incarnate "subtler language" that "opens new paths, 'sets free' new realities."[149]

Taylor mentions Jean Vanier as the founder of such a community, L'Arche, a worldwide group of communities where people with and without intellectual disabilities share life together in community.[150] In *Leurs regards perce nos ombres—Their Look Pierces our Shadows*, Vanier and Julia Kristeva reflect on the nature of disability from the contrasting perspectives of Vanier's Christian faith and Kristeva's humanist-atheist philosophy.[151] Kristeva is also the mother to David, who was born with a neurological disability. The title of the exchange of letters is a reference

---

145. Taylor, *A Secular Age*, 701.
146. Taylor, *A Secular Age*, 703.
147. Taylor, *A Secular Age*, 643.
148. Shearn, "Charles Taylor, Nietzsche and Theology," 278–80.
149. Taylor, *A Secular Age*, 758.

150. After revelations that have affected the reputation of Jean Vanier it would be a double tragedy if the work of the L'Arche communities were to be similarly tainted and if what they teach us about how we can live and think were to be lost.

151. Kristeva and Vanier, *Leur Regard Perce nos Ombres*.

CHAPTER 6: AMBIVALENCE AND DISCIPLESHIP

to the play *Little Eyolf* by the Swedish dramatist Henrik Ibsen, in which tragedy befalls a family when their disabled son drowns. Grieving the loss of her son, the mother in Ibsen's play declares that it is the memory of the look in Eyolf's eyes that has the capacity to penetrate the depth of her humanity. Kristeva asks Vanier if their mutual understanding of disability could be encapsulated by the mother's insight into the unique encounter she has had with her son and the capacity of this encounter to reveal her humanity. "These words bring us back to our ambition," writes Kristeva, "yours and mine, to change the gaze of the non-disabled on persons with disability.... Ibsen helps us to do this by reversing the perspective: it is Eyolf who looks at us, it is the look of the little boy with a disability that counts, for it is he who will pierce our shadows."[152]

Kristeva sees something in Vanier and his community that she desires within her own humanism with its language of rights and equality but is unable to bring about. She admits that her real concern is to find people who are able to accompany the disabled, such as her son, in such a way that they grow in freedom. Struck by the humanity, respect, and joy she perceived in the interactions between the handicapped members of Vanier's community and those who have freely chosen to share their lives with them, she writes in her first letter to him:

> It is not easy to be in an intimate proximity to irreparable physical and mental wounds ... Yet the humanity of your L'Arche neither denies nor exalts these irreparable failures and wounds. You are happy to welcome, if I dare say, because this corresponds to the wounds of each one of us... How do you do it?[153]

One of the novelties of Vanier's experience of L'Arche is his understanding that "encounter" must be at the heart of an adequate understanding of agape. Vanier stresses that in the encounter with the disabled, the young volunteers who come to L'Arche begin to discover and respect their own humanity and its vulnerabilities and desires, and with this new awareness of what unites them, are able to "share" life together. His deeply trinitarian understanding of agape brings to the fore the radical dignity of the person and his or her call to love, the tension between belonging and freedom, and each one's desire for fruitfulness that perhaps in the past have been neglected under the guise of doing "good works." Vanier says that L'Arche

---

152. Kristeva and Vanier, *Leur Regard Perce nos Ombres*, 67.

153. Kristeva and Vanier, *Leur Regard Perce nos Ombres*, cited in Roderick, "Their Look Pierces Our Shadows."

does not exist to do good things for people but to participate in the mission of Jesus who says to each person: "I love you as you are, I have confidence in you, I want to help you to discover how beautiful you are, that you are capable of giving your life for others."[154]

Eutrapelia

Ivan Illich, upon whose critique of modernity Taylor's account of the making of a secular age depends, re-proposed an ancient virtue whose practice offers a way for Christians to be faithful to their ancient ambivalence about the world.

In the *Summa Theologica*, II, II, in the 186th question, article 5, Thomas Aquinas deals with disciplined and creative playfulness. In his third response, he defines the now degraded word "austerity" as a virtue, which does not exclude all enjoyments, but only those which are distracting from or destructive of personal relatedness. For Thomas, "austerity" is a complementary part of a more embracing virtue that he calls friendship or joyfulness. It is the fruit of an apprehension that things or tools could destroy rather than enhance *eutrapelia* (or graceful playfulness) in personal relations.[155]

One question to address in making a rule of life might be to try to discern what is destroying and what is enhancing this *eutrapelia*. For both Aristotle and Aquinas, the *eutrapelos* is the person who strikes the happy mean between *bomolochos* the buffoon, and *agroikos* the humorless boor who never even smiles.[156] He or she is both serious and serene. In the *Summa*, this piece of Greek wisdom is given a place at the very heart of the Christian art of life. Knowledge of this virtue could be a healing necessity for those trapped in the barren solemnity of a purely utilitarian view of life. Hermann Hesse recognizes this in *The Glass Bead Game*. For Hesse, a true human being must be a creature of light-hearted, carefree play, a creature whose play is filled with the spirit. This freedom is received through the monastic severity of the spiritual discipline with which they turn their life into a game. The image of this game is the dancing chorus of heaven. The world is no longer hated with reforming earnestness or loved with an acceptance of its exclusive preoccupation with itself. A light-hearted relaxation of the

---

154. Kristeva and Vanier, *Leur Regard Perce nos Ombres*, 203.
155. Illich, *Tools for Conviviality*, xxiv–xxv.
156. Rahner, *Man at Play*.

mind and a certain smiling contempt for mundane things, are possible if the world is no longer regarded as a thing whose reality lies wholly in itself. They are possible for those whose minds are open to God. They are possible for those who anticipate eternity in the way they shape their lives. They are possible for those who, as it were, push the world away from them with the grace of a dancer, and yet hold it close to their hearts because God the Creator can be seen in its transparency.

Bibliography

Adorno, Theodor. "Commitment." In *Notes to Literature, Volume Two*, edited by Rolf Tiedemann and translated by Shierry Weber Nicholsen, 348–63. New York: Columbia University Press, 1974.

———. *Minima Moralia: Reflections on Damaged Life*. Translated by E. Jephcott. London: Verso, 1975.

Agamben, Giorgio. *The Time That Remains. A Commentary on the Letter to the Romans*. Stanford, CA: Stanford University Press, 2005.

Alexandrova, Alena, and Ignaas Devisch, eds. *Retreating Religion: Deconstructing Christianity with Jean-Luc Nancy*. New York: Fordham University Press, 2011.

Appleby, David. "'Bodily Need is a Kind of Speech:' Human Dignity and Bodily Necessity According to Bernard of Clairvaux." In *A Companion to Medieval Christian Humanism: Essays on Principal Thinkers*, edited by John P. Bequette, 122–41. Leiden: Brill, 2016.

———. "Humanism, Christian." In *Encyclopedia of Monasticism*, edited by W. Johnston, 617–21. London: Routledge, 2015.

Archbishops' Council. "Developing discipleship." *The Church Of England*. General Synod 1977. https://www.churchofengland.org/sites/default/files/2017-12/gs%201977%20-%20developing%20discipleship.pdf

Arendt, Hannah. *Between Past and Future: Eight Exercises in Political Thought*. New York: Viking, 1961.

———. "*The Deputy*, Guilt by Silence?" In *Amor Mundi: Explorations in the Faith and Thought of Hannah Arendt*, edited by James William Bernauer, 51–58. Boston, MA: Martinus Nijhoff, 1987.

———. *Eichmann in Jerusalem: A Report on the Banality of Evil*. New York: Viking, 1963.

———. *The Human Condition*. New York: Doubleday, 1959.

———. *Love and Saint Augustine*. Edited by Joanna Vecchiarelli Scott and Judith Chelius Stark. Chicago, IL: University of Chicago Press, 1985.

———. *Men in Dark Times*. New York: Harcourt Brace and Company, 1968.

———. *The Origins of Totalitarianism*. London: George Allen and Unwin, 1958.

———. "World Alienation." In *The Human Condition*, 248–57. New York: Doubleday, 1959.

Atkinson, Tyler. *Singing at the Winepress: Ecclesiastes and the Ethics of Work*. Edinburgh: T&T Clark, 2015.

Augustine. *City of God*. Translated by Henry Bettenson. New York: Penguin, 1972.

———. *City of God*. Translated by George McCracken, William Green, David Wiesen, Philip Levine, and Eva Sanford. 7 vols. Cambridge, MA: Harvard University Press, 1957–1972.

———. *Confessions*. Translated by Edward Pusey. Oxford: John Henry Parker, 1991.

———. *Expositions on the Book of Psalms*. Translated by Henry Walford. Oxford: John Henry Parker, 1857.

———. *Homilies on the First Epistle of John*. Translated by Boniface Ramsey. New York: New City, 2008.

Ayres, Lewis. *Nicaea and its Legacy: An Approach to Fourth Century Trinitarian Theology*. Oxford: Oxford University Press, 2004.

Balmer, Randall. "Between God and the Führer." Book Review, *The New York Times*, August 8, 2014. https://www.nytimes.com/2014/08/10/books/review/strange-glory-a-life-of-dietrich-bonhoeffer-by-charles-marsh.html.

Balthasar, Hans Urs Von. *The Christian State of Life*. Translated by Sister Mary Frances McCarthy. San Francisco, CA: St Ignatius, 1983.

———. *My Work in Retrospect*. Translated by Brian McNeil. San Francisco, CA: Ignatius, 1993.

Barre, Jean-Luc. *Jacques et Raissa Maritain*. Paris: Stock, 1997.

Batallion, Louis-Jacques, and Jean-Pierre Jossua. "Le Mepris du Monde. De l'interet d'une discussion actuelle." *Revue des Sciences philosophiques et theologiques* 51 (1967) 23–38.

Batany, Jean. "L'Eglise et le Mepris du Monde." *Annales* 20 (1965) 218–28.

BeDuhn, Jason. "'The Metabolism of Salvation': Manichean Conceptions of Human Physiology." In *The Light and the Darkness: Studies in Manichaeism and its World*, edited by Paul Mirecki and Jason BeDuhn, 3–37. Leiden: Brill, 2001.

———. "'Not to Depart from Christ': Augustine between 'Manichean' and 'Catholic' Christianity." *Theological Studies* 69 no. 1. DOI: https://hts.org.za/index.php/hts/article/view/1355/3434.

Bellah, Robert Neelly. "Religious Evolution." *American Sociological Review* 29 (1964) 358–74.

Berkowitz, Roger. "'The Love of the World,' Amor Mundi." The Hannah Arendt Centre for Policy and Humanities, November 22, 2012. https://hac.bard.edu/amor-mundi/the-love-of-the-world-2012-10-22.

Berman, Harold. *Law and Revolution: The Formation of the Western Legal Tradition*. Cambridge, MA: Harvard University Press, 1983.

Bernard of Clairvaux. *Selected Writings*. New York: Paulist, 1987.

Bernauer, James William. "Bonhoeffer and Arendt at One Hundred." *Studies in Jewish-Christian Relations* 2 no.1 (2007) 77–85.

Bernauer, James William, ed. *Amor Mundi: Explorations in the Faith and Thought of Hannah Arendt*. Boston, MA: Martinus Nijhoff, 1987.

Bethge, Eberhard. "The Challenge of Dietrich Bonhoeffer's Life and Theology." In *The World Come of Age*, edited by Ronald Gregor Smith, 22–88. London: Collins, 1967.

———. *Dietrich Bonhoeffer: A Biography*. Revised and edited by Victoria Barnett. Minneapolis, MN: Fortress, 2000.

Bielik-Robson, Agata. "Being-Towards-Birth." In *Another Finitude Messianic Vitalism and Philosophy*, 75–102. London: Bloomsbury Academic, 2019.

BIBLIOGRAPHY

———. "Love Strong as Death—Jews against Heidegger, On the Issue of Finitude – Part 2." http://jcrt.org/religioustheory/2016/08/01/love-strong-as-death-jews-against-heidegger-on-the-issue-of-finitude-part-2-agata-bielik-robson/.

———. "A Matter of Faith: Derrida, Žižek, and the Fourth 'Overcoming of Gnosis.'" In *Theology and World Politics: Metaphysics, Genealogies, Political Theologies*, edited by Vassilios Paipais, 75–104. London: Palgrave, 2020.

Bielik-Robson, Agata, and Daniel Whistler, eds. *Interrogating Modernity: Debates with Hans Blumenberg*. London: Palgrave Macmillan, 2020.

Blakeney, Edward Henry, trans. *The Epistle to Diognetus*. London: SPCK, 1943.

Blumenberg, Hans. *The Legitimacy of the Modern Age*. Translated by Robert M. Wallace. Cambridge, MA: MIT Press, 1953.

Boersma, Hans. *Embodiment and Virtue in Gregory of Nyssa*. Oxford: Oxford University Press, 2013.

———. *Heavenly Participation. The Weaving of a Sacramental Tapestry*. Grand Rapids, MI: Eerdmans, 2011.

———. *Nouvelle Theologie and Sacramental Ontology: A Return to Mystery*. Oxford: Oxford University Press, 2009.

Bonhoeffer, Dietrich. *The Cost of Discipleship*. Translated by Reginald Fuller. London, SCM, 2001.

———. *Creation and Fall: A Theological Exposition of Genesis 1–3*. Edited by John de Gruchy and translated by Douglas Bax. Dietrich Bonhoeffer Works 3. Minneapolis, MN: Fortress, 1997.

———. *Ethics*. Translated by Neville Smith. London: Collins, 1964.

———. *Letters and Papers from Prison*. Dietrich Bonhoeffer Works 8. Edited by John de Gruchy and translated by Isabel Best, et al. Minneapolis, MN: Fortress, 2010.

———. *No Rusty Swords: Letters, Lectures and Notes from the Collected Works Volume I*. Edited by Edwin Robertson. London: Fontana, 1970.

———. *A Testament to Freedom*. Edited by Geoffrey Kelly and Burton Nelson. San Francisco, CA: Harper Collins, 1995.

Borgmann, Albert. "Contemplation in a Technological Era: Learning from Thomas Merton." *Philosophy Faculty Publications*. https://www.asa3.org/ASA/PSCF/2012/PSCF3-12Borgmann.pdf.

Bouyer, Louis. *Christian Humanism*. Translated by A. V. Littledale. Westminster, MD: Newman, 1959.

———. *Christian Initiation*. Translated by J. R. Foster. Providence, RI: Cluny Media, 2018.

———. *Introduction to Spirituality*. Collegeville, MN: Liturgical, 1961.

———. *Introduction to the Spiritual Life*. Translated by Mary Perkins Ryan. Notre Dame, IN: Ave Maria, 2013.

———. *Le Métier de Théologien: Entretiens avec Georges Daix*. Paris: Ad Solem Editions, 2005.

Bowes, Kim. *Private Worship, Public Values and Religious Change in Late Antiquity*. Cambridge: Cambridge University Press, 2008.

Brewitt-Taylor, Sam. "From Religion to Revolution: Theologies of Secularisation in the British Student Christian Movement, 1963–1973." *Journal of Ecclesiastical History* 66 no. 4 (October 2015) 792–811.

Brient, Elizabeth. "Hans Blumenberg and Hannah Arendt on the 'Unworldly Worldliness' of the Modern Age." *Journal of the History of Ideas* 61 (2000) 513–30.

———. *The Immanence of the Infinite. Hans Blumenberg and the Threshold to Modernity.* Washington, DC: Catholic University of America Press, 2002.
Brittain, Christopher. *Adorno and Theology.* London: Bloomsbury, 2010.
Brown, Callum. "What was the Religious Crisis of the 1960s?" *Journal of Religious History* 34 no. 4 (December 2010) 468–79.
Brown, Peter. *Augustine of Hippo: A Biography.* London: Faber and Faber, 1967.
———. "Introducing Robert Markus." *Augustinian Studies* 32 (2001) 181–87.
———. *Power and Persuasion in Late Antiquity: Towards a Christian Empire.* Madison, WI: University of Wisconsin Press, 1992.
———. *The Rise of Western Christendom.* Oxford: Oxford University Press, 2003.
Bruno, Michael. *Political Augustinianism. Modern Interpretations of Augustine's Political Thought.* Minneapolis, MN: Fortress, 2014.
Burkart, Eugene. "From Economy to Friendship: My Years Studying Ivan Illich." In *The Challenges of Ivan Illich. A Collective Reflection*, edited by Lee Hoinacki and Carl Mitcham, 153–61. New York: State University of New York Press, 2002.
Burton-Christie, Douglas. *The Blue Sapphire of the Mind: Notes for a Contemplative Ecology.* Oxford: Oxford University Press, 2013.
———. "Christianity (4)—Early Church (Fathers and Councils)." In *The Encyclopedia of Religion and Nature*, edited by Bron Taylor, 324–26. London: Continuum, 2005.
Buss, Andreas. "The Evolution of Western Individualism." *Religion* 30 (2000) 1–26.
Bynum, Caroline. "Why All the Fuss about the Body? A Medievalist's Perspective." *Critical Inquiry* 22 no. 1 (Autumn 1995) 1–33.
Cacciari, Massimo. *Europe and Empire: On the Political Forms of Globalization.* Edited by Alessandro Carrera and translated by Massimo Verdicchio. New York: Fordham University Press, 2016.
Cameron, Averil. "Ascetic Closure and the End of Antiquity." In *Asceticism*, edited by Vincent Wimbush and Richard Valantasis, 147–61. Oxford: Oxford University Press, 1998.
Cantor, Norman. "The Crisis of Western Monasticism, 1050–1130." *American Historical Review* 66 (1960/1) 46–67.
Cayley, David. *The Rivers North of the Future: The Testament of Ivan Illich.* Toronto: Anansi, 2004.
Chapman, Mark. "Theology in the Public Arena: The case of South Bank Religion." In *Redefining Christian Britain: Post 1945 Perspectives*, edited by Jane Garnett, et al., 92–105. London: SCM, 2007.
Chesterton, G. K. *Orthodoxy.* http://www.gkc.org.uk/gkc/books/orthodoxy/.
Christianson, Eric. "Ecclesiastes in Premodern Reading Before 1500 CE." In *The Words of the Wise Are Like Goads: Engaging Qohelet in the 21st Century*, edited by Mark Boda, Temper Longman, and Christian Rota. University Park, PA: Eisenbrauns, 2013.
Christianson, Eric S. *Ecclesiastes Through the Centuries.* Oxford: Blackwell, 2012.
Clair, Joseph. "The Concept of the Secular in Augustine's City of God." In *Rethinking Secularisation: Philosophy and the Prophecy of a Secular Age*, edited by Herbert de Vriese and Gary Gabor, 27–56. Newcastle: Cambridge Scholars Publishing, 2009.
Clark, Mary. "World." In *Augustine Through the Ages: An Encyclopedia*, edited by Allan Fitzgerald, 892–94. Grand Rapids, MI: Eerdmans, 1999.
Cloots, Andre, Stijn Latre, and Guido Vanheeswijck. "The Future of the Christian Past: Marcel Gauchet and Charles Taylor on the Essence of Religion and its Evolution." *The Heythrop Journal* 565 no. 6 (November 2015) 958–74.

Coakley, Sarah. *God, Sexuality and the Self: An Essay on "the Trinity."* Cambridge: Cambridge University Press, 2013.

———. *The New Asceticism. Sexuality, Gender and the Quest for God.* London: Bloomsbury Continuum, 2015.

Coakley, Sarah, and Jessica Martin, eds. *For God's Sake: Re-Imagining Priesthood and Prayer in a Changing Church.* Norwich: Canterbury, 2016.

Colorado, Carlos. Review article on *A Secular Age. Touchstone* 28 no. 2 (May 2010) 57–68.

Constable, Giles. *The Reformation of the Twelfth Century.* Cambridge: Cambridge University Press, 1996.

Coolman, B. Taylor. *The Theology of Hugh of St Victor: An Interpretation.* Cambridge: Cambridge University Press, 2010.

Corrington-Streete, G. "Trajectories of Ascetic Behaviour." In *Asceticism*, edited by Vincent Wimbush and Richard Valantasis, 119–26. Oxford: Oxford University Press, 1998.

Coyne, Ryan. *Heidegger's Confessions: The Remains of Saint Augustine in Being and Time and Beyond.* Chicago, IL: University of Chicago Press, 2015.

Critchley, Simon. *The Faith of the Faithless: Experiments in Political Theology.* London: Verso, 2012.

Cunningham, Lawrence. *Thomas Merton and the Monastic Vision.* Grand Rapids, MI: Eerdmans, 1999.

Daiker, Angelika. *Beyond Borders: Life and Spirituality of Little Sister Magdalene.* Makati City: St. Pauls, 2010.

Damian, Peter. *Letters of Peter Damian 151–180.* The Fathers of the Church: Medieval Continuation, vol. 7. Translated by Owen Blum and Irven Resnick. Washington, DC: Catholic University of America Press, 2005.

———. *Vita Romualdi, Camadolese Spirituality.* Bloomingdale, OH: Holy Family Hermitage, 2007.

Day, Dorothy. *On Pilgrimage.* Grand Rapids, MI: Eerdmans, 2004.

De Lubac, Henri. *A Brief Catechism on Nature and Grace.* San Francisco, CA: Ignatius, 1984.

———. *Aspects of Buddhism.* Translated by G. Lamb. London: Sheed and Ward, 1953.

———. *La Rencontre du Bouddhisme et de l'Occident.* Paris: Cerf, 2000.

Delumeau, J. *Sin and Fear: The Emergence of a Western Guilt Culture, 13th–18th Centuries.* Translated by E. Nicholson. New York: St. Martin's, 1990.

Dodaro, Robert. *Christ and the Just Society in the Thought of Augustine.* Cambridge: Cambridge University Press, 2004.

———. "Ecclesia and Res Publica: How Augustinian are Neo-Augustinian Politics?" In *Augustine and Post Modern Thought: A New Alliance Against Modernity?*, edited by L. Boeve, M. Lamberigts, and M. Wise, 257–71. Leuven: Peters, 2008.

Dostoevsky, Fyodor. *The Brothers Karamazov.* Translated by Richard Pevear and Larissa Volokhonsky. New York: Random House, 1990.

Dreher, Rod. *The Benedict Option: A Strategy for Christians in a Post-Christian Nation.* New York: Sentinel, 2017.

Drew, Rose. *Buddhist and Christian? An Exploration of Dual Belonging.* London: Routledge, 2013.

Dumont, Louis. *Essays on Individualism: Modern Ideology in Anthropological Perspective.* Chicago, IL: University of Chicago Press, 1986.

BIBLIOGRAPHY

Elm, Susanna. *Virgins of God. The Making of Asceticism in Late Antiquity.* Oxford: Clarendon, 1994.

Eusebius, *Oration in Praise of Constantine*, sections 4–5. Translated by Ernest Cushing Richardson. In *Nicene and Post-Nicene Fathers*, Second Series, Vol. 1, edited by Philip Schaff and Henry Wace. Buffalo, NY: Christian Literature Publishing Co., 1890. Revised and edited for New Advent by Kevin Knight. http://www.newadvent.org/fathers/2504.htm.

Fagerberg, David. *Consecrating the World: On Mundane Liturgical Theology.* Kettering, OH: Angelico, 2016.

———. *On Liturgical Asceticism.* Washington, DC: Catholic University of America Press, 2013.

Finley, James. *Merton's Palace of Nowhere.* Notre Dame, IN: Ave Maria, 1978.

Foltz, Bruce. *The Noetics of Nature: Environmental Philosophy and the Holy Beauty of the Visible.* New York: Fordham University Press, 2013.

Frank, Thomas. *Commodify Your Dissent: The Business of Culture in the New Gilded Age.* New York: Norton and Company, 1997.

Fraser, Giles. *Redeeming Nietzsche: On the Piety of Unbelief.* London: Routledge, 2002.

Frick, Peter. "The *Imitatio Christi* of Thomas à Kempis and Dietrich Bonhoeffer." In *Bonhoeffer's Intellectual Formation*, edited by Peter Frick, 31–52. Tubingen: Mohr Siebeck, 2008.

Gauchet, Marcel. *The Disenchantment of the World: A Political History of Religion.* Translated by Oscar Burge. Princeton, NJ: Princeton University Press, 1997.

Gillespie, Michael. *Nihilism before Nietzsche.* Chicago, IL: University of Chicago Press, 1995.

———. *The Theological Origins of Modernity.* Chicago, IL: University of Chicago Press, 2008.

Gordon, Peter. "The Place of the Sacred in the Absence of God: Charles Taylor's *A Secular Age*." *Journal of the History of Ideas* 69 no. 4 (October 2008) 647–73.

Gorman, Michael J. *Apostle of the Crucified Lord. A Theological Introduction to Paul and his Letters.* Grand Rapids, MI: Eerdmans, 2004.

Gregory, Brad. *The Unintended Reformation. How a Religious Revolution Secularized Society.* Cambridge, MA: Harvard University Press, 2012.

Gregory, Eric. *Politics and the Order of Love: An Augustinian Ethic of Democratic Citizenship.* Chicago, IL: University of Chicago Press, 2008.

Gregory of Nyssa. "On Virginity." In *St. Gregory of Nyssa, Ascetical Works*, 6–75. Translated by Virginia Woods Callahan. Washington, DC: Catholic University of America Press, 1967.

Guarino, Thomas. "For the Secular." *First Things* (August 2006). https://www.firstthings.com/article/2006/08/for-the-secular.

Gur-Ze'ev, Ilan. *Diasporic Philosophy and Counter-Education.* Rotterdam: Sense, 2010.

Habermas, Jürgen. "Consciousness Raising of Rescuing Critique." In *Philosophical-Political Profiles*, translated by F. Lawrence, 99–110. London: Heinemann, 1983.

Harris, Elizabeth J. "Detachment and Compassion in Early Buddhism." http://www.accesstoinsight.org/lib/authors/harris/bl141.html.

Harvey, Barry. *Taking Hold of the Real. Dietrich Bonhoeffer and the Profound Worldliness of Christianity.* Eugene, OR: Cascade, 2015.

Hauerwas, Stanley. *In Good Company: The Church as Polis.* Notre Dame, IN: University of Notre Dame Press, 1995.

BIBLIOGRAPHY

Healy, Nicholas J., Jr. "Evangelical *Ressourcement.*" *First Things* 213 (May 2011). https://www.firstthings.com/article/2011/05/evangelical-ressourcement.

Heinitz, Michael. Introduction. In *Introduction to the Spiritual Life*, by Louis Bouyer, translated by Mary Perkins Ryan, 1–11. Notre Dame, IN: Ave Maria, 2013.

Herdt, Jennifer. "The Authentic Individual in the Network of Agape." In *Aspiring to Fullness in a Secular Age: Essays on Religion and Theology in the Work of Charles Taylor*, edited by Carlos Colorado and Justin Klassen, 191–216. Notre Dame. IN: University of Notre Dame Press, 2014.

Hill, Wesley. "The Full This-Worldliness of Life." http://www.booksandculture.com/articles/2014/sepoct/full-this-worldliness-of-life.html.

Hinson, Glenn. "Contemptus Mundi—Amor Mundi: Merton's Progression from World Denial to World Affirmation." *Cistercian Studies* 26 (1991) 339–49.

Horkheimer, Max, and Theodor Adorno. *Dialectic of Enlightenment*. Translated by John Cummings. London: Verso, 1979.

Hotam, Yotam. "Overcoming the mentor: Heidegger's present and the presence of Heidegger in Karl Loewith's and Hans Jonas' postwar thought." *History of European Ideas* 35 (2009) 253–64.

Howard, Donald R. *The Three Temptations: Medieval Man in Search of the World*. Princeton, NJ: Princeton University Press, 1966.

Howard-Brook, Wes. *"Come Out, My People!" God's Call Out of Empire in the Bible and Beyond*. Maryknoll, NY: Orbis, 2010.

Howe, John. *Before the Gregorian Reform: The Latin Church at the Turn of the First Millennium*. Ithaca, NY: Cornell University Press, 2016.

Illich, Ivan. "Health as One's Own Responsibility—No Thank You!" http://www.davidtinapple.com/illich/.

———. "Philosophy . . . Artifacts . . . Friendship." https://www.pudel.samerski.de/pdf/Illich_1429id.pdf.

———. *Tools for Conviviality*. London: Marion Boyars, 2001.

Inchausti, Robert. *Thomas Merton's American Prophecy*. New York: State University of New York Press, 1998.

Iogna-Prat, Dominique. *Order and Exclusion: Cluny and Christendom Face Heresy, Judaism and Islam (1000–1150)*. Translated by Graham Edwards. Ithaca, NY: Cornell University Press, 1998.

Jonas, Hans. *Mortality and Morality*. Evanston, IL: Northwestern University Press, 1996.

———. *The Phenomenon of Life: Toward a Philosophical Biology*. New York: Harper and Row, 1966.

———. "Technology and Responsibility: Reflections on the New Tasks of Ethics." In *Ethics and Emerging Technologies*, edited by Ronald Sandler, 37–47. New York: Palgrave MacMillan, 2014.

Kant, Immanuel. *Groundwork of a Metaphysics of Morals*. Translated by James Ellington. Indianapolis, IN: Hackett, 1993.

Karris, Robert J., and Campion Murray. *Commentary on Ecclesiastes*. 1st ed. New York: Franciscan Institute, 2005.

Kaspar, Walter. "Charles de Foucauld, the Mission in the Desert of Today." http://www.jesuscaritas.info/jcd/fr/charles-de-foucauld-mission-desert-today.

Kelly, Geoffrey. "Kierkegaard as 'Antidote' and as Impact on Dietrich Bonhoeffer's Conception of Christian Discipleship." In *Bonhoeffer's Intellectual Formation*, edited by Peter Frick, 145–65. Tubingen: Mohr Siebeck, 2008.

———. "Prayer and Action for Justice: Bonhoeffer's Spirituality." In *The Cambridge Companion to Dietrich Bonhoeffer*, edited by John de Gruchy, 246–68. Cambridge: Cambridge University Press, 1999.

Kierkegaard, Soren. *Journals*. Edited and translated by Alexander Dru. London: Fontana, 1958.

Kiess, John. *Hannah Arendt and Theology*. London: Bloomsbury T&T Clark, 2016.

Kirkpatrick, Matthew. *Attacks on Christendom in a World Come of Age: Kierkegaard, Bonhoeffer, and the Question of "Religionless Christianity."* Eugene, OR: Wipf and Stock, 2011.

Kopp-Oberstebrink, Herbert, and Martin Treml, eds. *Apokalypse und Politik: Aufsatze, Kritiken und kleinere Schriften*. Munich: Wilhelm Fink, 2017.

Kreider, Alan, ed. *The Origins of Christendom in the West*. Edinburgh: T & T Clark, 2001.

Kristeva, Julia, and Jean Vanier. *Leur Regard Perce nos Ombres*. Paris: Fayard, 2011.

Kroeker, Travis. "Messianic Ethics and Diaspora Communities: Upbuilding the Secular Theologically from Below." In *Religious Voices in Public Places*, edited by Nigel Biggar and Linda Hogan, 110–30. Oxford: Oxford University Press, 2009.

Kroll, Joe Paul. *A Human End to History? Hans Blumenberg, Karl Lowith, and Carl Schmitt on Secularization and Modernity*. https://www.academia.edu/6598589/A_Human_End_to_History_Hans_Blumenberg_Karl_Löwith_and_Carl_Schmitt_on_Secularization_and_Modernity.

Lacoste, Jean-Yves. *Experience and the Absolute: Disputed Questions on the Humanity of Man*. Translated by M. Raftery-Skeban. New York: Fordham University Press, 2004.

Ladner, Gerhart. *Cosmos and Humankind: The World of Early Christian Symbolism*. Translated by Thomas Dunlap. Berkeley, CA: University of California Press, 1955.

———. "*Homo Viator*: Mediaeval Ideas on Alienation and Order." *Speculum: A Journal of Mediaeval Studies* XLII.2 (1967) 233–59.

Laird, Martin. *Into the Silent Land: A Guide to the Christian Practice of Contemplation*. Oxford: Oxford University Press, 2006.

Landes, Richard, Andrew C. Gow, and David C. Van Meter, eds. *The Apocalyptic Year 1000: Religious Expectation and Social Change, 950–1050*. Oxford: Oxford University Press, 2003.

Lapidot, Eliad. "The Legitimacy of Nihilism: Blumenberg's Post-Gnosticism." In *Interrogating Modernity: Debates with Hans Blumenberg*, edited by Agata Bielik-Robson and Daniel Whistler, 37–59. London: Palgrave Macmillan, 2020.

Lazier, Benjamin. *God Interrupted: Heresy and the European Imagination between the World Wars*. Princeton, NJ: Princeton University Press, 2008.

Leclercq, Jean. *Aspects of Monasticism*. Kalamazoo, MI: Cistercian, 1978.

———. "Postface." In *Aspects of Monasticism*, 327–41. Kalamazoo, MI: Cistercian, 1978.

Lemna, Keith. *The Apocalypse of Wisdom: Louis Bouyer's Theological Recovery of the Cosmos*. New York: Angelico, 2019.

Leyser, Conrad. *Authority and Asceticism from Augustine to Gregory the Great*. Oxford: Oxford Historical Monographs, 2000.

Lilla, Mark. *The Stillborn God: Religion, Politics and the Modern West*. New York: Knopf, 2007.

Lowrie, Walter. *A Short Life of Kierkegaard*. Princeton, NJ: Princeton University Press, 1942.

Lukacs, Georg. *The Destruction of Reason*. Translated by Peter Palmer. Atlantic Highlands, NJ: Humanities, 1981.

MacIntyre, Alasdair. *After Virtue*. 2nd ed. Notre Dame, IN: University of Notre Dame Press, 1984.
Malesic, Jonathan. *Secret Faith in the Public Square: An Argument for the Concealment of Christian Identity*. Grand Rapids, MI: Brazos, 2009.
Malits, Elena. *The Solitary Explorer: Thomas Merton's Transforming Journey*. Eugene, OR: Wipf and Stock, 2014.
Maritain, Jacques. *The Peasant of the Garonne*. Translated by Michael Cuddihy and Elizabeth Hughes. London: Geoffrey Chapman, 1968.
Markus, Robert. "Church Reform and Society in Late Antiquity." In *Reforming the Church before Modernity. Patterns, Problems and Approaches*, edited by Christopher Bellitto and Louis Hamilton, 3–19. Aldershot: Ashgate, 2005.
———. *The End of Ancient Christianity*. Cambridge: Cambridge University Press, 1990.
———. *Saeculum: History and Society in the Theology of St Augustine*. Cambridge: Cambridge University Press, 1980.
Marrou, Henri-Irénée. *Saint Augustin et la Fin de la Culture Antique*: "*Retractatio.*" Paris: Editions de Boccard, 1958.
Marsh, Charles. *Strange Glory: A Life of Dietrich Bonhoeffer*. London: SPCK, 2014.
Matthews, Charles. *A Theology of Public Life*. New York: Cambridge University Press, 2007.
McCready, William David. *Odiosa sanctitas. St Peter Damian, Simony and Reform*. Toronto: Pontifical Institute of Medieval Studies, 2011.
McCurry, Jeffery. "To Love the World Most Deeply: The Phenomenology of the World as Gift in Augustine's *Confessions*." *New Blackfriars* 92 (January 2011) 46–54.
McKenzie, Bridget. "Turning for Home." https://www.appropedia.org/New_Public_Thinking_(2011)/Turning_for_home_-_Bridget_McKenzie
Mcleod, Hugh. *The Religious Crisis of the 1960s*. Oxford: Oxford University Press, 2007.
Meeks, Wayne A. *The Origins of Christian Morality: The First Two Centuries*. New Haven, CT: Yale University Press, 1993.
Merton, Thomas. *Basic Principles of Monastic Spirituality*. Springfield, IL: Templegate, 1996.
———. *Conjectures of a Guilty Bystander*. Garden City, NY: Doubleday, 1966.
———. *Contemplation in a World of Action*. New York: Doubleday, 1971.
———. *The Inner Experience: Notes on Contemplation*. San Francisco, CA: Harper Collins, 2003.
——— "Marxism and Monastic Perspectives." In *The Asian Journal of Thomas Merton*, edited by Patrick Hart, James Laughlin, and Naomi Burton Stone, 326–43. New York: New Directions, 1973.
———. *The Monastic Journey*. Edited by Patrick Hart. New York: Doubleday, 1978.
———. *New Seeds of Contemplation*. New York: New Directions, 1961.
———. *Raids on the Unspeakable*. New York: New Directions, 1966.
———. *Seeds of Contemplation*. New York: New Directions, 1962.
———. *The Seven Storey Mountain*. New York: Harcourt, Brace, Jovanovich, 1948.
———. *Survival or Prophecy?: The Letters of Thomas Merton and Jean Leclercq*. Edited by Patrick Hart. New York: Farrar, Straus and Giroux, 2002.
Miccoli, Giovanni. "Monks." In *Medieval Callings*, edited by Jacques Le Goff and translated by Lydia Cochrane, 37–73. Chicago, IL: University of Chicago Press, 1987.
Morris, Theresa. *Hans Jonas's Ethic of Responsibility: From Ontology to Ecology*. Albany, NY: State University of New York Press, 2013.

BIBLIOGRAPHY

Murray, John Courtney. "Is It Basket Weaving? The Question of Christian and Human Values." In *We Hold These Truths: Catholic Reflections on the American Proposition*, 175–96. Oxford: Sheed and Ward, 2005.

Nemo, Philippe. *What is the West?* Pittsburgh, PA: Duquesne University Press, 2006.

Newhauser, Richard. *The Early History of Greed: The Sin of Avarice in Early Medieval Thought and Literature*. Cambridge: Cambridge University Press, 2000.

Newman, Barbara. "Eliot's Affirmative Way: Julian of Norwich, Charles Williams, and *Little Gidding*." *Modern Philology* 108 no. 3 (February 2011) 427–61.

Nirenberg, David ."Choosing Life." *New Republic,* November 5, 2008. https://newrepublic.com/article/64504/choosing-life.

Northcott, Michael. "'Who am I?': Human Identity and the Spiritual Disciplines in the Witness of Dietrich Bonhoeffer." In *Who Am I? Bonhoeffer's Theology through His Poetry*, edited by Bernd Wannenwetsch, 11–30. London: T&T Clark, 2009.

O'Donnell, James J. *Augustine: Confessions*. Vol. III: Commentary on Books 8–13. Oxford: Clarendon, 1992.

O'Donovan, Oliver. *The Desire of the Nations: Rediscovering the Roots of Political Theology*. Cambridge: Cambridge University Press, 1996.

Oliver, Simon. "Introducing Radical Orthodoxy: From Participation to Late Modernity." In *The Radical Orthodoxy Reader*, edited by John Milbank and Simon Oliver, 3–27. London: Routledge, 2009.

O'Regan, Cyril. *Gnostic Return in Modernity*. Albany, NY: State University of New York Press, 2001.

Origen. *The Song of Songs, Commentary and Homilies*. Translated and annotated by R. P. Lawson. New York: Paulist, 1957.

Pascal, Blaise. *Pensees and Other Writings*. Translated by Honor Levi. Oxford: Oxford University Press, 2008.

Pope Benedict XVI. *Church Fathers and Teachers: From Saint Leo the Great to Peter Lombard*. Vatican City: Libreria Editrice Vaticana, 2010.

Pope Gregory VII. *The Correspondence of Gregory VII: Selected Letters from the Registrum*. Translated by Ephraim Emerton. New York: Columbia University Press, 1999.

The Project on Lived Theology. "Overview." http://www.livedtheology.org/overview/.

Rahner, Hugo. *Man at Play*. Translated by Brian Battershaw and Edward Quinn. London: Burns and Oates, 1965.

Ramfos, Stelios. *Like a Pelican in the Wilderness*. Brookline, MA: Holy Cross Orthodox, 2000.

Rauh, H. D. "Eschatologie und Geschichte." In *The Use and Abuse of Eschatology in the Middle Ages*, edited by W. Verbeke, D. Verhelst, and A. Welkenhuysen, 333–58. Louvain: Louvain University Press, 1988.

Rebillard, Eric. *Christians and Their Many Identities in Late Antiquity, North Africa 200-450 CE*. Ithaca, NY: Cornell University Press, 2012.

Rensberger, David. *Overcoming the World*. London: SPCK, 1989.

Robinson, James M. "'World' in Modern Theology and in New Testament Theology." In *Soli Deo Gloria*, edited by J. McDowell Richards, 88–110. Richmond, VA: John Knox, 1968.

Robinson, John. *Honest to God*. London: SCM, 1963.

Roderick, Ellen. "Their Look Pierces Our Shadows." *Humanum Review* 3 (2014). https://humanumreview.com/articles/their-look-pierces-our-shadows.

BIBLIOGRAPHY

Rose, Matthew. "Tayloring Christianity." *First Things* (December 2014). https://www.firstthings.com/article/2014/12/tayloring-christianity.
Rousseau, Philip. "Ascetics as Mediators and as Teachers." In *The Cult of Saints in Late Antiquity and the Middle Ages: Essays on the Contribution of Peter Brown*, edited by James Howard-Johnston and Paul Anthony Hayward, 45–59. New York: Oxford University Press, 1999.
Ruddy, Christopher. "What is the *Opus Dei?*: Christian Humanism on the Eve of Vatican II." *Proceedings of the Catholic Theological Society of America* 73 (2018) 1–19.
The Rutba House. *School(s) for Conversion: 12 Marks of a New Monasticism*. Eugene, OR: Cascade, 2005.
Sawicki, John. "Towards a Politics of Apathy: Baudrillard, Bartleby, and Adorno." MA Thesis, University of Western Ontario, 1997. https://www.collectionscanada.gc.ca/obj/s4/f2/dsk2/ftp01/MQ28657.pdf
Schmemann, Alexander. *For the Life of the World: Sacraments and Orthodoxy*. New York: St. Vladimir's Seminary Press, 1982.
Schmitt, Carl. *Roman Catholicism and Political Form*. Translated by G. L. Ulman. Westport, CT: Greenwood, 1996.
Scott, Joanna Vecchiarelli. "What St. Augustine Taught Hannah Arendt about 'How to Live in the World': Caritas, Natality and the Banality of Evil." https://helda.helsinki.fi/bitstream/handle/10138/25821/008_03_Scott.pdf;sequence=1.
Segovia, Fernando F., ed. *Discipleship in the New Testament*. Philadelphia, PA: Fortress, 1985.
Shaw, Amanda. "Contemptus Mundi and the Love of Life." *First Things* (May 2008). https://www.firstthings.com/article/2008/05/contemptus-mundi-and-the-love-of-life.
Shearn, Samuel. "Charles Taylor, Nietzsche and Theology." In *Working With a Secular Age: Interdisciplinary Perspectives on Charles Taylor's Master Narrative*, edited by Florian Zemmin, Colin Jager, and Guido Vanheeswijck, 263–82. Berlin: Walter De Gruyter, 2016.
Sigurdson, Ola. *Theology and Marxism in Eagleton and Žižek. A Conspiracy of Hope*. New York: Palgrave Macmillan, 2012.
Silber, Ilana F. *Virtuosity, Charisma, and Social Order: A Comparative Sociological Study of Monasticism in Theravada Buddhism and Medieval Catholicism*. Cambridge: Cambridge University Press, 1995.
Slane, Craig. *Bonhoeffer as Martyr: Social Responsibility and Modern Christian Commitment*. Grand Rapids, MI: Brazos, 2004.
Smalley, Beryl. "Review of R. Bultot," *Christianisme et Valeurs Humaines*. *The Journal of Theological Studies* 16 no.1 (April 1963) 234–35.
Smith, James K. A. *How (Not) to be Secular: Reading Charles Taylor*. Grand Rapids, MI: Eerdmans, 2014.
Spaemann, Robert. *Philosophische Essays*. Stuttgart: Philip Reclam, 1994.
Staniforth, Maxwell, trans. *Early Christian Writings: The Apostolic Fathers*. London: Penguin, 1968.
Stewart-Kroeker, Sarah. *Pilgrimage as Moral and Aesthetic Formation in Augustine's Thought*. Oxford: Oxford University Press, 2017.
Storey, David. "Charles Taylor's *A Secular Age*: Breaking the Spell of the Immanent Frame." In *Rethinking Secularization: Philosophy and the Prophecy of a Secular Age*, edited by H. de Vriese and G. Gabor, 177–208. Newcastle: Cambridge Scholars Publishing, 2009.

BIBLIOGRAPHY

Styfhals, Willem. *No Spiritual Investment in the World: Gnosticism and Postwar German Philosophy*. Ithaca, NY: Cornell University Press, 2019.

Surin, Kenneth. "*Contemptus mundi* and the disenchanted world: Bonhoeffer's 'discipline of the secret' and Adorno's 'strategy of hibernation'." In *The Turnings of Darkness and Light: Essays in Philosophical and Systematic Theology*, 180–200. Cambridge: Cambridge University Press, 1989.

———. *The Turnings of Darkness and Light: Essays in Philosophical and Systematic Theology*. Cambridge: Cambridge University Press, 1989.

Swenson, David. "Soren Kierkegaard—a Danish Socrates." In *Something About Kierkegaard*, 34–69. Macon, GA: Mercer University Press, 2003.

Tardif, Mary, ed. *At Home in the World: The Letters of Thomas Merton and Rosemary Radford Ruether*. Maryknoll, NY: Orbis, 1995.

Tawney, R. H. *Religion and the Rise of Capitalism*. New Brunswick: Transaction, 1998.

Taylor, Charles. *A Secular Age*. Cambridge, MA: Harvard University Press, 2007.

———. *Sources of the Self. The Making of Modern Identity*. Cambridge: Cambridge University Press, 1989.

Thomas à Kempis. *The Imitation of Christ*. Translated by L. Shirley Price. London: Penguin, 1952.

Thompson, Phillip. *Returning to Reality: Thomas Merton's Wisdom for a Technological World*. Eugene, OR: Wipf and Stock, 2012.

Thurston, Bonnie. *Hidden in God: Discovering the Desert Vision of Charles de Foucauld*. Notre Dame, IN: Ave Maria, 2016.

Ticciati, Susannah. "Ecclesiastes, Augustine's *Uti/Frui* Distinction, and Christ as the Waste of the World." In *Reading Ecclesiastes Intertextually*, edited by K. Dell and W. Keynes, 253–67. London: Bloomsbury, 2014.

Torrance, Alexis C. *Repentance in Late Antiquity: Eastern Asceticism and the Framing of the Christian Life, c. 400–650 CE*. Oxford: Oxford University Press, 2013.

Tuttle, Howard. *The Crowd is Untruth: The Existential Critique of Mass Society in the Thought of Kierkegaard, Nietzsche, Heidegger and Ortega Y Gasset*. New York: Peter Lang, 1996.

Tyson, Paul. *Returning to Reality: Christian Platonism for Our Times*. Eugene, OR: Cascade, 2014.

Vanheeswicjk, Guido. "The End of Secularization?" In *Rethinking Secularization: Philosophy and the Prophecy of a Secular Age*, edited by H. de Vriese and G. Gabor, 1–26. Newcastle: Cambridge Scholars Publishing, 2009.

Vatter, Miguel. *The Republic of the Living: Biopolitics and the Critique of Civil Society*. New York: Fordham University Press, 2014.

Vernon, Mark. "Freedom—by giving stuff up." In *The Good Life: 30 Steps to Perfecting the Art of Living*, 51–57. London: Hodder Education, 2010.

Vogel, Lawrence. "The Responsibility of Thinking in Dark Times: Hannah Arendt versus Hans Jonas." *Critical Theory Today, Special Issue, Graduate Faculty Philosophy Journal*, New School for Social Research 29 no. 1 (2008) 253–73.

Volpe, Medi Ann. *Rethinking Christian Identity: Doctrine and Discipleship*. Oxford: Wiley-Blackwell, 2012.

Walsh, Sylvia. *Kierkegaard: Thinking Christianly in an Existential Mode*. Oxford: Oxford University Press, 2009.

Ward, Benedicta, trans. *The Sayings Of The Desert Fathers: The Apophthegmata Patrum: The Alphabetic Collection*. Kalamazoo, MI: Cistercian Studies, 1975.

Ward, Bruce. "Transcendence and Immanence in a Subtler Language: The Presence of Dostoevsky in Charles Taylor's Account of Secularity." In *Aspiring to Fullness in a Secular Age: Essays on Religion and Theology in the Work of Charles Taylor*, edited by Carlos Colorado and Justin Klassen, 262–90. Notre Dame, IN: University of Notre Dame Press, 2014.

Ware, Kallistos. "Afterword." In *A Silent Action: Engagements with Thomas Merton*, by Rowan Williams, 87–90. Louisville, KY: Fons Vitae, 2011.

Weber, Max. *The Protestant Ethic and the Spirit of Capitalism*. Translated by Talcott Parsons. London: Routledge Classics, 2001.

Weill, Marie-David. *L'humanisme eschatologique de Louis Bouyer: De Marie, Trone de la Sagesse, a l"Eglise, Espouse de l'Agneau*. Paris: Les Editions du Cerf, 2016.

Weiss, Monica. *The Environmental Vision of Thomas Merton*. Lexington, KY: University of Kentucky Press, 2011.

Westphal, Merold. *Kierkegaard's Critique of Reason and Society*. Macon, GA: Mercer University Press, 1987.

Wiese, Christian. *The Life and Thought of Hans Jonas: Jewish Dimensions*. Translated by Jeffrey Grossman and Christian Wiese. Waltham, MA: Brandeis University Press, 2007.

Williams, Charles. *The Descent of the Dove: A Short History of the Holy Spirit in the Church*. London: Longmans, Green and Co., 1939.

Williams, Rowan. "The Benedict Option: A New Monasticism for the 21st Century." *New Statesmen*, May 30, 2017. https://www.newstatesman.com/politics/religion/2017/05/benedict-option-new-monasticism-21st-century.

———. "Defining Heresy." In *The Origins of Christendom in the West*, edited by Alan Kreider, 313–35. Edinburgh: T & T Clark, 2001.

———. "The New Evangelisation for the Transmission of the Christian Faith." Address to the Synod of Bishops in Rome, October 10, 2012. http://rowanwilliams.archbishopofcanterbury.org/articles.php/2645/archbishops-address-to-the-synod-of-bishops-in-rome.html.

———. *On Augustine*. London: Bloomsbury Continuum, 2016.

———. "'The Only Real City': Monasticism and Social Vision." In *A Silent Action: Engagements with Thomas Merton*, edited by Rowan Williams, 53–68. London: SPCK, 2011.

———. "Politics and the Soul." In *On Augustine*, 107–30. London: Bloomsbury Continuum, 2016.

———. "Secularism, Faith and Freedom." In *Faith in the Public Square*, 23–36. London: Continuum, 2012.

———. *A Silent Action: Engagements with Thomas Merton*. Louisville, KY: Fons Vitae, 2011.

———. *Why Study the Past? The Quest for the Historical Church*. London: Darton, Longman and Todd, 2005.

———. *The Wound of Knowledge*. London: Darton, Longman and Todd, 1979.

Wimbush, Vincent L. *Paul the Worldly Ascetic: Response to the World and Self-Understanding according to 1 Corinthians 7*. Macon, GA: Mercer University Press, 1987.

BIBLIOGRAPHY

Winter, Bruce W. *Seek the Welfare of the City. Christians as Benefactors and Citizens.* Grand Rapids: Eerdmans, 1994.

Wolin, Richard. *Heidegger's Children: Hannah Arendt, Karl Löwith, Hans Jonas, and Herbert Marcuse.* Princeton, NJ: Princeton University Press, 2001.

Wolin, Sheldon. *The Presence of the Past: Essays on the State and the Constitution.* Baltimore: John Hopkins University Press, 1989.

Yap, Joaquin. "'Word' and 'Wisdom' in the Ecclesiology of Louis Bouyer." https://pdfs.semanticscholar.org/4861/36fbc618f5340a0572bb6fe65b6361ac06e9.pdf.

Index of Subjects

acceptance, of love from others, 144
"accepting life on their terms," meaning of, 127
"active love," 143
active purgation, stage of, xii
adaptation and relevance, anxious concern with, 132
admiratio mundi, versus *contemptus mundi*, 37
Adorno, Theodor, xviii, 94, 95, 97, 101, 117, 123
"aesthetic existence," 132
affirmation, as possible with *agape*, 144
"the affirmation of ordinary life," 62, 67, 117
Agamben, Giorgio, 103
agape, 125, 136, 138
agapic love, 143
aggression, 145
alien God, 78
alienation, experienced by Jesus, 6
all is vanity, 39
"the allurements of the world" (*blandimenta saeculi*), 26
always-the-same, unrelenting barbarism of, 99
Alyosha Karamazov, 121, 143, 146
Ambitio seculi, defeating humility, 47
ambivalence
about the world (*mundus*), xv–xvi, xviii, 5, 7, 17, 29, 115

Christian, 34, 55, 119
communities of, 1–11
delivering Augustine from apocalyptic hostility to Rome, 24
Dietrich Bonhoeffer faithful to, 115–16
of *saeculum*, 30
theology of, 18–24
amor mundi
Arendt and, 77, 84, 86–87, 91
in Dostoevsky's *The Brothers Karamazov*, 121
of each citizen, 93
overcoming the "dilemma of mutilation," 140
return to the Great Tradition of Christian, 112
those graced with called "to set it right," 85
tradition of, 16
"angelism," attitude leading to, 125
anima mundi (world soul), *logos* as, 15
Antaeus, lost contact with the earth, 116
Antichrist, 50–51, 52
anti-cosmic dualism, of Gnostics, 69
Antony, 16, 99
Apologeticum de contemptu saeculi (Damien), 52
apologists, insisting on unsuspected unities, 13

INDEX OF SUBJECTS

approfondissement, of *contemptus mundi*, 128
Aquinas, Thomas, 73, 148
Arendt, Hannah, xvii
   on Augustine's vision of Christian life, 18
   blaming Augustine for a worldlessness, 91
   on Christian love "going public," 90
   critical dialogue with Augustine, 77
   on Eichmann, 92–93
   focus on ordinary practices, 87
   learning from and criticizing Augustine, xviii
   love of the world, 117
   on political evil, 81
   responses to modern worldlessness, 76
   sharing Augustine's sense of human temporality, 93
   showing modern persons how to love the world, 94
   on "unequalled worldlessness," 74
aristocratic laity, imposing ascetic norms on, 31
aristocratic patrons, in medieval Christendom, 59
Aristotle, 148
Arkandiziplin, protecting the church from the corruption of the world, 119
ascetic closure, as the end of ancient Christianity, 27–32
ascetic ideals, 103
ascetic virtuosi, emerging from Buddhism, 49
asceticism, xv, 30
   inner-worldly, 9, 65
   new, 115
   worldly, 7–10
ascetics, 34
"astounding faith," of Pope John XXIII, 94
atheism, close to being inconceivable, 57
atomic war, resorting to, 79
atomistic individuals, 66
Augustine
   Arendt on, xviii, 87

brief exposition of Ecclesiastes in *City of God*, 40
on Christian ambivalence about the world, 18
on a Christian being a citizen, 88
on creation as a whole, 20
dealing with Manichaeans, 20–21, 22, 93
distinction of the transitory and the permanent, 40
distinguishing between *res* (things) and *signa* (signs), 41
on enjoyment of God, 41
on how the body of Christ lives, 91
on how to love the world, 43
inspired Arendt to challenge Heidegger, 92
on the number of the saved as very small, 51
redefinition of the public, 88–89
rejected eternal recurrence, 92
on the struggle for immortality, 89
on the things of the "world," 47
use of Platonic ontology, 19
on using the things of this world, 63
"austerity," defined as a virtue, 148
authenticity, age of, 135
authority, sliding away from a hierarchy, 60
Autpert, Ambrose, 44–45
avarice, 47
average Christian, as an ideal, 117
awakening, within the moment of hibernation, 102
awareness, in contemplative prayer, 130
Axial Age, 55, 136
"axiomized ambiguity," of a Christian, 54

Babylon, 2–4, 28
Balthasar, Hans Urs Von, 101–2n75, 112
beauty, 18, 19
Being, 80, 112
Being and Time (Heidegger), 80
belonging to a community, sense of, 88
"belonging wholly to the earth," Bonhoeffer on, 116
Benedict, saw a celestial light, 46

INDEX OF SUBJECTS

Benedict Labre, 108
Benedict Option, Dreher defended, 101n75
The Benedict Option (Dreher), 101n75
Bernard of Clairvaux, 38
Bethge, Eberhard, 116, 119, 122
biblical love, of the world, 1
Bielik-Robson, Agata, on the finite human life, 92n51
birth and death, 83
birth of the New Man, Paul on, 21
Black Christians, compared to John's community, 6
the Black Death, 73
Blumenberg, Hans, xvii, 78n10
Boccaccio's *Decameron*, 73
Bodhisattva, delaying nirvana, 125
bodily discipline, transformation of the soul and, 30
Bonaventure, 43, 44
bonds, between persons, 88
Bonhoeffer, Dietrich
    aesthetic existence and, 132
    on ancient Christian ambivalence, 119
    on Christ and the world, 121
    on the "discipline of the secret," 134
    engaged but imprisoned, 122
    faith of, 116–23
    faithful to ambivalence, 115–16
    not accepting Nazism "on its own terms," 127
    on Protestant reengagement with monasticism, 118
    reacting against Barthian radicalism, 126
    rethinking the doctrine of *contemptus mundi*, 123
    revisionary reading of, xviii
Bonhoeffer, Karl-Freidrick, 119
bourgeois moral code, Christianity increasingly identified with, 67
Bouyer, Louis, xiii, xiiin5
Brethren of the Common Life, 60
A Brief Catechesis on Nature and Grace (de Lubac), 110–11

British Student Christian Movement, collapse of, 105
The Brothers Karamazov (Dostoevsky), 121, 142
Buddhist meditative practices, 48, 49
Buddhist societies, laity feeding the monks, 59
"buffered identity," transformed view of, 65
"buffered self," 60, 66, 135
built environment, of Arendt, 81
Bultot, Robert, 35
bureaucracies, based on rationality and rules, 138
Byzantine mosaic, at the Mausoleum of Galla Placidia, 15

Caesarius of Arles, 31
Calvinism, turning the world into a monastery, 64
"capacity of man," Augustine on, 92
capitalism, 124
capitulation to mass culture, 102
cardiac cycle, two phases of, 101n75
caritas, 88
Carmen de contemptu mundi (Roger of Caen), 36
Carnival, inverting ordinary order of things, 58
categorical imperative, of Kant, 80
"categorical societies," 137
categories, shaping our lives, 138
Catherine of Siena, 19
Catholic Christianity, rejected gnostic dualism, 69
Catholic dominance, normativizing processes consolidating, 22
celibacy, "impossibility" of, 113
celibate clergy, for a married laity, 58
"cemetery contemplations," monk encouraged to undertake, 49
charity, Augustine on, 89
chaste love, for the world, 44
chastity, 48
"cheap grace," Bonhoeffer's expression of, 118
Chesterton, G. K., 54

INDEX OF SUBJECTS

child playing with dice, of Nietzsche, 11
children, loving, 86
Christ. *See also* Jesus
    as both the way and the end, 19
    choosing the world as it really is in Him, 131
    as the "sacrament of the world," 111
    seeking without the world, 121
    as the source of justice, 91
    true identity found in the presence of, 6
    wholeness of as the Logos, 35
    as the Word of God, 15
Christ, Mary, and the saints, painting as human beings, 62–63
Christ-centered justice, 91
"Christendom," Kierkegaard's attack on, 117
Christian ambivalence. *See* ambivalence
Christian anxiety, to recompose the world, 69
Christian asceticism, relativizing as an "inner-worldly asceticism," 9
Christian community, 5, 6
Christian congregations, flood of half-converted Romans into, 30
Christian culture, 32, 105
Christian discipleship, re-envisaging, xviii
Christian faith, identification with civilizational order, 139
Christian God, as immanent as well as transcendent, xii
Christian life. *See also* life
    ascetic models of, 30
    dangerous capacity to shake the world, 94
    as a duty laid on every Christian living in the world, 118
    for those engaged in human flourishing, 63
Christian monastic tradition, 15
Christian political theologies, 22
Christian respect, for the transiency of the world and the structure of the church, 126
Christian revolution, described, 10–11

Christian tradition, ambivalence of its responses to the "world," 34
Christian unworldliness, 17, 93
Christianitas, struggle to establish, 51
Christianity
    acquired its empire accidentally, 22
    anxious to put Humpty-Dumpty together again, 13, 69
    Arendt fiercely critical of, 87
    as a bulwark of "civilization," 67
    calling persons out of the existing social order, 136
    comparing with the Indian *sannyasin*, 10
    distinct "Eastern" and "Western" trajectories of, 20
    as life in the world outside the world, 10
    modernity as a mutation of, 54–55
    tackling issues of continuity and stability, 13
    temporalization of, 108
    this-worldliness of, 119–20
    on the world as the good creation, 100
Christianization of the Empire, Augustine's response to, 23
Christians
    called to participate in worldliness, 122
    commanded to turn over all things, 104
    compelled by a new guilt and fear, 62
    conceiving themselves and the natural world apart from divine purposes, 67
    conquering society, 22–23
    on the hostility of modern civilization to Christianity, 107
    as modern civilization's "loyal opposition," 139
    not completely rejecting the world, 54
    relationship to the world, 3
    as resident aliens, 2
    torn between belonging and distancing, 11

INDEX OF SUBJECTS

Chronicle of Two Cities (Otto of Freising), 52
Church
  as like a sacrament, 111
  as not outside the world, xv
  passing into the self-transcendent mission, 101n75
  on pilgrimage toward the heavenly city, 25
  unity of as the truth of the Eucharist, 111
church fathers, on the Eucharist, 17
church governance, restoring right order to, 50
Church of England, reform and renewal program, xi
Church statements, silence against the fate engulfing European Jews, 94
Cicero, 70
cities, of late antiquity, 36
citizenship, as the everyday task of making a common world, 93
city, reimagined as "a creative and pastoral community," 89
city of God, 25, 88
City of God (Augustine), 23, 27–28
civitas Dei, as a substitute for the public realm, 88
civitas peregrina, creating an ambivalent this-worldly space, 29
Clement of Alexandria, 14, 15
clergy, restoring moral purity to, 50
clown, Eichmann as a, 93
Cluniac alliance, between monasticism and the papacy, 49
Coakley, Sarah, 113, 114–15
colonial empires, persecuting societies became, 68
coming of Christ, making true community possible, 137
commandment, of Jesus to love one another, 6
commitment, tension of division of, 9
commodity principle, as deep-rooted, 97
"common of the world," chosen by God, 8
common world, 81, 82
Communion of Saints, 136

communities
  of ambivalence, 1–11
  deploying foundational stories and images, 14
  envisioned by divine affirmation, 146
  held together in agapic love, 143
  Paul's fundamental rule for, 8
community of love, initiated by divine love, 137
compassion, 49, 125, 142
compassionate love, independent reality of, 143
complementarity, between authentic individuality and the need for community, 136
compromise, between acceptance and rejection, 11
concentration camps, Arendt's analysis of, 83
Concluding Unscientific Postscript (Kierkegaard), on monasticism as a false solution, 117
concupiscentia carnis, 47
concupiscentia oculorum, 47
Cone, James, 6
Confessing Church, small illegal seminary for, 118
Confessions, lesson of the story in Augustine's, 42
Congar, Yves, 112
Conjectures of a Guilty Bystander (Merton), 125
consciousness, 133, 134
conservation, element of, 85
conservatives, divine mandate to dominate, 125
Constantine, 22, 23
consumer society, approaching all things as goods, 83
contemplation, 109, 128, 134
contemplative community, as "the only real city," 132
contemplative prayer, practice of, 130
contemplative vocations, promise of, 115
contemplatives, earthly critique of, 67
contempt, 44
"contempt of the world," 46, 51

INDEX OF SUBJECTS

contemptus mundi
   from Adorno, 94–104
   as *approfondissement* rather than abandonment, 125
   Augustinian account of, 43–44
   balancing *amor mundi*, 124
   as a compassion for the transient world, 126
   corruption and abuse of the tradition of, 49–50, 51
   cultivating to remain very much in the world, 53
   literature of, 38
   referring to both a world view and a literary genre, 33
   as a refusal to compromise with an unjust, violent society, 37
   as a rejection of the false self, 132
   secularized version of, 94
   as a sense of the end time, 52
   teaching of used in the effort of Reform, 62
   on the "world," xvii
contemptus mundi tradition, 38, 40, 45, 46
Contract, Herman, 36
Corinthian church, factiousness, 8
corrupted Christianity, 138, 139
cosmic cross, 15
cosmos, 14, 17, 19, 70. *See also* kosmos
created matter, serving eucharistically, 17
created order, anchoring of in the eternal Logos, 16
created world, as an imperfect image of God, xii
creation
   as better than the higher things alone, 20
   corrupted by sin, 108
   as good by definition, 71
   participatory doctrine of, 113
   redeemed and recreated in Christ, 120
Creation and Fall (Bonhoeffer), 123
creative subjectivity, spiritual advent of, 140
creator, versus the renewal of creation, 43

creator God himself, as the source of evil, 69
creatures, used as signs of God, 41
"cretinization of the masses," ensuring, 96
"The Crisis of Education" (Arendt), 85
crisis of secularization, spiritual source of, 106
critique of modernity, philosophy as, 76
the Cross, xiv–xv, 108
crucifixion, 9, 10
cultural anxiety, negotiating, 114
culture, xi, 7, 83, 135
"culture industry," 95–96
"culture of the Theopolis," 35

Damian, Peter, 1, 36, 52, 64
"The Damnable Exit from the Human Condition," 53
Danielou, Jean, 112
"dark times," 84, 94
De cupiditate (Autpert), 44
De doctrina christiana (Augustine), 40
de Lubac, Henri, 110, 111–12
De Miseria Condicionis Humane, by Cardinal Lotario dei Segni before he became Pope Innocent III, 52–53
De vanitate mundi, of Hugh of St Victor, 45–46
"death" of God, in modernity, 78
demons and spirits, powers of, 60
The Deputy (Hochhuth), 94
"desacralizing secularization," 111
de-sacramentalized society, 110
desert, alive with the power of the *logos*, 16
Desert Fathers, on Zacharias, 34
desire, 114, 115
"despised [of the world]," God has chosen, 8
destruction, in the name of the faith, 141
The Destruction of Reason (Lukacs), 75
destructive ideals, directing to genuine goods, 140
detachment, 48, 65, 129
deus absconditus, 78–79
"de-worldification," 80, 81

INDEX OF SUBJECTS

"Dialectic of Enlightenment," 95, 97
Dialectic of Enlightenment (Horkheimer and Adorno), 95
diffusive Christianity, phenomenon of, 135
dignity of man, affirming, 45
"dilation," phenomenon of, 46
dilemma of mutilation, 140, 145, 146
disability, reflecting on the nature of, 146
disabled son, drowning, 147
disciple of Christ, set apart from the world, 122
discipleship
    as both a way of affirmation and a way of negation, xvi
    demanding a very definite attitude towards the "world," 4
    embracing the world and pushing it away, xi
    as paradoxical, xii
    as participation in Christ's suffering, 123
    reality of Christian identity as, 115
    report on the development of in the Church of England, xi
Discipleship (Bonhoeffer), 118
disciplinary society, 65, 66
discipline, 61
"discipline of the secret," 119, 123
disciplined existence, as necessary, 134
disciplined society, instead of a network of agape, 137
"disembedded" selfhood, 65
dis-embedding religion, Christianity's contribution to, 137
"disenchanted" world, critique of, 95, 96
disenchantment, 61
disobedience, circle of, 2
disordered loves, healing, 90
dispossession, of secular vocation, 104
disruptive moment, systematized into a theory of "anti-history," 13
divine *logoi*, earth revealed as a nexus of, 121
Divine Love, required for a fallen creation, xv
divine neighbor, revelation of God as, 90
divine power, use and misuse of, 145
Dostoevsky, Fyodor, 56, 141, 142, 143
double meontology, of Paul, 9
downfall of the world, 70
dualisms, Jonas's studies of, 79
dukkha, suffering, satisfaction, and disease, 48
Dumont, Louis, 10
dying to our false self, to discover our true self, 131

Eagleton, Terry, 100
early Christianity, 12, 113
early Christians, 2, 3
early church, as a community marginalized, 87–88
earth
    as it is in heaven, 121
    remaining our mother, 116
earthly affection, as a melody of life, 122
earthly city, created by self-love, 25
earthly kingdoms, grounded in a heavenly kingdom, 57
earthly things, developing a taste for, 18
Eastern Patristic tradition, eschatological orientation of, xiii n5
ecclesia, 37, 51
Ecclesiastes
    Augustine's interpretation of, 40
    Jerome's interpretation of, 38
    on the meaning of Christian vocations, 66
    message of, 40
    reading of taking *vanitas* as its leading word, xvii
    as Solomon's manual for penitents, 39
    as understood from Jerome's commentary, 102
    weakness of perishable things seen clearly in, 38
ecclesiastical world, as transient, 126
economic imperative, of limitless growth, 83
education, 85, 86
ego, 96
Eichmann, Adolf, 92
Eliot, T. S., xii

INDEX OF SUBJECTS

emancipatory practice, as foolishness and insanity, 98
embedded religion, 136
embodied existence, Manichaean understanding of, 22
Emperor of this world, instead of Heavenly Father, 108
empirical identity, making into the false self, 130
enchanted or "charged" objects, powers of, 60
"enchanted world," inhabited by spirits and demons, 56
"encounter," at the heart of an understanding of agape, 147
end of the world, anticipation of, 88
the "enemy," Merton discovered as himself, 128
"English Bonhoefferism," 105, 106
enjoyment (*frui*), 40, 41
Enlightenment, as disenchantment of the world, 95
Enlightenment naturalism, 140
Ennead VI (Plotinus), 19
Ephesians, on assimilation to God, 4
episcopal authority, evolving, 13
equilibrium
    between acceptance and rejection of the world, 54
    accepting that masses of people were not going to live up to the demands of perfection, 59
    based on complementarity of functions, 58
    of *contemptus mundi* and *amor mundi*, 125
    between negative and affirmative ways, xiii, xv
    between sacred and profane demands, 58
"eschatological humanism," xiii, xiv, xv
eschatological orientation, of Augustine, 18
eschatological reign of the God of Israel, 120
eschaton, anticipation of, 47
eternal life, xv

eternal things of God, directing one's love to, 40
ethical presuppositions, centering on, 135
Ethics (Bonhoeffer), 126
Eucharist, 16, 17, 111
Eusebius, 23
eutrapelia (graceful playfulness), 148
"everyone for himself," as the common battle cry, 79
evil
    as describable only negatively, 93
    as nothingness, 71
    as only a turning away to separateness, 19–20
    saints opposing totally, 108
    struggle against generating evil, 136
"excarnation," 61, 138
"exclusive humanism," 56, 66
Exhortatio ad Contemptum Temporalium et Desiderium Eternorum (Anselm), 37
Exhortatory Poem on the Contempt of the World (Contract), 36
existence of God, 66
existentialists, 78
external nature, domination and manipulation of, 95
eyes, lust of, 47

faith, 2, 43, 121–22, 146
fallen world, 2
false self, 129, 130, 132
Farewell Discourse, of John 14–17, 6
Fathers of the Church, as sources for renewal of Christian theology, 112
feminists, on excluding women, 140
finite human mind, deciding to trust in itself, 73n52
finite life, affirmation of, 92n51
finite will, act of against infinite voluntarism, 73nn52
first churches, far from being world affirming, 4
flesh, 21, 47
flight from the world, tied to the salvation of the world, 2

INDEX OF SUBJECTS

flood of down-coursing waters," thinking of the entire world as, 46
"foolish of the world," chosen by God, 7–8
"for this world," not living, 25
Fortunatus, Manichaean presbyter and missionary, 21
Foucauld, Charles de, 109–10
Foucault, Michel, 140
Four Quartets, of T. S. Eliot, xii–xiii
frameworks, of Arendt, 81
Francis of Assisi, 108
freedom, 78, 87, 98
friend, as a kind of substitute for God, 42
friend of the world, as an enemy of God, 4
friendship, 139, 148
frui and *uti* (enjoyment and use), 40–41, 42
"the full this-worldliness of life," taken from Europe, 122

Gauchet, Marcel, 10, 11, 54, 55
Gaudium et spes, "incarnational humanism" in, xiv
genealogy, of our secular age, xvi
Girard, Rene, 55, 145
The Glass Bead Game (Hesse), 148
gluttony, 47
"gnostic" cluster of systems, 13
gnostic creation, 79
gnostic separation, 14
Gnosticism
    Augustine's overcoming of, 92
    having no need of theodicy, 69–70
    modern age as the second overcoming of, 69
    not overcome by Augustine's solution to the problem of evil, 71
    resistance to modern, 77
    revival of, 76
    salvation as liberation from a world of oppression, 100
    as an understanding of existence, 80
"Gnosticism, Existentialism, and Nihilism" (Jonas), 78
gnostics, 69, 70, 78

God
    acted to save the world, 7
    of Augustine as a worldly God, 90
    as basic and "desire" the precious clue, 114
    cannot become a sign, 41
    on the connection between violence and divinity, 145
    contrasts between "the world" and, 7
    creation of as very good, 1
    humankind taking pleasure in praising, 43
    as immanent as well as transcendent, xii
    as the most generous giver, 43
    of the New Testament as an "alien god," 69
    not understood by human reason, 72
    as the only proper "object" of enjoyment for Augustine, 40–41
    as the "supreme thing" (*summa res*) for Augustine, 41
    willed a sensory world from which Christians must separate themselves, 54
    word of putting the world into uproar, 94
God and man, as competitors in a relation of power, 112
God's people, calling to come out of Babylon, 4
Goethe's women, sense of life radiated by, 102
the Good, 19
"good things," offered by the affluent society, 127
goodness, 93, 133, 144
grace, 21, 107, 142
Grand Inquisitor, 142, 143
grasping and attachment, causing us to suffer, 48
"great compassion" (*mahaakarunaa*), 129
"great disembedding," of society, 65
Greek notion, of the cosmos, 70
Gregory, Eric, 88, 89–90, 91
Gregory of Nyssa, 17
Gregory the Great, 46, 47–48

INDEX OF SUBJECTS

Pope Gregory VII (Hildebrand), reforms of, 50–51, 55–56
grief, of Augustine, 42
"guilty bystander," Merton adopting the role of, 133
"The Guilty Progress of the Human Condition," listing man's futile ambitions, 53

Habermas, Jürgen, 96, 101–2
hating the world, xvi, 1, 2
Hauerwas, Stanley, 100
heart of the world, the Church as, xv
Heavenly City, 25, 29
Hegel, 97–98
Heidegger, Martin
    on the connection between Gnosis and modernity, 80n14
    existentialism failed to help, 79
    fatal flaw in teachings of, 80
    hidden debt to Augustine, 77n4
    Jewish students of, xvii, 76
helpless conformity (*Anpassung*), producing, 96
"heresy," 13–14
Hesse, Hermann, 148
hibernation, of Adorno, 102, 103
hierarchical complementarity, falling back into, 64
Hochhuth, Rolf, 94
holiness, 12, 67
Holocaust, "non-redemptive apocalypse" of, 77n3
holy longing, life of a good Christian as, 28
homoeroticism, 114
"homosexuality," 115
hope, 141
Horkheimer, Max, 95
hos me, "as if not" or "as not" repeated by Paul, 8
Hoskyns, Edwyn, 9–10
household, becoming a "laboratory of the spirit," 89
Hugh of Cluny, 37
Hugh of St Victor, 45–46
human affairs, results of, 35–36

human beings
    doctrine of centered on the heart rather than the mind alone, 35
    enjoying the creature instead of the creator, 25
    as exiles from their true homeland, 18
    new model of, 66
    as an ontological beginning, 92
    in this most inhuman of ages, 133
human capacities, fragility of, 93
The Human Condition (Arendt), 77, 88, 132
human embodiment and sexuality, Augustine on, 20
human fulfillment, the cross as the principal means of, xv
human identity, question of ultimate, 129
human life, 23, 27
human mind, meaning situated within, 60
human nature, metaphysical roots of violence in, 136
human praxis, as an illusion, 96
human self-assertion, 68, 69
human subject, reification of, 95
human suffering, 71, 101
human will, 5
humanism, 127
Humanisme Integral (Maritain), 139–40
humanisms, xiii–xiv, xiv
humanity, 65, 145
humankind, sinking into barbarism, 95
humility, 25, 27, 47, 91, 132
Humpty Dumpty, having another great fall, 13, 69

I See Satan Fall Like Lightning (Girard), 55
Ibsen, Henrik, 147
iconicity, of the earth, 121
"ID" story, 68, 73
"ideal statesman," 24
identities in time, stabilizing, 83
identity
    buffered, 65
    Christian, 115
    human, 129

INDEX OF SUBJECTS

in the presence of Christ, 6
social, 2–3
"identity thinking," 97
ignorance (*avidya*), 134
Illich, Ivan, 137, 139, 148
illusory self, 128, 130, 133
images, xii, 11
imagination, 144
Imitatio Christi (Thomas à Kempis), 118
"immanent frame," 56
"immanentism," of de Lubac, 110
immigrants, ancient Christians as, 2
immortality, striving for, 89
imperative, of Jonas, 80
imperium, compared to *sacerdotium*, 53
imprisonment, escaping from on earth, 77
"incarnational humanism," xiii, xiv
Incarnational spirituality, 63
incognito, of Kierkegaard's knight of faith, 119
The Individual and the Church: Concerning Luther and Protestantism (Kierkegaard), 118
individual liberty, at the price of a personal split, 11
"an individual outside-the-world," 10, 11
indulgences, sale of, 60
inevitable progress, 98
infinite, relating to while existing in the finite, 117
inner detachment, as necessary, 9
"inner-worldly asceticism," 9, 65
Pope Innocent III, 45, 52–53
"insane mistake," of kneeling before the world, 108
insanity, of instrumental reason, 98
instrumental reason, 65, 98
"Intellectual Deviation story," xvii, 68
"intending," politics of, 87
internal nature, domination of, 95
Investiture Controversy, 56
Irenaeus, 14
Islam, tradition of political theology, 22
Ivan Karamazov, 142

James, on assimilation to God, 4

Jeremiah, 3
Jerome, 38, 39–40
Jerusalem, 25, 28
Jesus. *See also* Christ
fulfilling prophecy but reconstructing it, 12
on the love of God and the love of creation as united, 120
retelling the story of, 5
saying to each person: "I love you as you are," 148
Jewish understandings, of the "world," 12
John
on being in the world but not of the world, 5–7
on the world, 1
on "And the world did not know him," 25
John of Fecamp, 36, 45
John of the Cross, xii, xiii, 109
Pope John XXIII, 93–94
John's Gospel, 6, 7
Jonas, Hans
belief in a God as he who wills life, 81
condemning his teacher, Heidegger, 80
link between defending Judaism and defending life, 81
reading modernity as super-gnostic, 78n10
responses to modern worldlessness, 76
revaluing the world in the face of an absent God, 78
on a revival of Gnosticism, xvii–xviii
on the unity of the cosmos and God, 70
victory against Gnosticism in the (modern) West, 77
Journals (Kierkegaard), on the monastery, 117
Judaism, defense of as a defense of life itself, 81
judgment, of the world, 7
Julian of Norwich, xii, xiii
justice, 91, 98

INDEX OF SUBJECTS

Kant, Immanuel, Jonas following, 80
karunaa, "true compassion," exercising, 48–49
Kharkov famine, perpetrated by atheists, 140
Kierkegaard, Soren, 117
Kierkegaardian "repetition," 10
Killing Fields, perpetrated by atheists, 140
kingdom of God, 56, 125, 137
kneeling, before the world, 105–10
kosmos, 7. *See also* cosmos
Kristeva, Julia, 146–47

Ladner, Gerhart, 59
Lapidot, Eliad, 78n10
L'Arche, 146, 147–48
"large 'R'" reformers, 60
late bourgeois society, everything as a commodity, 97
late capitalist society, relations of production of, 96
Lateran Council of 1215, 51
Latin Christendom
    contemptus mundi as the ideology of, xvii, 53
    reforms of Pope Gregory VII (Hildebrand), 55–56
lay society, 51, 52
lay state of life, as a life without grace, 36
lay world, in canonical Buddhism, 49
Leclercq, Jean, 35, 37, 44
legal and moral codes, becoming idolatrous traps, 139
The Legitimacy of the Modern Age (Blumenberg), xvii, 68, 74
Letter to Diognetus, 3
Leurs regards perce nos ombres—Their Look Pierces our Shadows (Vanier and Kristeva), 146
Lialine, Clement, xiiin5
liberals and conservatives, Western Christians dividing into, 105
libido dominandi (lust for power), pride turning into, 24
license, people permitted forms of, 58
life. *See also* Christian life
    claiming freedom and subjectivity, 78
    in the last age, 27
    pride of, 47
    removing ourselves from the culture industry, 102
    rendering artificial, 77
    without God as imaginable, 67
    in the world, 9, 75, 82
Life of Antony (Athanasius), 16
limits, of the Church as those of the world itself, 51
"linear master narrative," 55
Little Brothers of Jesus, in Toulouse, 109
Little Eyolf (Ibsen), 147
Liturgy and Contemplation (Maritain), 109
"living life" (*zhivaya zhizn*), 142, 144
logos (Word of God), 14, 15
the Logos, the Son of God, 5
loneliness, 84
loss of ordering, an "Ordnungsshwund," 68
love
    as constitutive of being human, 90
    determining our home, 87
    finding the same ground of in everything, 131
    having a real presence in the world, 143
    of the world, 1, 28, 84
    the world as a product of our, 93
love of God (*amor dei*), as humility, 25
love of self (*amor sui*), as pride, 25
loving, an eternal and incomprehensible God, 90
"loving the eternal," *caritas* meaning, 88
Lukacs, Georg, 75
lumen Christi, bringing into the world, 111
Luther, Martin, 60–61, 66

magic, primacy of before a secular age, 60
"magical" sacramentality, of the corrupt hierarchical church, 61
magna monasterium, of Calvin's Geneva, 64

INDEX OF SUBJECTS

Mahaakassapa, a disciple of the Buddha teaching, 129
making money, 124
man born blind, confuting the Pharisees, 6
Mani, found key alignments between Christ, Zoroaster, and the Buddha, 20
Manichaean doctrine, Augustine on, 22
Manichaeanism, as an alternative, and indeed "true" Christianity, 20
mankind, not remaining bound to the earth forever, 77
man-made world, distinguishing from nature, 82
Marcion, on the creator God of the Old Testament, 69
Maritain, Jacques, xviii, 106, 109
Maritain, Raissa, 109, 115
Mark (gospel of), portraying an alternative social order, 4
martyrs, cult of, 31
Marx, dialectical thought, 97–98
Marxist view, of change, 133
masked Manichaeism, superimposed on the Christian faith, 107
"mass society," modern unfreedom of, 84
material existence, pervading Augustine's thinking on sin, 21
material preconditions, for the existence of a liberated society, 95
material realities, xvi–xvii
material things, 34
material world, as sacramental, 14, 133
materialistic society, 124
meaning, in the enchanted medieval world, 60
medieval balance, between a Christian world order and alienation from the world, 57
medieval Catholicism, "decentered centrality" of, 49
medieval Catholics, on the number of the saved as very small, 51
medieval Christians, 31, 47, 58, 62
medieval persons, within a complex web of arrangements, 58

medieval teaching, to the laity about married sexuality, 63
medieval visionaries, seeing the world as God sees it, 46
medievalists, "una querelle di vaste proporzioni" among, 35
men, loving as men should be loved, 42
mendicant friars, disciplines of monasticism and, 62
meontology, Paul preaching, 9
merit and achievement, *caritas* indifferent to, 88
Merton, Thomas, xviii, 115–16, 123–34
messianic life, most rigorous definition of, 103
messianic use of the world, 104
"metaphysical optimism," balancing with a "historical pessimism," xiv
metaphysics, Arendt's suspicion of, 81
Middle Ages, failed to produce a positive theology of worldly realities and activities, 35
Milbank, John, 112–13
Minima Moralia (Adorno), 102
"The Miserable Entrance of the Human Condition," 53
missionary disciples, halting declining Church numbers, xi
misunderstanding, of making practical truth speculative, 107
modern age, 76, 77
modern alienation from nature, 79
modern humanism, on compassion, 142
modern moral order, emergence of, 65
modern rationality, exemplified by the development of science, 73n52
modern science, predicated on an objective stance, 74
modern world, as guilty and fallen, 127
modern worldliness, attended by world alienation, 75
modernity
 critiques on, 100
 as a mutation of Christianity, 54–55
 resistance to the "world" of, xviii
 taking form within Christian tradition, 72

INDEX OF SUBJECTS

modernity *(continued)*
    Taylor's analysis of the paradox of, 141
monastery, as the only refuge for those with contempt of the world, 36
monastic and Christian life, concern with total inner transformation, 134
monastic attitude, to the world, xvi, 1
monastic church, merging with the universal church, 49
monastic communities, as communities of ambivalence about the world, xvi
monastic culture, 35
monastic schools, giving fearlessness, 118–19
monastic search for God, necessity for the purification of the heart in, 37
monastic separation, as a paradoxical invitation to be close to the world, 125
monastic spirituality, association with otherworldliness, xi
monastic system, disintegration of, 51
monastic theologians, seeing no intrinsic worth in created things, 35
monastic tradition, eschatological orientation of, xiiin5
monastic vows, 48, 52
monasticism
    Buddhist and Christian, 133–34
    intractable oddity of, 99
    offering a space for the cultivation "aesthetic existence," 132
    as the only true humanism, xv
    returned to the cities of the Empire, 31
monk(s)
    on the claims of the world as fraudulent, 133
    dwelling in the center of society, 134
    of the Egyptian desert, 15–16
    and nuns devoted themselves to the demands of eternity, 57–58
    renounced the world, 48
    sought: a kind of paradise, 16

surviving in the modern world and dissenting from it, 132
vocation of in the modern world as prophecy, 126
moral and spiritual aspirations, for human beings, 136
"moral forces," embedded in the lived environment, 56
moral responsibility, requiring engagement with spiritual disciplines, 134
morality, taking precedence over theology, 107
mortal person, loving, 42
mundus. See the world (*mundus*)
Murray, John Courtney, xiv
music, importance of polyphony in, 122
mutability, of things of the visible world, 46
mutual love, community of confronting the world, 6
mystical truth, 106, 107

natality, 85, 86
"natural" matter, Christ came to restore it, 120
nature, 17, 65, 79, 126
Nazi era, disintegration of churches, 118
"negative dialectics," Adorno's commitment to, 97
Negative Dialectics (Adorno), 97
negative way, converging with the affirmative way, xii
neighbors, loving actively and tirelessly, 143
Neo-Stoicism, embodied by Lipsius and Descartes, 65
network of *agape*, 137–38
networks of living concern, centering our lives in, 139
"new asceticism," offering a "lived theology," 115
new Christian worldliness, of Irenaeus, 14
new otherworldliness, Augustine exemplifying, 20

INDEX OF SUBJECTS

new *paideia*, bound to a concept of repentance, 35
New Testament, 120, 136
new worldliness, 17, 31
newcomers, 85, 86
Nicene tradition, of Augustine, 21
Nicene-Catholics, as crude semi-Christians, 20
Nicodemus, 6
Nietzsche, 10–11, 116, 140, 146
nihilism, 34, 99
nominalist God, fearful in his omnipotence, 73
Nominalist philosophy, 65
Nominalist revolution, against Scholasticism, 72–73
Nominalist theology, 68
nonattachment, 48
non-disabled, gazing on persons with disability, 147
nonidentity thinking, negative dialectics striving to achieve, 97
non-place, occupying, 46
Notes from Underground (Dostoevsky), 102

obedience, 48
objectifying standpoint, on everything, 138
obligations, a vicious circle of, 11
"an old layman," questioning himself about the present time, 106
Old Man, as not really conscious and responsible, 21
On Christian Doctrine (Augustine), 24–25, 26
On Virginity (Gregory of Nyssa), 17–18
ontic dualism, 74
ontological realists, 72
ontology, 81
ontosophic truth, 106, 107
optimism, in regard to the created order, xiv
ordinary householder, living in all the practices and institutions of flourishing, 63
ordinary life, affirmation of, xvii, 64–65

organic life, containing the ethics that we need to learn, 80
Origen, 15, 38, 39
The Origins of Totalitarianism (Arendt), 92
Orthodoxy (Chesterton), 54
otherworldliness, xi, 33, 40, 43
Otto of Freising, 52
out-worldly individual, in India, 10
own self, as the obstacle to realizing true self, 130

pagan empire, yielding before Christ's army, 23
paganism, Augustine on, 26
paidagogos, world of, 35
paideia, 35, 119
painting, moving out of the orbit of the icon, 62
papacy, eschatological events and, 50
parents, educating their children, 85
partial truths (*logoi*), of pagan knowledge, 35
Pascal, Blaise, 79
"passing away," of the world, 103
passions, 17, 30
passive purgation, phase of, xii
"pastoral of fear," fostered a spirituality of death, 62
patristic era, reform as personal, 50
Paul
    appearing as a "fool," 12
    concerned with the integrity of a community, 10
    exhorting the Romans on renewal of mind, 50
    recommending relativizing of all the things in the world, 9
    referring to the world as a dung hill, 106
    on "remaining in the calling in which you have been called," 103–4
    worldly asceticism of, 7–10
The Peasant of the Garonne (Maritain), xviii, 106, 109
Peguy, Charles, 112

INDEX OF SUBJECTS

Pelagius, Augustine opposed the rigorism of, 31
penitential provenance, of Ecclesiastes, 39n20
peregrinatio, signifying a journey to the homeland (a pilgrimage), 18
perfection, demanded of all, 31
personal and social relationships, distorted accepted as natural and unchangeable, 96
personality, relationships making, 129
"the perversity of this world" (*perversitas saeculi*), 26
pessimism, about human sinfulness, xiv
Peter the Venerable Abbot of Cluny, 37–38
The Phenomenon of Life (Jonas), 78
philanthropy, 141–42
Philippians, on the surrendering of all personal entitlements, 4
Pickstock, Catherine, 112–13
piety, enfleshed forms of, 61
Pope Pius XII, Arendt reflecting on, 93–94
Platonic ontology of transcendence, 17
Platonic tradition of "desire," 114
Platonist Christianity, 116
Platonist-Christian synthesis, 17, 113
Platonist-Christian theology, of Eusebius, 23
Platonist-Christian tradition, theoretical framework of, 71
Platonist-Christian vision, of the world, xvi
Platonists, on evil, 71
pleasures of the flesh, neglecting the judgment of God, 62
Plotinus, 19
poet, on worldly life, 36
point of nothingness (*le point vierge*), at the center of our being, 131
political power, for a reformed and reforming Church, 53
political sphere, Arendt not welcoming human passion into, 90
political theology, of Augustine, 23
politics, 29, 87

polyphony of life, losing, 122
porous selves, turned to "good magic," 60
"portability," of ascetic practice, 30
positive references, to the world in John 1–12, 5
poverty, opposed to the desire for riches (lust of the eyes), 48
power, temptation of as too strong, 56
practical truth, lived by the saints as a contempt for the world, 106
praising God, as thanking God for the world, 43
predestination, Augustine's doctrine of, 71
pride
  of life, 47
  rooted in self-love, 24, 25
primitive separatism, reinscribing as the cause of anxiety, 14
private realm, of Arendt, 81
"profane values," of cities of late antiquity, 36–37
progress, confusing with the coming of a new creation, 111
Protestant Reformation, contribution of, 61
Protestantism, making certain pious practices absolutely general, 64
Proto-Reformations, series of, 60
psychic petrification, resisting the process of, 98
public realm, 81–82, 87, 88
pure glory of God in us, 131

Qoheleth, in Ecclesiastes, 39–40

Rabinbach, Anson, 77n3
Radical Orthodoxy, on the metaphysics of *methexis*, 112
"rage for order," relieving tension between loving and hating the world, 64–65
Raisa, Maritain's wife, 109, 115
rationality, 97
"real" world, having to do with inner life, 128

INDEX OF SUBJECTS

"realism," in religious painting, 62
reality, 68, 69, 121, 134
reason, 72, 97
"reasonable insanity," 98, 99
rebellion, against the ascetic demands of religion, 140
"recalcitrant logic," 55
recapitulation, doctrine of, 14
redemption, xiv, 100
reductio atrium ad theologiam (leading of secular disciplines back to theology), humanism assuming, 35
Reform, 50, 59, 68
"Reform Master Narrative," 55–67, 106
Reformatio, in the early centuries of the church, 50
Reformation, subjecting Christianity to a movement towards "excarnation," 61
reformers, seeking to carry the ascetic into the world itself, 51
reformers and Reformers, attempts to restore and revitalize the lives of the faithful, 59–60
refusal, to accept things as they are, 108
reified society, 99
reified world, 98
rejection of images, xii
religion, 55, 135, 140
religious crisis, of the 1960s, 136
religious faith, as dangerous, 145
religious meaning, as not merely "in the mind," 57
renunciation, building into ordinary life, 64
resident aliens
  Christians as, 2, 3
  seeking to recompose the world, 12–18
respect, giving to our whole person in spiritual life, 130
ressourcement, xviii, 112
restoration of the church, coming from a new kind of monasticism, 119
resurrection, 139

Revelation (book of), rejection of Rome, 4
"revolt against escapism," plea for a determined, 77
revolution, joining to guarantee Christianity will survive, 126
rich and powerful, acquisitive greed of, 44
Robinson, John, 127
Roger of Caen, 36
Romanesque art, images of an age hardened to unalleviated pain, 37
Romuald, 64
rule of God, 22
rules, prescribing treatment for categories of people, 138
"rules of faith," evolving, 13

sacerdotium (spiritual function), seeking to rule in worldly matters, 53
sacramental ontology
  Christian synthesis expressed in, 16
  danger of an imbalance, 17
  encouraging turning from sign to reality, 18
  on the natural world as a cosmos, 56–57
  in the Platonist-Christian synthesis, 112
  postconciliar decline of, 110
sacraments, 60, 61, 121
saeculum, 24–27, 29, 30
saints, 107, 108
salvation, 2, 21, 23
samsara, mundane life, 49
samsara, the "world," 48
sanctification, 61
sanctified life, 64
saraga, "attachment," 48
Satipatthana Sutta, on mindfulness, 49
satisfaction, of the desire for beauty, 18
"scapegoat mechanism," described by Rene Girard, 145
Schillebeeckx, Edward, 111
Schmemann, Alexander, 120–21
Schmitt, Carl, 2, 76n3
schola, Christian ascetics and, 35

INDEX OF SUBJECTS

Scholastic view, of humankind, 71
Scholasticism, struggles with
    Nominalism, 72
schools, drawing students out of their
    families, 85
science, modern, 73n52, 74
scientific modernity, terror of, 79
Scotus, Duns, 112–13
Scripture, reading of, 15
the "secular," 26, 29, 56
secular age, as a mutation or corruption
    of Christianity, xvi
A Secular Age (Taylor), xvii, 54, 135,
    144–45
secular modernity, as unable to
    recompose the world, 75
"secular" space, beginning of, 29
"secular theology," constructing, 105
secular vocations, 104
secular world, emergence of, 58–59
secularism, transient world of, 126
secularist temptation, as strong, 110
secularists and unbelievers, against
    Christian faith itself, 67
secularity, as a corruption or mutation of
    Christianity, 54
secularization, xvii, 55, 105, 106
self, 34, 57, 75, 129
self-assertion, 73n52
self-conception, as users of tools, 138
self-conscious inner-worldly withdrawal,
    strategy of, 99
self-control, 30, 42
"selfhood," possessing, 78
self-possession, of a secure inner mental
    realm, 66
self-realization and flourishing, breaking
    down barriers to, 135
"self-transcendence," tension with, 57
sensory world, distancing ourselves from,
    11
The Seven Storey Mountain (Merton),
    123–24
sexual "orientation," orientation to God
    and, 115
sexual union, as a "type" of God's relation
    to Israel or church, 113

"sexuality" and the "self," trinitarian God
    and, 115
Sexuality and the Self (Coakley), 113
shared meanings, work of establishing, 87
signs, for Augustine, 41
Abba Silvanus, 34
sin, 21–22, 23, 42, 138
sinful or fallen world, organized against
    God, 2
sinners, warning against the horrors of
    the tomb, 52
Sloterdijk, Peter, 73
small "r" reformers, 59
smashing, the multispeed dispensation,
    60
social body, 57, 58
social identity, 2–3
social life, 23–24, 98–99
social order, 23
social reality, demystifying, 96
society
    creation of a free and economically
        productive, 95
    enslaved to idolatrous
        objectifications, 84
    founded on covenant, 136
    grounded in higher reality, 57
    providing a context of
        unremitting delusion,
        Verblendzusammenhang, 96
sole fide, of Luther, 60
Solomon, 38, 39
Song of Songs, 38, 39
Sources of the Self (Taylor), 140, 141, 144
"space for appearing," 82, 83
spell, of a seemingly objective "second
    nature," 96
spiritual autonomy, winning, 11
spiritual ideals, 66, 140
spiritual life, rhythms of, 16
spiritual realities, 17
spiritual visions, of human history, 140
spirituality of monks, imposing upon all,
    51–52
"spring of remembrance," 84
Stalin's universal terror, 73
the "statesman," a new model of, 91

INDEX OF SUBJECTS

state-sponsored oppression, standing up for the victims of, 118
Stoic teaching, on *logos* God permeating the cosmos, 14–15
"strategy of hibernation," of Adorno, 101
stripped down secular outlook, involving "mutilation," 141
Styfhals, Willem, 76–77n3
subjectivity, 60, 78
suffering, 4, 103
Summa Theologica (Thomas Aquinas), 148
supernatural power, everyday objects "charged" with, 57
"supreme thing," God to be enjoyed as, 41
Surin, Kenneth, 96
survival, in a temporal or worldly sense, 126
Sutz, Erwin, 118
Symposium (Plato), 113

Taubes, Jacob, 76n3
Taylor, Charles
  on the dilemma of mutilation, 135–48
  on medieval equilibrium between otherworldliness and worldliness, 54
  reimagining contemporary Christianity, 135, 140
  on secularization, xvii, 55
  using insights of Dostoevsky, 144
  wanting to rehabilitate Christianity, 145
technical civilization, unintended dynamics of, 79
technological advances, consequences of, 75
technological and ideological achievements, as destructive illusions, 123
technological evil, critique of modernity dealing with, 81
"Technology and Responsibility: Reflections on the New Tasks of Ethics" (Jonas), 80

techno-scientific project, foundation of the modern, 77
telos, securing, 57
tempora christiana, Christian times, of Augustine, 22
temporal structures, Christian renewal of, 108–9
temporal things, as not inherently bad, 26
temptations, presented in the first epistle of John, 47
tending, 87
tension
  between loving and hating the world, 37
  between two types of cities and love, 25
Saint Teresa of Avila, 109
Tertullian, 14
theistic affirmation, of being, 144
theocratic temptation, in the past, 110
theodicy, Augustine's Christian response to the problem of, 71
theologians, 105, 107
theological absolutism, of late medieval Nominalism, 68
theological polarizations, of the second century, 13
theology, of ambivalence, 18–24
Theopolis, culture of, 35
Theravada Buddhism, "decentered centrality" of, 49
Saint Thérèse of Lisieux, 109
things, inordinate love of, 26
things that are not (*ta me onta*), bringing to naught those that are (*ta onta*), 8
this-worldliness, of Christianity, 119–20
Thomas à Kempis, 39
"thrownness," into the voidness of the world, 80
tightrope dancer, of Nietzsche, 11
time-bound human life, frailty of, 27
"total history of a specific contingency," of Taylor, 55
traditional religions, transforming and liberating the truth, 134

INDEX OF SUBJECTS

transfiguration, as an effective seeing-as, 144
transient things of this world, placing one's love in, 40
transitory world, 42
a tribe, church community becoming, 137
true God, as an alien God, 70
true self, 128–29, 130
truth
    of the Eucharist, 111
    mystical, 106, 107
    ontosophic, 106, 107
    partial, 35
    practical, 106, 107
    traditional religions seeking to transform and liberate, 134
    withered by the reified world, 98
"turning toward the world," 124, 128
two- "speed" model, Latin Christendom's dissatisfaction with, 59

ugliness, of sickness and suffering, 128
"unbearable lightness of being," miracle of, 130–31
"unequalled worldlessness," of the modern age, 74
"Unheimlichkeit," of modern reality, 74
unity, 13, 111
universals, reality of, 72
universe, form of the cross upon, 15
"the Unspeakable," Merton confronting, 133
"unsystematic systematics," of Coakley, 115
unworldliness, Christian, 17, 93
unworldly life, lived in the world, 94
"unworldly worldliness," paradox of, 74
upadhiviveka, as absence of lust, desire, and craving, 48
urban Christians, taught to develop an earthly and a heavenly focus, 3
urban mob violence, directed against pagans, 30
use (*uti*), defined by Augustine, 40
usus facti, of the early Franciscans, 104

uti, rendering the transitory world as ephemeral, 42
utilitarian view of life, 148

vainglory, the pride of life, brought Adam to consent to sin, 47
values, accepting the Platonist hierarchy of, 17
Vanier, Jean, 146, 146n150
vanitas vanitatum, 37–47
vanity, of the "world," xvii
vanity of vanities [*vanitas vanitatutum*], 39, 45
vice, 45, 47
view of ourselves, 138
vigilance, of those awaiting the Parousia, 9
violence
    complicity with, 139
    directed against pagans, 30
    problem of, 136
    redirected toward sinful acts and attitudes, 145
    testing agapic love against, 143
"virtual" reality, denying the lived body, 138
virtue, demands of periodically suspended, 58
virtues, separating from vices, 146
visible beauty, provoking Christian minds, 46
visible church, distinguished from the true community of the saved, 60
vision in Louisville, of Merton, 131
viveka, meaning separation, aloofness, or seclusion, 48
vocation
    contemplative, 115
    Ecclesiastes on the meaning of, 66
    of monk(s) in the modern world, 126
    of monks, 132
    secular, 104
    as that of the friend, 139
volunteers, coming to L'Arche, 147

way of affirmation, xii

INDEX OF SUBJECTS

way of negation, xii
the "weak of the world," chosen by God, 7–8
Weber, Max, 74, 103
wedding ring, simile of, 43–44
Western Christianity, transformation of beginning in medieval society, 56
Western conceptions, of equality and individualism, 10
Western painting, after the High Middle Ages, 62
Western society, 135
Who Am I, prayerful asking of, 129
the will, as the engine of moral change, 65
Williams, Charles, xii
Williams, Rowan, 88, 89, 91, 101n75
Wolin, Sheldon, 87
women, 102, 114, 140
Word of God, 14, 15, 16
words, not pointing to real universal entities, 72
works of art, as the most worldly objects, 82
the world (*mundus*)
    adaptations to for Merton, 126
    affirming the modern, xi
    ambivalence about, xv–xvi, xviii, 5, 17, 115
    appearing in its totality from afar, 46
    attitude toward including rejection, 4
    besieged by the lures of, 47
    as both a material and a linguistic reality, 12
    bracketed so that the eschatological kingdom can appear, 46–47
    characterized by *vanitas*, 48
    as the dehumanized surface, 128
    disenchantment of, 61
    endemic mistrust of and its prince (and princes), 33
    enduring, 82
    enduring context outlasting our lifespan, 82
    failing to distinguish as creation from our modern world, 100
    fighting back the demands of, 55
    first disciples both loved and hated, 1
    hating those who Jesus chooses, 5
    imminent dominion of God over, 50
    individuals inwardly isolated from, 11
    interpreting nontheistically, 67
    kneeling before, 105–10
    living on as a space for human activity, 83
    loving as a gift from a loving giver, 43
    made through Jesus, 5
    made worldly by eschatology, 52
    "making use" of in a manner appropriate, 103
    needing care and refreshing, 86
    negative sense of, 55
    as not intrinsically evil, 48
    not regarding as a thing whose reality lies wholly in itself, 149
    as an obstacle to God, 106–7
    in a pejorative sense, 25
    in the power of the evil one, 1
    present form of passing away, 8
    "reassembling," 13
    recomposed as "saeculum," 24–27
    referring to society, the human world, culture, 7
    referring to what is to be used rather than enjoyed, 24
    as the reign of Satan, 36
    rejected Jesus and hated his disciples, 6
    representing a rival power structure, 53
    as a rival sacred order to the *ecclesia*, 37
    as saturated with God for Augustine, 29
    seeking without Christ, 121
    as something to be mastered, 68
    taking away the sins of, 7
    tension between loving and hating, xvi
    in terms of the three temptations of 1 John 2:16, 47

the world (*mundus*) (*continued*)
    as the "in-between" that connects us all, 86
    transcendent visions and impulses against, 4
    unclean because of our sin, 1–2
    as vain when considered in abstraction, 42
world alienation, 74, 84
"world come of age," after Christendom, 123
world loss, ever growing sense of, 74
world view, originating in elements of a conflict, 33
worldlessness, 68–75
worldliness
    Augustine's conception of, 26
    of Bonhoeffer, 127
    as the characteristic of the modern age, 73–74
    of Christianity, 121
    dealing with a secular age, 123
    as involvement in technological culture, 132
    provoking a new otherworldliness, 51
    seeing the world redeemed in Christ, 127
worldly asceticism, of Paul, 7–10
worldly domain, *saeculum* as, 27
worldly in-between, mediating relations, 84
world's renewal, contributing to, 86

Zacharias, 34
Zen koans, of Marton, 125
zero-sum game, 90
zero-sum realities, xiv
Žižek, Slavoj, 100, 101
Zossima, 143

Index of Ancient Sources

Old Testament

Genesis	15

Psalms

137	28
150	45

Proverbs	38
Ecclesiastes	xvii, 38, 39, 40, 42, 43, 47, 48, 66
1	39
8:14	40

Song of Songs	38, 39, 113
7:6	122

Isaiah

63:3	108

Jeremiah

29:7	3

Deuterocanonical Books

Wisdom of Solomon

11:22	46

New Testament

John	4, 6
1:1	14
1:9–12	5
1:10	25
1–12	5
1:29	7
3:16	1, 5
3:19	7
4:42	5
6:29	6
6:33	5
12:46	7
12:47	5
13–20	5
13:34–35	6
14–17	6
15:12	6
15:18	5
15:19	5
16:33	7
20:21–23	7

INDEX OF ANCIENT SOURCES

Romans	
1:1	103
6:11–13	9
12:2	50

1 Corinthians	
1:18	7
1:20	7
1:25	7
1:26–31	7
1:28	8
4:6–13	8
7:17	8, 104
7:29–31	103
7:29–35	8
7:35	9
8:3	104

Galatians	
1:10	103
6:14	9
6:15	10

Ephesians	4
2:18	2

Philippians	4
3:8	106
3:20	3

Hebrews	
11:16	3
12:22	3
13:14	3

James	4
4:4	4
4:6	27

1 Peter	4
1:1	2
2:11	2
2:11—3:17	3
5:5	27

1 John	5
1:15–16	47
2:15–16	1
2:16	47, 48
3:2	28
5:19	1

Revelation	
18:4	4

Apostalic Fathers—Writings

Didache

10th chapter	120

Epistle to Diognetus

5:4, 5, 8	3

Early Christian Writings

Anselm of Canterbury

Exhortatio ad Contemptum Temporalium et Desiderium Æternorum — 37

Antony	99

Athanasius

Life of Antony — 16

Augustine	18, 71, 91, 119

On Christian Doctrine

1.12.12	25

INDEX OF ANCIENT SOURCES

1.2.2	41
1.4:4	24
1.4.4	40–41
1.5.5	41
2.3.3	25
5.17–18	26
book 1	40–41

City of God — 23, 27
1.Preface	25, 27
1.35	25
10.6	26
11.28	90
12.15	27
12.20	92
14.28	25
18.40	26
19	27
19.14	29
19.17	29
19.8	27
20.3	40, 42

Confessions — 43, 47
1.1.1	43n27
4.12.18	43n27
4.4.9	43n26
4.4.9, p. 50	42n25
4.4.9–4.7.12	42
10.30.41	47n37
VII.xiii.19	20

Expositions
168–73	28n27

Homilies
69	28n26

Autpert Ambrose

Conflictus viriorum atque virtutum (Combat between the vices and the virtues) — 44

De cupiditate
1: CCCM 27B, 963	44
1:CCCM 27B, 978	45

Bernard of Clairvaux

Selected Writings
210–11	38n19

Song of Songs	38

Bonaventure

Works of St. Bonaventure
9.28	44

Catherine of Siena	19
Clement of Alexandria	14, 15
Damian, Peter	36

Apologeticum de contemptu saeculi — 52

Letters
225	52n52

Vita Romualdi
37.78	64n31

Eusebius

Oration in Praise of Constantine
sections 4–5	23n17

Gregory of Nyssa

On Virginity — 17–18
11.292.12–13	18n6

Gregory the Great — 48n39

Dialogues
II.35	46

Moralia	47

INDEX OF ANCIENT SOURCES

Pope Gregory VII
(Hildebrand) 55
Collected Letters
9.46 50–51

Herman Contract
*Exhortatory Poem on
the Contempt of the World* 36

Hugh of St. Victor 45
Archa Noe 46n34

Innocent III
*De Miseria Condicionis
Humane* 45, 52–53

Irenaeus of Lyons 14, 15n3, 132

Jerome 39, 66
Ecclesiastes 38

John of Fecamp 36
De Vanitate Mundi 45n33

John of the Cross xii, xiii

Justin Martyr 13

Marcion 69, 70

Origen 15, 66
de Principiis
1.4.5 39
Ecclesiastes 38
The Song of Songs
45, 46 38, 38n18

Pelagius 31

Peter the Venerable
Abbot of Cluny
Epistle
58 37–38, 38n17

Plotinus
Ennead
VI 19

Roger of Caen
Carment de contemptu mundi 36
*The Sayings of the
Desert Fathers*
5 99n68
233 34n4

Tertullian 14

Thomas à Kempis 39
Imitatio Christi 118

Thomas Aquinas 57, 73
Summa Theologica
II, II, 186th question, article 5 148

Greco–Roman Literature

Aristotle 148

Cicero
De Natura Deorum
2.11–14 70

INDEX OF ANCIENT SOURCES

Heraclitus 13

Plato
Symposium 113

Plotinus
Ennead
I.viii.5 19

Socrates 13

Asian Religious Literature

Satipatthana Sutta 49

www.ingramcontent.com/pod-product-compliance
Lightning Source LLC
Chambersburg PA
CBHW021731220426
43662CB00008B/799